Perestroika

King's College Research Centre Project on Soviet History
and Politics 1988–1991

Perestroika
The Historical Perspective

Edited by Catherine Merridale
Research Fellow, King's College, Cambridge

and Chris Ward
Lecturer in the Department of
Slavonic Studies, Cambridge

Edward Arnold
A division of Hodder & Stoughton
LONDON NEW YORK MELBOURNE AUCKLAND

First published in Great Britain

Distributed in the USA by Routledge, Chapman and Hall, Inc.
29 West 35th Street, New York, NY 10001

British Library Cataloguing in Publication Data

Merridale, Catherine
  Perestroika: the historical perspective.
  I. Title   II. Ward, Chris
  947.085

ISBN 0–340–55789–3

Typeset in 10½ /11½ Times by Anneset, Weston-super-Mare, Avon
Printed and bound in Great Britain for Edward Arnold, a division
of Hodder and Stoughton Limited, Mill Road, Dunton Green,
Sevenoaks, Kent TN13 2YA by Biddles Ltd, Guildford & King's
Lynn.

Contents

Contents

Notes on Contributors

Francesco Benvenuti
Francesco Benvenuti graduated from the University of Florence in 1974. He is now a Senior Lecturer in the Department of History of the University of Bologna. He has held research posts at the Universities of Essex and Birmingham. His publications include *The Bolsheviks and the Red Army 1918–1922* (1988).

Mary Buckley
Mary Buckley has been a Lecturer in Politics at the University of Edinburgh since 1983. She is the author of *Women and Ideology in the Soviet Union* (1989), editor of *Soviet Social Scientists Talking* (1986), and co-editor of *Women, Equality and Europe* (1988). She is currently writing a book entitled *New Soviet Agendas* and editing another on *Perestroika and Soviet Women*.

Julian Cooper
Julian Cooper is Director of the Centre for Russia and East European Studies (CREES) at the University of Birmingham. His publications include *Industrial Innovation in the Soviet Union* (1982), *Technical Progress and Soviet Economic Development* (1986), and many articles on Soviet technology and the Soviet economy. He is currently working on the changing role of the Soviet defence industry.

Julie Curtis
Julie Curtis is Lecturer in Russian at the University of Oxford and Fellow of Wolfson College, Oxford. From 1986 to 1989 she held a British Academy Post-doctoral Research Fellowship at Cambridge University's Department of Slavonic Studies. She was also a Fellow of Robinson College. Her publications include *Bulgakov's Last Decade – The Writer as Hero* (1987) and *Manuscripts Don't Burn. Mikhail Bulgakov: A Life in Letters and Diaries* (1991).

Alexander Dallin
Alexander Dallin is Raymond A. Spruance Professor of International History and Professor of Political Science at Stanford University. He is the author of a number of books and articles on Soviet affairs and international relations, including *German Rule in Russia* (1957 and 1981); *The Soviet Union at the United Nations* (1962); *The Soviet Union and*

Disarmament (1965); *Political Terror in Communist Systems* (1970), and *Black Box: KAL 007 and the Superpowers* (1985).

R. W. Davies
R. W. Davies is Emeritus Professor of Soviet Economic Studies at CREES and was the Director of the Centre from 1963 to 1978. He is the author of *The Development of the Soviet Budgetary System* (1958) and *Soviet History in the Gorbachev Revolution* (1989), and co-author, with E. H. Carr, of volume 1 of *Foundations of a Planned Economy 1926–1929* (1969). He is currently writing a multi-volume history of Soviet indus-trialization, the third volume of which, *The Soviet Economy in Turmoil 1929–1930*, was published in 1989.

Ernest Gellner
Ernest Gellner is William Wyse Professor of Social Anthropology at the University of Cambridge and a Professorial Fellow of King's College, Cambridge. He has written widely on philosophy, religion and ethnicity. He spent the year 1988–89 in Moscow as a guest of the Institute of Ethnography of the Academy of Sciences of the USSR. His publications in the Soviet field include *State and Society in Soviet Thought* (1988).

Leonid Gordon
Leonid Gordon is a Professor at the Institute of the International Workers' Movement in Moscow. He has published extensively on social history and sociology, and takes a particular interest in the miners' and other workers' movements of the 1990s.

Caroline Humphrey
Caroline Humphrey is a Lecturer in Social Anthropology at the University of Cambridge and a Fellow of King's College. Her publica-tions include *Karl Marx Collective: Economy, Society and Religion in a Siberian Collective Farm* (1983). She is now working on contemporary Mongolia.

David Lane
David Lane is a Lecturer in Sociology at the University of Cambridge and a Fellow of Emmanuel College. He has written on socialism, social stratification and political power in the Soviet Union. His recent publications include *Soviet Economy and Society* (1985), *Soviet Labour and the Ethic of Communism* 1987), and *Soviet Society Under Perestroika* (1990 and 1991). He is currently working on the structure and composition of elites in the USSR.

Moshe Lewin
Moshe Lewin was born in Wilno in 1921. As a young man he worked in a Soviet factory and served in the Soviet Army during the Second World War. Since 1978 he has been Professor of History at the University of Pennsylvania. His publications include *Lenin's Last Struggle* (1968); *Russian Peasants and Soviet Power* (1968); *Political Undercurrents in*

Soviet Economic Debates – from Bukharin to Modern Reformers (1974); *The Making of the Soviet System* (1985), and the *Gorbachev Phenomenon* (1988).

Catherine Merridale
Catherine Merridale is a Senior Research Fellow of King's College, Cambridge. She was a research student at CREES from 1982 to 1987 working on the history of the Moscow Communist Party in the 1920s. Her book, *Moscow Politics and the Rise of Stalin 1925–1932* was published in 1990. She is currently working on a biography of the Bolshevik leader L. B. Kamenev.

Judith Shapiro
Judith Shapiro, Senior Lecturer in Economics at Goldsmiths College, University of London and the National Secretary of the British Association for Soviet, Slavonic and East European Studies, is the author of articles on Soviet economic history and the present day Soviet Union. Her book on unemployment during the New Economic Policy will be published in 1992.

Graham Smith
Graham Smith is a Fellow of Sidney Sussex College and Lecturer in Geography at the University of Cambridge. He has published on the nationalities question and territorial politics in the Soviet Union. His most recent publication is *Planned Development in the Socialist World* (1989). He is also editor of *The Nationalities Question in the Soviet Union* (1990). His next book, *The Baltic Republics in Revolt: National Separatism in Estonia, Latvia and Lithuania*, will be published shortly.

Robert C Tucker
Robert Tucker is Professor of Politics Emeritus at Princeton University. He worked in the United States Embassy in Moscow after the Second World War. He has written extensively on Soviet political history. Titles include *The Soviet Political Mind* (1963) and 1971); *The Marxian Revolutionary Idea* (1969); *Stalin as Revolutionary 1879–1929* (1973); *Political Culture and Leadership in Soviet Russia from Lenin to Gorbachev* (1987), and *Stalin in Power: The Revolution from Above 1928–1941* (1990).

Chris Ward
Chris Ward works in the Department of Slavonic Studies at the University of Cambridge and is a Fellow of Robinson College. He was an ESRC Research Fellow at CREES from 1986 to 1987. His book, *Russia's Cotton Workers and the New Economic Policy*, was published in 1990. He is currently preparing a textbook entitled *Russia Under Stalin*.

Stephen White
Stephen White is Professor in Politics and a member of the Institute of Soviet and East European Studies at the University of Glasgow. The

most recent of his many writings on Soviet history and politics are *The Bolshevik Poster* (1988) and *Gorbachev in Power* (1990). He is currently investigating Gorbachev's anti-alcoholism campaign, and working on an ESRC-funded study of the composition of the Soviet Communist Party's Central Committee from 1917 to the present.

Acknowledgements

This book is the fruit of a three-year project organised in the Research Centre of King's College, Cambridge. The project consisted of a series of seminars and discussions, culminating in a workshop which was held in King's in July 1990. Although very much a team effort, the project was steered by John Barber, who has continued to offer valuable support and advice to the editors of the present volume. The other organisers, apart from ourselves, were Jonathan Haslam and Hiroaki Kuromiya.

The King's College Research Centre has generously funded the project throughout its three years. We are grateful to the Provost and Fellows of King's College for this support, and to the Research Centre's managers, especially Professor Geoffrey Lloyd and Dr Martin Hyland. We are also indebted to Catherine Marinkovic and Rosemarie Baines, successive secretaries of the Research Centre. Rosemarie Baines in particular not only helped with the organisation of the workshop, but has given invaluable assistance with the preparation of the papers presented here.

We are also grateful to the people who contributed to and attended our regular seminars. Many are represented in this volume, but in addition we should like to thank Professor John Dunn and Dr Simon Franklin, both of whom also acted as discussants at the workshop. Among the other discussants not represented here we should like to mention Professor Gertrude Schroeder and Dr. Lilia Shevtsova; their comments are reflected in the final versions of many of the papers.

The workshop was funded mainly by the King's College Research Centre. We should also like to acknowledge the generosity of the trustees of the Ford Foundation for a grant which helped to cover the expenses of our four Soviet participants. Special thanks for helping with the logistics of the workshop are due to Chris Costa, Lynn Mainland, Susan Moody and Vinayak Srivastava. Finally we must record our gratitude to Fiona Wilson, who patiently and efficiently typed the text, and to Rachel Gomme for her translation of Leonid Gordon's paper.

Catherine Merridale
Chris Ward

Introduction

Catherine Merridale and Christopher Ward

In July 1990, some five years after the appointment of Gorbachev as General Secretary of the Communist Party of the Soviet Union, a group of academics and other specialists drawn from several disciplines and countries was invited to a workshop at King's College, Cambridge to examine the phenomenon of perestroika. It was the first time that a group of this kind included academics from the Soviet Union, all of whom were directly involved in the Soviet political process. The participants met at a crucial turning-point in Soviet political history. The twenty-eighth party congress, which met in Moscow in July 1990, saw the first official split in the Communist Party since 1912. And only 5 months before, article six of the Soviet Constitution had been abolished, permitting, for the first time since 1922, the formation of political parties to rival the Communist Party. These exciting developments inside the Soviet Union provided a dramatic context for the meeting in Cambridge.

The workshop itself was the culmination of a series of seminars and informal discussions held at King's College over the previous two years. Those who took part were convinced that perestroika could be understood only by taking account of Russian and Soviet history. The papers published here, most of which were originally presented at the workshop, were written with this in mind. Their authors include historians, economists, political and social scientists, anthropologists, geographers and specialists in Soviet culture. They express a wide range of different approaches to the question of perestroika and the uses of history, and they also reflect a number of different political standpoints. The editors have not attempted to gloss over the differences between the participants. The variety of perspectives and interpretations which emerged reflects the heterogeneous and contradictory nature of political, social and economic reform in the largest country in the world.

Rapid change often provokes a fundamental reassessment of the past. Nowhere is this more apparent than in the study of Russia and the Soviet Union. At one extreme, there are those who now dismiss the entire Soviet experiment as a cruel and futile interlude, characterised by the profligate waste of resources, the needless sacrifice of lives and the criminal neglect of opportunities. For these people, perestroika signals the resumption, after a break of 73 years, of Tsarist Russia's economic and political progress, the course of which was so disastrously and peremptorily interrupted in the early twentieth century by Lenin's

Revolution. At the other extreme are those who credit the Soviet experiment with many positive and progressive elements, and who consider its collapse to be a mortal blow to their cherished ideal of socialism. A third group holds that perestroika does not mark a complete negation of the Soviet Union's past, or of the socialist experiment, and that many of its elements can be found in previous periods of Soviet history. Viewed in this way, perestroika cannot be seen as signalling the USSR's final 'convergence' with the capitalist west. There are, of course, many different points of emphasis within these broad lines of approach, but in all cases history is brought to bear on the interpretation of the present, and conversely the interpretation of the present influences the writing of history.

One of the controversies that emerges from the papers presented in this book is precisely this intimate relationship between historical and political interpretation, between the past and the present. At its simplest, this can be reduced to the drawing of historical parallels. Some of the papers collected here have identified cycles of reform and reaction over centuries of Russian and Soviet history; others have taken specific moments in the past and compared them to current events. The most common precedents for perestroika cited in the papers are the Great Reforms of the 1860s, the 1905 Revolution and the brief interlude of the Duma Monarchy, and the Revolutions of 1917. In the post-revolutionary years, where parallels are perhaps easier to draw, two phases of reform have attracted special attention: the New Economic Policy of the 1920s (which Gorbachev himself has used as a reference for contemporary reforms), and the Khrushchevian 'thaw' of the late 1950s and early 1960s.

However, although it is interesting, entertaining and even thought provoking to draw historical parallels like these, the exercise may raise as many questions as it solves. The comparative method explicitly informs much contemporary sociological and historical theory. But does comparing the past with the present have any value, and if so, how can such comparisons and values be defined and tested? If each historical event is unique, the comparative method has little validity outside the realm of metaphor. Pushed to its logical conclusion, this argument leaves us with nothing except a business-like empiricism. There is much to commend this approach; indeed, it has long been one of the staples of the British sovietological profession. The problem is that when empiricists begin to disavow theory, they often lose sight of the implicit theoretical foundations upon which their research is based. What they write may be perfectly plausible, but the reader has no way of engaging with the assumptions that underlie their work.

These familiar problems of history and social science are now matters of urgent concern for students of the Soviet Union. Many of us have for too long identified ourselves in terms of area studies, shirking the theoretical debates that have transformed so many other fields of intellectual life. But it is no longer possible to carry on in the old way. The upheavals of the last five years took almost all Soviet specialists by surprise.

Long-established models, which purported to explain the Soviet polity, fell apart in our hands. The organising concepts of so much historical enquiry – class, ideology, and the nature, structure and functioning of the party-state – are now under challenge from all directions. For political and social scientists the well-worn notion of totalitarianism, along with its successor theories of corporatism and institutional pluralism, has similarly become obsolete.

To some degree the changes themselves have suggested the direction this reassessment should take. A number of themes recur in many of the papers. Prominent among these is the idea of civil society. A few years ago, the term was seldom used by scholars writing about Soviet-type societies. By the end of 1989, however, it had become a commonplace of the analysis of change in Soviet and East European politics. As Ernest Gellner and Moshe Lewin demonstrate, there is no consensus about the meaning of the term in the Soviet context, and insufficient critical attention has so far been paid to it. Pluralism is another controversial concept explored in several papers, especially those of Catherine Merridale and Stephen White. Here again each contributor takes a different view of the extent and meaning of the term. One central question is the degree to which some form of pluralism was predetermined by long-term changes in Soviet society. Merridale argues, for example, that pluralism was not simply the product of social change; and conversely that even an industrial and urban society, such as the Soviet Union's has largely become, need not necessarily develop into a western-style democracy. Perestroika must be viewed as a complex and reversible set of political events. The theory of modernisation, which suggests that social change invariably produces a certain type of political reform, provides a point of contrast between the contributions of White and Merridale on the one hand and David Lane on the other.

No less significant than these political issues are those surrounding society and social structure. Mary Buckley's essay, which discusses the issue of gender, highlights the need for new thinking to challenge the idea of class as a primordial organising concept. She demonstrates, among other things, that even in the 1920s gender was never as serious a political issue as it has become in the past five years. Leonid Gordon issues another challenge, this time to Soviet scholars: their understanding of the Soviet working-class and the wellsprings of its political activity has for too long been conditioned by the crude Marxist models originally developed under Stalinism. Gordon's paper is evidence that now, at last, western and Soviet scholars can begin to engage in genuine debates using a common intellectual framework.

The relationship, which Gordon touches on, between the Great Russian heartland and the provinces, between Moscow and the republics, has long been of interest to specialists in Russian and Soviet studies. Here it would seem that history, in the form of the 'return' of repressed cultural traditions, was at last wreaking its revenge on Moscow. But in fact, as Caroline Humphrey shows in her paper, many of the problems that are now collected under the 'ethnic' heading derive largely from the economic difficulties of the last few years. Because 'glasnost' has given the republics the chance to express a multitude of dissatisfactions in the brute language of resistance to Great Russian chauvinism, it often appears that the issue is simple, when in reality the 'nationalities problem' is an amalgam of many different problems. Consequently, nationality, which for so long seemed a dead issue in the study of the Soviet Union, has suddenly and spectacularly revived, and obliged specialists to engage with the question of ethnicity.

Moreover, if, as is often suggested, the Soviet Union is the last of the great territorial empires of Europe; and if, as seems apparent, the empire is now disintegrating, an urgent question for the future is what shape the successor states may take. Few candidates for statehood, for example, have existed as discreet nation-states in the modern period. Those that have often include within their borders sizeable minorities whose claim to special status is bound to create problems if and when Russian imperialism is finally overturned. The difficulties that bedevilled European diplomats throughout the nineteenth century and the first half of the twentieth century seem set to reappear in the Soviet Union, as indeed they already have in Central and Eastern Europe.

No less severe than the ethnic crisis is the collapse of the Soviet economy. In many ways this lies at the root of the country's present turmoil. R. W. Davies and Judith Shapiro tackle the complex question of economic reform. Both draw heavily on historical precedents. As both agree, the 'command–administrative system' of economic development which evolved in the Stalin period is no longer able to fulfil the demands placed on it by the state, still less to meet the material aspirations of Soviet citizens. The economic and social costs of changing this system may, however, be too high for Soviet citizens to bear. As Shapiro indicates, previous reform efforts, including the mixed economy experiment of the 1920s, brought in their wake unemployment, inflation and social discontent arising from conspicuous inequalities – here the parallels with the present may be all too obvious. At a more fundamental level there is the question of whether or not a specifically *socialist* political economy is possible. Davies's essay focuses on the changing Soviet view of economic reform, and on Soviet perceptions of the relationships between the market, planning, state ownership, socialism and capitalism. He suggests that, current fashions notwithstanding, the free market will not entirely displace planning.

Planning may survive, but it seems doubtful whether the idea of Soviet-style socialism, the ideology, or, in Gellner's view, the state religion, which has dominated the Soviet Union since 1917, can do so. Julian Cooper, stressing the links between Marxism and the Enlightenment, goes so far as to argue that 'Bolshevik–Marxist–Leninist' ideology has always been utopian. He contrasts 'socialist ideology' with the concept of 'civilisation' and concludes that the latter idea may be emerging as a result of the challenge to ideology represented by perestroika. Gordon draws a similar contrast; between the 'civilised norm' on the one hand, which he defines as the market and democracy, and the 'extreme' on the other, the Stalinist system of universal state control – or, as he puts it, 'the organisation of everyone and everything.'

Perestroika, or more exactly glasnost', has also had a profound effect on literature, a liberation, as Julie Curtis suggests, of a special kind – not so much a thaw as a loss of purpose. For much of the nineteenth and twentieth centuries Russian literature functioned as the chief vehicle of social and political criticism, especially so in the Soviet period. Now, with the rapid development of glasnost' and the collapse of the hegemony of Soviet socialism, most Soviet writers have been deprived of their traditional themes. This, in Curtis's view, has created the opportunity for a new kind of literature, one which must be judged on equal terms with that of the rest of world.

The future of perestroika remains uncertain and the term may now be losing its meaning. Indeed, in the months since the workshop was convened, the prospects for a peaceful resolution of the Soviet Union's manifold problems may have receded still further. In the short term there are many possibilities – civil war, military coup, the disintegration of the Union – but at the moment they remain possibilities. If perestroika ends in one of these ways, the temptation to dismiss the Gorbachev era as another of Russia's sporadic and painful interludes of liberal reform, sandwiched, inevitably, between decades of reaction, will be too strong for many to resist. The danger of arguing along these lines – and still more of pursuing a foreign policy based on the assumption that the Soviet Union can never be reformed – is that the prophecy may turn out to be self-fulfilling.

Our contributors display a wide range of views on the course of perestroika. They are united, however, in their conviction that contemporary events must be understood in terms, not only of the present, but also of the past. History has bequeathed many problems to the Soviet Union, but only limited resources for tackling them. Whether the diverse peoples of the Union will be able to transcend their particular cultural inheritance is open to question. On the other hand, what is striking – and it can only be appreciated against the backdrop of Russian and Soviet history – is the astonishing speed with which many long-established traditions are being challenged, and in some cases overturned. This process continues. From the perspective of the present, it would be foolhardy to try to predict any final outcome.

I Politics

1
Political Reform in Historical Perspective
Stephen White

There were two key issues involved in perestroika, Gorbachev told his audience on the 70th anniversary of the October Revolution in November 1987: the 'democratisation of all public life and a radical economic reform'.[1] Economic reform, so far, has made little headway beyond plans and proclamations. But reform of the Soviet political system has been advancing at an accelerating pace since the plenary meeting of the CPSU Central Committee in January 1987, and has already brought about what Gorbachev and others have described as the greatest advance in socialist democracy since the October Revolution itself.[2] Addressing the January plenum, Gorbachev made clear that economic reform was conceivable only in association with far-reaching changes in the political system. Control 'from above' would remain, and even be strengthened; but it was likely to prove effective only when combined with control 'from below', based upon the widest possible popular participation. There were still 'forbidden' subjects, officials who did their best to suppress criticism, and stagnation and corruption at leading levels of party and state. All of this, in Gorbachev's view, argued the need for a 'profound democratisation' of Soviet society, designed to ensure that ordinary people once again felt themselves to be masters of their own destinies.[3]

Gorbachev elaborated upon the reasons for these changes in subsequent speeches. Democratisation, he told the Soviet trade union congress in February 1987, was a 'guarantee against the repetition of past errors, and consequently a guarantee that the restructuring process is irreversible'. There was no choice – it was 'either democracy or social inertia and

[1] M.S. Gorbachev, *Izbrannye rechi i stat'i*, 6 vols. (Moscow, 1987–89), vol. 5, p. 411. The discussion that follows draws in part upon Stephen White, ' "Democratisation" in the USSR', *Soviet Studies*, vol. 42, No. 1 (January 1990), pp. 3–24, and Stephen White, *Gorbachev in Power* (Cambridge, 1990). For further discussion of the contemporary process of political reform, see for instance Michael E. Urban, *More Power to the Soviets* (Aldershot, 1990), and Elizabeth Teague and Dawn Mann, 'Gorbachev's dual role', *Problems of Communism*, vol. 39, No. 1 (January–February 1990), pp. 1–14.
[2] Gorbachev, *Izbrannye*, vol. 5, p. 411.
[3] *Materialy plenuma TsK KPSS 27–28 yanvarya 1987 goda* (Moscow, 1987), pp. 11–15, 24–25.

conservatism'.[4] The June 1987 Central Committee plenum agreed with his proposal that a party conference – the first for nearly 50 years – should be called in the summer of 1988 to consider further democratising measures. Addressing the conference, Gorbachev called for 'radical reform' of the Soviet political system, not just 'democratisation', and argued that it was 'crucial' to the solution of all the other problems that faced Soviet society. The political system established by the October Revolution, he maintained, had undergone 'serious distortions', leading to the development of 'administrative–command' rather than democratic forms of management. A massive bureaucratic apparatus had developed, which had begun to dictate its will in political as well as economic matters. Many millions of working people, elected to state and non-state bodies, had been 'removed from real participation in handling state and public affairs'. Public life had become unduly governmentalised, and ordinary working people had been 'alienated'. It was this 'ossified system of government' that was now the main obstacle to perestroika.[5]

The process of political reform has involved both a critique of the Stalinist past and an attempt to delineate the democratic socialist future. In 1986, responding to a question from *L'Humanité*, Gorbachev refused to accept that there could be such a phenomenon as Stalinism. But in 1987, in his speech on the 70th anniversary, there were references to the 'wanton repression' of the 1930s, and shortly afterwards a Politburo commission was set up which, by the spring of 1989, had already rehabilitated 47,000 victims of the purges.[6] The vision of the future has been much less clear; but broadly speaking, Gorbachev and the reformers have called for a new model of socialism, one that discloses the creative potential of the Soviet people and the socialist system, one that is centred on society rather than the state, and one that involves co-operation with societies elsewhere in the resolution of common problems. Central to the achievement of such a society is a political system that is responsive to its citizens, not simply to its rulers, and this in turn explains the priority that has been attached to political reform since at least the January 1987 plenum. What mechanisms of popular control have been developed over this period? And how do they relate to the Soviet political experience over the longer term, and to the delicate balance between Leninist direction 'from above' and popular control 'from below'?

Reforming the Political System

The political reforms that have now been agreed include, in the first place, an entirely new electoral law, approved on 1 December 1988.[7] The faults of the existing system were apparent not just to outside

[4]Gorbachev, *Izbrannye*, vol. 4, p. 31.
[5]*Materialy XIX Vsesoyuznoi konferentsii KPSS* (Moscow, 1988), pp. 35–37.
[6]*Pravda*, 26 September, 1989, p. 1.
[7]Text in *ibid.*, 4 December 1988, pp. 1–3.

observers but also, and increasingly, to Soviet citizens themselves. Most obviously, perhaps, there was no choice of candidate, still less of party or programme. At the last national elections under the old system, in March 1984, not even this degree of choice obtained, as one of the nominated candidates died just before the poll, leaving the remaining 1499 candidates to fight it out for the 1500 seats available.[8] The single slate of candidates was often all but entirely unknown to the electorate, not surprisingly as many of them had little connection with the constituency for which they had been nominated (in a survey of October 1988, for instance, only 5 per cent of those who were taking part in a by-election could even name the candidate).[9] Nor could this situation easily be remedied, as the right of nomination was reserved under the Constitution for the CPSU and other party-controlled organisations.

Voters could, in theory, delete the name of the single candidate, and at the local level there were occasional defeats of this kind in response to particularly unpopular nominations. Such a practice, however, was strongly discouraged by the need to make use of the screened-off booth for this purpose, and at the national level no candidate had ever been unsuccessful since the first elections under this system were held in 1937. The candidates, moreover, were chosen so that they conformed to certain centrally specified guidelines. This 'modelling' could be alarmingly precise. One local official, for instance, told *Izvestiya* what his 'programme' was in this respect: he was to ensure that 4.6 per cent of the successful candidates were enterprise directors, 1.1 per cent were to be employed in culture and the arts, and 45.9 per cent were to be returned for the first time.[10] In another instance, reported by an émigré source, a notorious prostitute had to be returned as she was the only person in the constituency who satisfied the relevant criteria: female, aged between 35 and 40, unmarried, and a factory worker.[11] If all this failed, the results were simply falsified: Stalin, in an early exercise, once secured a vote of over 100 per cent (voters in other constituencies, it was explained, had insisted on casting their votes in his favour),[12] and there was abundant evidence in more recent times of family members voting on each other's behalf and officials voting for anyone who seemed likely to 'spoil the percentages'.[13]

There had been expressions of dissatisfaction with these arrangements for some time and Gorbachev, in his speech to the twenty-seventh Party Congress in February 1986, promised that the 'necessary correctives' would be made. A limited experiment took place in the local elections

[8]See Stephen White, 'Noncompetitive elections and national politics: the USSR Supreme Soviet elections of 1984', *Electoral Studies*, vol. 4, No. 3 (1985), p. 222.
[9]*Moscow News*, 1989, No. 3, p. 8.
[10]*Izvestiya*, 10 February 1987, p. 2.
[11]Mark Ya. Azbel, *Refusenik* (Boston, 1981), p. 154.
[12]John Maynard, *The Russian Peasant*, 2 vols. (London, 1942), vol. 2, p. 438.
[13]For a fuller discussion of these and other matters, see Stephen White, 'Reforming the electoral system', in Walter Joyce *et al.*, *Gorbachev and Gorbachevism* (London, 1989), pp. 1–17.

in June 1987, by which more candidates were nominated than seats available in about 1 per cent of all constituencies,[14] and a new electoral law, published in draft in *Pravda* on 23 October and adopted in its final form on 1 December 1988, has since made these practices universal. The right to nominate has been extended to electors' meetings of 500 or more, and an unlimited number of candidates may be nominated. Deputies must 'as a rule' live or work in the area they represent, and they cannot hold governmental posts at the same time (how, it was asked, could ministerial deputies be expected to hold themselves to account?)[15] Candidates are now required to present a 'programme of their future activity' to the electorate, and have the right to appoint up to ten campaign staff to assist them. Electors, for their part, have to pass through a booth and must cast an 'active' rather than a 'passive' vote by marking the ballot paper in line with their preferences, unless (exceptionally) there is just a single candidate. The new law was to apply to all future elections, beginning with the national elections in March 1989; these, the Central Committee promised at its meeting in November 1988, would be 'unlike all those that had preceded them'.[16]

The Central Committee, in fact, can hardly have guessed how different the new electoral arrangements would prove to be. A whole series of party and state leaders were successfully returned, and there were some striking victories for individual first secretaries: the Tambov party secretary, for instance, won more than 90 per cent of the vote, and the first secretary in earthquake-stricken Spitak took more than 93 per cent. The proportion of party members among the new deputies was substantially higher than in the outgoing Supreme Soviet, and slightly higher even than the level of party membership among the candidates that had been nominated. Much more striking, however, were the defeats suffered by official candidates, even when there was no direct competitor. The prime ministers of Latvia and Lithuania were both defeated, and the mayors of Moscow and Kiev, and about 38 district and regional party officials. The most spectacular defeats were in Leningrad, where the list of casualties included the regional first secretary (a candidate Politburo member), the regional second secretary, the chairman of the city soviet and his deputy, the chairman of the regional soviet and the city party secretary.[17] Many party leaders, understandably, found that the heavy burdens of office prevented them from standing in the republican and local elections which took place in 1990.

The process of reform could scarcely limit itself to the electoral system: at least as important, the deputies that were elected would have to have a

[14]See *Ibid.*, and Jeffrey Hahn, 'An experiment in competition: the 1987 elections to the local soviets', *Slavic Review*, vol. 47, No. 2 (Fall, 1988), pp. 434–47.
[15]Boris Strashun in *Izvestiya*, 30 January, 1987, p. 3.
[16]*Pravda*, 29 November 1988, p. 1.
[17]For a general account, see Stephen White and Gordon Wightman, 'Gorbachev's reforms: the Soviet elections of 1989', *Parliamentary Affairs*, vol. 42, No. 4 (October 1989), p. 93.

meaningful role to perform. The old Supreme Soviet had met for three or four days a year, making it among the world's least frequently convened assemblies. Its members, all of them working on a part-time basis, had approved every proposal of the Soviet Government without a dissenting voice at least since 1955, when there was a single abstention.[18] The same was true at local levels. Nominally, under this system, all power belonged to the people themselves through the soviets of deputies to which they elected their representatives. In reality these arrangements meant the virtually unconstrained power of the apparatus, who served for lengthy periods of office with scarcely any need to defend their decisions or their personal integrity. The result, inevitably, was incompetence and inertia, and sometimes straightforward crime. Hardly less significant, the policies that emerged from such a system were often misconceived and wasteful. One of these misconceived decisions was the Baikal-Amur railway, a grandiose and politically inspired proposal which has never been justified by the volume of traffic it has generated. Another was the long-standing plan to divert the Siberian rivers (the same ministry, *Izvestiya* reported, had even made plans to irrigate the Sahara Desert).[19] The new objective was 'all power to the soviets', but this time in real rather than formal terms, so that state bodies would exercise the full range of powers with which they had nominally been invested.

The soviets, in Gorbachev's view, had served as the basis of a genuinely socialist democracy during the revolutionary years, but had then fallen victim to bureaucratisation and over-detailed regulation by party commit-tees. One of the problems was the often honorific character of the mem-bership of such bodies. In the 1984 Supreme Soviet, it was calculated, at least 39 per cent of the deputies owed their place to the official function they performed. These *ex officio* deputies, mostly party and state bureau-crats, were balanced by large numbers of manual workers, leaving very few deputies to represent the white collar professions. Would it be so bad if there were fewer milkmaids and party secretaries in the new Supreme Soviet, but rather more popular and articulate economists, historians, actors and writers?[20] Three jurists, Barabashev, Sheremet and Vasil'ev, pointed out that surveys had found low levels of satisfaction with the work of the soviets; and even deputies themselves appeared to be unsure of their own usefulness. They had access to legislation only in its final stages, sessions were far too brief, and even the plan and budget could scarcely be seriously considered.[21] According to Boris Kurashvili, writing in *Kommunist* in May 1988, nothing less than 'Soviet parliamentarianism' was needed, backed up by a separation of powers, a constitutional court and a system of smaller, full-time soviets staffed by salaried politicians.[22]

A number of these proposals found favour in Gorbachev's speech to

[18]Wolfgang Leonhad, *The Kremlin since Stalin* (London, 1965), p. 93.
[19]*Izvestiya*, 19 June, 1989, p. 5.
[20]*Ibid.*, 29 April 1988, p. 3.
[21]*Sovetskoe gosudarstvo i pravo*, 1988, No. 5, pp. 3–13.
[22]*Kommunist*, 1988, No. 8, pp. 28–36.

the nineteenth Party Conference a month later and were duly passed into law in the package of constitutional amendments that was approved by the Supreme Soviet in December 1988 after some weeks of public discussion. The reforms that were agreed included a Committee of Constitutional Supervision (not quite a court) to monitor the legality of government actions. Judges, it was established, were to be elected by higher-level soviets and would hold office for ten rather than five years at a time in order to strengthen their independence. Soviets at all levels would be elected for five-year terms rather than for two and a half years at a time so that their deputies could accumulate a little more experience; and government officials were to hold office for two five-year terms at the most, subject to recall at any time if those who elected them decided accordingly. Deputies themselves could serve on no more than two soviets at the same time. Much more controversially, the soviets were to be given chairmen, elected deputies who would also be the party leaders of the area in question; this would, for the first time, expose them to the indirect control of ordinary citizens.[23]

The centrepiece of the new changes, however, was undoubtedly the formation of an entirely new representative body, the Congress of People's Deputies, which was based in turn upon the Congresses of Soviets that had exercised legislative authority in the 1920s and 1930s. The Congress of People's Deputies was to be elected by the population at large in three different ways. Ordinary constituencies were to return 750 members, as they had done before, and national-territorial areas such as the union republics would continue to return a further 750 members. They would, however, be joined by a wholly new group of deputies, again 750 in number, who were to be elected by a wide range of nationally-based organisations, including the Communist Party, the trade unions, and women's councils. The Congress of People's Deputies, which was to meet at least annually, would in turn elect from among its members a working Supreme Soviet of 542, a fifth of whom would retire every year. The new Supreme Soviet would meet for two three or four-month sessions every year and its members would 'as a rule' carry out their duties on a full-time basis. The Congress was also to elect to an entirely new post, the Chairmanship of the USSR Supreme Soviet, which would normally be combined with the party leadership. In March 1990, after a rather perfunctory public debate, the new state structure was completed with the institution of an executive Presidency with wide-ranging powers including the nomination of leading public officials, a suspensory veto on legislation and the right to rule by decree.[24]

The representative institutions that emerged from this process of reform were certainly very different from the 'supreme state organs' that they replaced. The proportion of women and workers was down

---

[23]For the text, see *Pravda*, 3 December, 1988, pp. 1–2 (the last–mentioned proposal has not been implemented).
[24]For the text, see *Trud*, 16 March, 1990, pp. 2–3.

by about half, but there were many more figures from the academic and cultural world, and the first-ever religious leaders, rural leaseholders and commercial co-operators. Gorbachev, as expected, was elected to the chairmanship of the Supreme Soviet, but after two candidates had been nominated to stand against him and by a less than unanimous vote. There were attacks upon the leadership, the party-state apparatus and the KGB – this last for 'crimes unprecedented in the history of humanity'.[25] An elaborate committee system covered glasnost' and citizens' rights, and defence and state security. An organisational base, with a library and electronic services, came into existence in central Moscow (together with the expenses of deputies, the new Parliament was expected to cost about 40 million rubles a year to run, as compared with seven million a year for its predecessor).[26] Organised caucuses of deputies began to emerge, particularly the Inter-Regional Group, whose first meeting drew an audience of nearly 400.[27] Not less important, the new institutions of government attracted a massive public audience through radio and television: from 61 per cent (in Alma-Ata) to 92 per cent (in Tbilisi) claimed to be following the first Congress of People's Deputies 'constantly' or 'more or less constantly', and very large majorities thought it was operating 'completely' or 'more or less democratically'.[28]

The Communist Party has undergone a corresponding process of political reform, the substance of which was agreed at the nineteenth Party Conference in mid-1988. The central thrust of these changes was, as *Kommunist* put it in an editorial in January 1988, that there should be a kind of 'division of labour' in which the party would stand aside from direct management of the economy and exercise a much more general co-ordinating role.[29] The discussion that preceded the Conference saw very widespread support for changes of this kind. There were calls, for instance, for party officials to spend more time working with ordinary people and less time in their offices, and for more frequent conferences of this kind. The most widely supported proposals, however, concerned democratic change in the party's own organisation. There should, for instance, be a choice of candidate at all elections to party office, and positions of this kind should be held for a limited period. There might even be age limits, such as 65 for Politburo and Secretariat members. More should be known about the party's finances. And there should be changes in the party's bureaucracy: it should be smaller, and less obviously duplicate the ministerial hierarchy.[30]

Most of these themes found a place in Gorbachev's speech to the Party Conference on 28 June, 1988. Democratic centralism within the party, he

[25]*Pravda*, 2 June, 1989, pp. 3–4.
[26]*Soviet Weekly*, 12 August, 1989, p. 4.
[27]*Pravda*, 31 July, 1989, p. 2.
[28]*Izvestiya*, 29 May, 1989, p. 8.
[29]*Kommunist* No. 1, 1988, p. 6.
[30]For this discussion, see Stephen White, 'Gorbachev, Gorbachevism and the Party Conference', in Joyce *et al.* (eds.), *Gorbachev and Gorbachevism*, pp. 132–6.

complained, had become bureaucratic centralism. The rank and file had lost control over the leadership that spoke in their name; an atmosphere of comradeship had been replaced by one of commands and instructions. The Conference agreed with his suggestion that the Party's whole existing membership should be reaccredited, so that the unworthy and inactive should be removed from its ranks. A less 'bureaucratic' approach to membership was to be adopted, with more emphasis being placed upon the personal qualities of new recruits than upon their social background. Central Committee members, it was agreed, must also be involved in a more regular way in the work of the leadership, and the rank and file more generally in the work of the leadership at all levels. Party officials, moreover, like their state counterparts, were to be elected by secret ballot from a choice of candidates, and were to hold office for no more than two five-year terms in a row. There was an eloquent plea to make an exception to this rule in Gorbachev's case; others, however, pointed out that exceptions, under Soviet conditions, inevitably became the rule, and Georgii Arbatov added that if such a provision had existed in earlier years, Stalin would have had to retire in 1934 (before the murder of Kirov) and Brezhnev in 1974, some time before he became decrepit.[31]

These changes, again, have become at least a partial reality. Six new commissions, for instance, were established under the auspices of the Central Committee in the autumn of 1988. Each of them headed by a senior member of the leadership, they were intended, at least in principle, to involve a wider party élite in the processes of Politburo decision-making.[32] The party apparatus was slimmed down from 20 to just nine departments, losing about a third of its staff in the process.[33] Much more information became available about the party's operations, not least for the benefit of its own members. The Party's finances, for instance, began to be reported in some detail (speakers at the Party Conference had complained that they knew more about the income of the British royal family than about the finances of their own party). The Central Committee journal *Izvestiya TsK* reappeared in 1989, covering all kinds of matters from unpublished Leniniana to the number of Eskimos that were party members.[34] The new party rules, adopted at the twenty-eighth Congress in 1990, extended these changes still further: party branches, for instance, have received a greater degree of independence, and a Control Commission, elected by the congress, restored the practice of the 1920s by which a body of this kind provided a continuing check on behalf of the membership over the actions of the central leadership.[35]

Finally and perhaps most fundamentally, the process of political reform has involved a reassertion of the rule of law in Soviet society, and more

[31]*Ibid.*, pp. 152–53.
[32]*Pravda*, 1 October, 1988, p. 1.
[33]*Izvestiya TsK KPSS*, No. 1, 1989, pp. 81–91.
[34]*Ibid.*, No. 7, p. 113.
[35]Onikov, in *Pravda*, 2 May, 1990, p. 3; for the new party statute, see *ibid.*, 18 July, 1990, pp. 1–2.

generally a greater place for political activity initiated by citizens rather than the state itself. Gorbachev, a lawyer by academic training, told interviewers from *Der Spiegel* that perestroika was as much a 'legal revolution' as a reform of the political system as such.[36] The changes that were involved centred around the concept of the 'socialist law-based state', first mentioned by Gorbachev at a meeting with media workers in May 1988 and later the centrepiece of a resolution on legal reform adopted at the nineteenth Party Conference. This called for 'large-scale legal reform' over the coming years, including a review of existing codes of law, greater safeguards for the independence of judges, and an extensive programme of legal education for the population at large.[37] Criminal and court reform took place during 1989, and Soviet penal and psychiatric institutions were opened to outside observers. Gorbachev's principle was that everything that was not prohibited by law should be allowed; recommending the changes in the Constitution that took place at the end of 1988, he argued that they represented a distinctive 'socialist system of checks and balances', protecting society at large from the abuse of power by those who held the highest executive offices of state.[38] It was certainly the most sustained attempt that has yet been made to institute a Soviet-style government of laws rather than men.

Leninism, 'socialist pluralism' and democracy

It must obviously be premature to judge a political system that is still under construction, with many laws still to be agreed, and with a commission at work drafting an entirely new constitution. Formal legislation may in any case be beside the point; for many reformers there can be no alternative to the slow process of 'learning democracy', developing a civic culture that can sustain processes of bargaining and accommodation rather than commands backed up by coercion. The evidence that is available suggests that the process of habituation to democratic norms has still some distance to travel.[39] Kurashvili, among Soviet reformers, has suggested that the transition from a harshly authoritarian to a democratic-authoritarian regime may take at least 10–15 years; a group of specialists at the Institute of State and Law has pointed out that the formation of the rule of law in capitalist countries had taken 'hundreds of years' and doubted if that period could be significantly reduced under Soviet conditions.[40] The evidence nonetheless suggests that a political order had developed in the Gorbachev years which was an uneasy amalgam of two conflicting principles: Leninism, or rule from above, which was what

[36]*Pravda*, 24 October, 1988, p. 2.
[37]*Materialy XIX konferentsii*, pp. 145–48.
[38]*Pravda*, 30 November, 1988, p. 3.
[39]See, for instance, the survey data reported in *Rabochii klass i sovremennyi mir*, No. 2, 1990, pp. 75–87.
[40]*Sotsiologicheskie issledovaniya*, No. 5, 1988, p. 11; *Pravda*, 2 August, 1988, p. 1.

the regime had been based upon since its inception, and democracy, or rule from below, which was the principle that animated the Gorbachev reforms and that had animated the Khrushchev reforms some years earlier.

The tension between these two principles was apparent in many ways. Voters, for instance, could reject party officials, but not (as yet) effect a change of regime. Deputies, reflecting the wishes of their electors, could resist unpopular policies such as a reduction in the subsidies on food, but, elected as individuals, could hardly put forward an alternative programme of government. The new representative system, with its inclusion of a range of organised interests, lent itself to the articulation of grievances rather than solutions. Tensions of this kind went back to the revolution itself, in which power had been taken in the name of the soviets but in fact by a small and organised Bolshevik minority. Article 2, in the 1977 Constitution, embodied the first of these principles with its references to popular sovereignty; but Article 6, until its reformulation in March 1990, embodied the rival principle of party monopoly. The tension between these two principles led to all kinds of questions, particularly after the 1989 elections had led to the defeat of so many of the party's official representatives. Why, it was argued, should the Communist Party have any guaranteed seats in the Congress of People's Deputies? Why should it have 100, when its numbers were so much smaller than the trade unions, which also had 100? And what was the relationship between the newly elected Congress and the CPSU: was the party subordinate to the Congress, or the Congress to the party?

The tension between these two principles, indeed, began to generate more than questions in the late 1980s and early 1990s. Deputies, for instance, began to reject the nominations to ministerial positions that were offered to them. At least ten of Ryzhkov's original list were voted down, and some positions (such as that of Minister of Culture) remained unfilled for months. Where did this leave the party's vital power of *nomenklatura*, or the right to fill such key positions? And how could it control the actions of officials when increasing numbers were outside the party's ranks and thus outside its disciplinary reach? There were conflicts on policy, with deputies, mandated to increase social spending and resist higher prices, voting extra funds for their constituents but refusing to accept the increase in prices that would be necessary to pay for measures of this kind. The bill on social security, for instance, approved in 1990, was amended by deputies so as to include a further 46 billion rubles of expenditure.[41] This increased the planned budget deficit by 76 per cent, but why should deputies worry when reconciling the priorities of government was someone else's responsibility? There were conflicts about the nature of the state itself, as nationalists in the Baltic and elsewhere secured a popular mandate to press for greater independence and even separation. The party leadership, armed with

[41]*Economist*, 19–25 May, 1990, p. 64.

the much less impressive mandate of history, had no alternative but to concede at least the principle of their demands.

This was, arguably, the tension upon which the Communist Party itself began to founder in the late 1980s and early 1990s. Having monopolised power throughout the Soviet period, the party monopolised the blame for the excesses it had belatedly acknowledged. As economic and other difficulties mounted, the party began to doubt its ability to guide the whole life of the society as it had done in the recent past. Some party members went on strike and rose to prominence in the popular fronts; others opposed them and called for discipline and central control. Members began to resign in significant numbers, the circulation of party papers began to fall and full time posts in the apparatus became increasingly difficult to fill. Factions began to develop, openly so after the twenty-eighth Congress, with as many as eight different groupings – including the 'silent majority' – identified in party writings.[42] The Party's standing in the wider society began to decline, and fewer and fewer professed to see an answer to the society's problems in the teachings of Marxism–Leninism. The biggest shortage of all, the Central Committee was told, was the 'deficit of trust' in the Party itself.[43] And this reflected a party that had begun to doubt its right to rule, perhaps even its ability to rule, in a society in which a wide range of other forces were appealing for public support.

The changes of early 1990, and the abandonment of the leading role in particular, represented the logical completion of these developments. There was virtually no opposition, within the Central Committee, to the abandonment of the party's monopoly; as Gorbachev pointed out in his opening speech, that monopoly had in fact already disappeared. A wide range of political forces had come into existence and could not be wished away; all the party could do was to recognise that reality and hope to retain a leadership position, co-operating with those 'healthy forces' that recognised the Constitution and the social order it embodied.[44] The aim, once again, was to reconcile Leninism and popular sovereignty, retaining party leadership but securing it by democratic consent. The outcome, in fact, was likely to be rather different: a demoralised and fragmented party losing its majority at the polls as most of its counterparts had done already in Eastern Europe. Reformers had called for 'socialist pluralist democracy under single-party conditions';[45] the experience of the Gorbachev years had shown how difficult it was to combine these various elements, and how little support remained for the Leninist alternative to democracy to which successive Soviet governments had been committed for more than 70 years.

---

[42]*Politicheskoe obrazovanie*, No. 18, 1989, p. 11 (I owe this reference to Ronald J. Hill).
[43]*Pravda*, 9 February, 1990, p. 2.
[44]*Ibid.*, 6 February, 1990, p. 1.
[45]Burlatsky, in *Moskovskaya pravda*, 23 September, 1989, p. 3.

2

Perestroika and political pluralism: past and prospects

Catherine Merridale

Historical perspectives have a special attraction for people who study Russia and the Soviet Union. Perhaps it is something about the grandeur of Russia – or the introspection of its intellectuals – that provokes even the most phlegmatic writers to speculate expansively about the whole sweep of Russian history from the Golden Horde to Gorbachev. Observers of a right-wing (or Slavophile) persuasion have always stressed Russia's uniqueness.[1] Left-wingers have used the excuse of Russia's past to explain why Marxism in the Soviet Union ended up as Stalinist dictatorship.[2] Confronted with a new reformer in the late 1980s, political scientists and historians again looked backwards in order to make sense of the present.[3] Gorbachev, however, made everything more difficult. The faster perestroika gathered pace, the less retrospection seemed to offer to its analysts. Indeed, by 1990, many of them had decided that the past, as far as the USSR was concerned, was definitely over.

But the past has continued to exert an influence in Soviet political life. For several years, indeed, history has been a cornerstone of glasnost'. The discussion of Stalinism, and latterly, of Leninism, has been important in itself ('we must have no more blank pages') and as an explanation for the current crisis of socialism in the USSR. History is a reference point for many of the USSR's reformers. It is also used as a grim example by those who fear that little can be done to avert another crisis. A pessimist, the joke goes in Moscow, is an optimist with a sense of history.[4] The past is not over, but its place in the analysis of current politics is unclear. In this paper I shall examine democratisation and the issues surrounding

[1]'The landscape of the Russian soul', wrote Nicolas Berdyaev, 'corresponds with the landscape of Russia, the same boundlessness, formlessness, reaching out into infinity, breadth.' *The Origin of Russian Communism* (1937), p. 3.
[2]As Feodor Burlatskii put it in 1988, 'Stalin borrowed two-thirds of his concepts about the grandeur of the state in our country, and the role of the leader, from the previous experience of Russia, and certainly not from Marxist sources.' Cited in R.W. Davies, *Soviet History in the Gorbachev Revolution* (London, 1989), p. 19.
[3]For some examples, see Robert O. Crummey (ed.), *Reform in Russia and the USSR: Past and Prospects* (Urbana and Chicago, 1989).
[4]Cited by Jonathan Steele, *The Guardian*, 28 August, 1987.

it – such as political pluralism and the concept of opposition – from the perspective of Soviet history. I shall argue that perestroika has no historical precedent. But the historical context in which current changes are often perceived, especially in the USSR, may nonetheless affect their outcome, and if it does, it is unlikely to do so in a beneficial way.

It is worth beginning with a reminder of how reform in Russia has often been viewed. Historians of Russia have favoured the theme of 'revolution from above'.[5] As Antonio Gramsci wrote,'In Russia, the state was everything, civil society was primordial and gelatinous'.[6] The model suggests that a straight line can be drawn between Ivan the Terrible, Peter the Great and Stalin. Strong leaders, usually impelled by their consciousness of Russia's relative backwardness, have been seen as painfully dragging the Russian people out of their accustomed world of mud and cockroaches, from the idiocy of rural life to the higher civilisation of the modern city.[7] Stalin himself seems to have been attracted by this idea. Eisenstein's film of Ivan the Terrible and Alexei Tolstoy's biography of Peter the Great underlined the continuities for all to see.

At least until the death of Stalin, post-revolutionary Soviet history fitted this scheme comfortably. The development of civil society, and with it, some form of public political life, seemed weaker than it had before the revolution. Adherents of the *plus ça change*, theory of Russian history attributed a good deal of this to the weak society-strong state pattern. And Leninism added another dimension to the original model. The strong state was now buttressed, if not superseded, by a 'guiding' party, which, in a society dedicated to the building of Communism, possessed, at least theoretically, the architects' drawings and the building expertise necessary to see it completed sooner rather than later. If Communist construction was desirable, and the party was the guiding force overseeing it, other parties could only be counter-productive.[8]

It is easy to see how this might lead to the rejection of factions within the ruling party. Leninists would argue that opposition was time-wasting, and that in conditions of capitalist encirclement and the deepening class-struggle, the Soviet Union had no time to spare. The multi-party system of 1917 was replaced by a Bolshevik monopoly. In 1921 factions within the ruling party were outlawed. By 1927 the very word 'opposition' had acquired a sinister overtone. Bolshevik dissidents like Bukharin refused

[5]For a recent exposition of the theory, see Vladimir Glotov's interview with Natan Eidelman, *Ogonek*, October 1988, No. 44, pp. 3–4.

[6]A. Gramsci, *Selections from the Prison Notebooks*, G. Hoare and G. Nowell Smith (eds.), (London, 1971), p. 238. According to Klyuchevsky, 'The state expands, the people grow sickly'. Cited in Berdyaev, *op. cit.*, p. 3.

[7]'In Russia', according to Boris Kagarlitsky, 'the ruling strata are always trying to impose some kind of western-style development, while the population is always resisting it, either actively or passively.' Interview in *New Statesman and Society*, 10 November, 1989.

[8]This view of the Communist Party's position is one of the themes developed by 'Z' in his polemic 'To the Stalin Mausoleum', *Daedalus*, vol. 119, No. 1 (Winter, 1990), pp. 295–340.

to allow the term to be applied to themselves, and went to considerable lengths to repel the charge of 'factionalism'.[9] Over the next four years, well before the Stalinist purges of the late 1930s, the idea of 'wreckers', 'enemies of the people' and even 'opposition centres' had taken a hold on the popular imagination.[10] There was less and less perceived difference between opposition and treason.

In its purest form, the weak society-strong state model combined with the image of the monopolistic ruling party to produce the totalitarian theory of Soviet politics. The image of the all-powerful, monolithic state and its atomised citizenry was a compelling one, and, applied to Stalinism, appeared satisfactory to most historians and political scientists until the 1950s. Even when the Stalinist system began to crumble (and the totalitarian thesis to lose its hold on scholarly imaginations), the evidence suggested that Soviet society was unlikely to be capable of autonomous political action. A number of social or religious organisations survived, especially in the national republics, but the possibility for applying sustained political pressure from outside the state or party structures was negligible.[11] When public discontent occasionally erupted on to the streets, most notably at Novocherkassk in 1962, the power of the centralised state to quell popular protest was clearly demonstrated. Some political scientists and sociologists argued that reform would have to come sooner or later, but their critics could argue with some justice that this was merely wishful thinking.[12]

These were some of the ways in which the continuities in Soviet history were understood until very recently. Gorbachev, at least initially, could be made to fit the model. His programme began as a revolution – or, at least initially, a reform package – from above. And many early elements of perestroika bore a close resemblance to previous phases in the party's history. Calls to breathe new life into existing party structures, and even to 'revitalise the Soviets', have been heard repeatedly since the Civil War.[13] Attacks on 'bureaucratism' recur from the 1920s onwards, and historically have often preceded campaigns of state-directed purging and its corollary, the crushing of opposition.[14] Observers who wished to conclude that Gorbachev was predestined to reproduce the dictatorial

[9]In his speech to the Central Committee Plenum on 18 April, 1929, Bukharin told his colleagues that 'Not one of us [the so-called 'Right'] will lead any kind of "new" or "newest" opposition'. *N.I. Bukharin, Problemy, teorii i praktiki sotsializma* (Moscow, 1989).

[10]See Catherine Merridale, *Moscow Politics and the Rise of Stalin*, (London, 1990), pp. 225–26.

[11]As a result, political scientists have preferred to classify Soviet society as 'institutional pluralist' or 'corporatist' rather than simply 'pluralist'.

[12]With characteristic vigour,' 'Z' accused 'mainline Sovietology' of rendering the 'extraordinary, indeed surreal, Soviet experience . . . banal to the point of triviality', *op. cit.*, p. 298.

[13]On the Soviets, see E.H. Carr, *Socialism in One Country, 1924–1926*, vol. 2, chapter 22 ('Revitalising the Soviets').

[14]See Mary McAuley,' 'Soviet Political Reform in a Comparative Context', *The Harriman Institute Forum*, vol. 2, No. 10, October 1989.

political structures of his predecessors could do so on fairly firm historical ground.[15] But the speed with which perestroika overtook the initial
predictions of its critics cast doubts on the validity of their assumptions.
People began to recall that Russian history had not in fact been an unin-
terrupted tale of society's total subordination to the state. One different
precedent – to which Gorbachev himself appealed – was the 1920s, the
period of the New Economic Policy, when Communist Party rule coin-
cided with the wide discussion of social issues, with economic and artistic
pluralism and, at least in Soviet terms, with short periods of relative
prosperity.[16]

The NEP period, moreover, was not the only time when Soviet citizens
exercised political initiative on a local scale. Those who interpret Russian
history as a record of enserfment for the people and absolute power for
the state ignore (or dismiss[17]) the evidence of decades of careful archival
research. They pass over the Revolution itself, with its spontaneously-
organised local soviets, citizens' militias, peasant self-organisation and
burgeoning local democracy. But the revolutionary period provides stun-
ning evidence of the speed with which tradition can be overturned in
moments of crisis. More controversial, but not lightly to be discounted,
is the debate about Soviet society after 1928. Many historians would now
argue that society in the Stalin era was more resilient than was once
imagined. The Stalinist state was obviously powerful, and inflicted great
suffering on many of its citizens. But society was not completely 'broken';
the persuasive image of 'large-scale theories versus small-scale realities'
applied to many aspects of Stalin's Russia.[18] The average Russian's deal-
ings with the central authorities involved a certain amount of cynicism
on both sides. Despite draconian laws for the punishment of deviance
and indiscipline, relations between central and local government were
complicated, with official directives ignored as often as they were implemented. Communism, moreover, was the religion of the elect. While
the majority of the population may have accepted much of the rhetoric
about 'enemies' and the danger of opposition, and may have mouthed the
familiar Stalinist slogans, it remained outside the party and the Communist belief system.[19] The Great Patriotic War, at least retrospectively, may
have strengthened the Communist Party's legitimacy, as, undoubtedly,

---

[15]For example, Walter Laquer, who devoted a whole book, *The Long Road to Freedom*, to
developing this theme, unwisely concluding (in 1989) that 'there is reason to believe that
the glasnost' era has reached its climax'.

[16]The significance of his reference to the re-introduction of 'something like a prodnalog' is
discussed in R.W. Davies, *Soviet History and the Gorbachev Revolution*, p. 49. See also
the discussion of Feodor Burlatsky's 1987 play, 'Political Testament', *ibid.*, pp. 34–36.

[17]For an example, see' 'Z', *op. cit.*, especially pp. 301–19.

[18]The phrase is Roger Pethybridge's (*The Social Prelude to Stalinism*, London, 1974), and
was originally applied to the 1920s. Evidence for the continuing tension between centre
and localities can be found even in the work of 'totalitarian' theorists such as Merle
Fainsod. See, for example, *Smolensk under Soviet Rule* (1958; reprinted Boston, 1989),
especially chapter 6.

[19]Merridale, *op. cit*, chapter 7 ('Political Education; Agitation and Propaganda').

did the mere passage of time. But no generation in the Soviet Union has fully subscribed to the Marxism–Leninism of Party textbooks.[20]

All this suggests that, at the very least, the assertion that 'too much freedom makes many Russians feel uncomfortable'[21] rests on a one-sided interpretation of history. At the same time, however, it is clear that perestroika has broken new ground. As the reforms gathered pace in the late 1980s, historical comparisons became less and less useful. That with NEP was of very limited value; there were no organised opposition parties in the 1920s and little public support for the various factions within the ruling party itself. Even the pre-revolutionary past was not really helpful. Gorbachev was not Stolypin,[22] the Congress of People's Deputies was not a Duma. There were – and remain – some parallels with 1917, which I shall discuss later, but even here the comparison does not bear close examination. There is little to be gained from ransacking the past for parallels to perestroika. The point needs to be made, because Russia's authoritarian past continues to throw a shadow forwards. It still influences the way in which some Soviet analysts discuss their country's future, and it clearly affects Western calculations about the reformability of the USSR.

One needs only an elementary sense of change over time to see how profoundly different the Soviet Union is now from the state bequeathed by Stalin. It is clear from the most superficial analysis that Gorbachev has not been reforming the Stalinist system, or even taking up the torch so brusquely knocked from Khrushchev's sturdy fists. Soviet politicians and publicists have occasionally obscured this fact. The revival or rediscovery of plays and novels written during the Khrushchev period contributed to the sense of continuity with previous periods of thaw. And it is true that most of perestroika's protagonists began their careers during the reforming late 1950s and early 1960s.[23] But they were changed by their experience over three decades, and the society which they were trying to reform was not the same as it had been thirty years before. Fundamental changes had been under way. Among the most striking were rapid urbanisation and mass literacy,[24] to which might be added increasing access to western ideas. These developments had been in gestation since the 1930s. Rapid social change characterised even Brezhnev's era of 'stagnation'. Further shocks are likely in the wake of computer and other communication technology. All this, as Moshe Lewin put it, must 'point to something deeper in the making'.[25] What that 'something' is, however, remains a controversial question.

[20]Donna Bahry, 'Politics, generations, and change in the USSR', in James R. Millar (ed.), *Politics, Work and Daily Life in the USSR* (Cambridge, Mass., 1987), pp. 61–99.
[21]Laqueur, *op. cit*, p. 8.
[22]Orlando Figes, writing in *The Guardian*, 23 December, 1989.
[23]Gorbachev himself represents this generation, as do Ryzhkov, Shevardnadze, and indeed Yeltsin.
[24]See Moshe Lewin, *The Gorbachev Phenomenon*, (London, 1988).
[25]*Op. cit*, p. 2.

There is, of course, at least one simple answer. Stephen White, writing in the 1970s, referred to it as 'the iron law of pluralism'.[26] His quotation from R.A. Dahl's *Polyarchy* sums up the idea. 'Because of its inherent requirements', Dahl wrote, 'an advanced economy and its supporting social structures automatically distribute political resources and political skills to a vast variety of individuals, groups and organisations'.[27] The conclusion to be drawn was that 'modernisation' in Communist states was bound, sooner or later, to threaten the hegemony of their ruling parties. This argument was made repeatedly in the 1970s by the numerous political scientists who scanned the Communist regimes of Eastern Europe for signs of potential liberalisation.[28] At the same time pluralism and modernisation were also being linked by dissidents like Andrei Sakharov, Roy Medvedev and Valentin Turchin. These three wrote a collective letter to Brezhnev, Kosygin and Podgorny at the end of the 1960s which called for many of the reforms Gorbachev subsequently put into operation. They stated that:

> 'there is an urgent need to carry out a series of measures directed toward the further democratization of our country's political life. This need stems, in particular, from the very close connection between the problem of economic and technological progress and scientific methods of management, on the one hand, and the problem of freedom of information, the open airing of views, and the free clash of ideas, on the other'.[29]

Pluralism fell out of fashion as a concept in the late 1970s, and until recently Western political scientists were wary of applying it to the USSR.[30] But the idea that a broadening of democracy must be inextricably linked to economic and social development revived in the late 1980s.[31] While the Soviet leadership saw democratisation and greater openness as essential preconditions for economic success, Western observers saw the modernisation that had already taken place as the motor behind political change. The idea was an attractive one for all concerned, and was not incompatible with the view of Russian history that we have examined. Civil society was no longer 'gelatinous',

---

[26]S. White, 'Communist Systems and the "Iron Law of Pluralism"', *British Journal of Political Science*, No. 8, January 1978, pp. 101–17.

[27]*Ibid*, p. 103.

[28]See, for example, Barbara Wolfe Jancar, 'Modernity and the Character of Dissent', in Charles Gati (ed.), *The Politics of Modernisation in Eastern Europe* (New York, 1974).

[29]'A Reformist Program for Democratization', reprinted from the samizdat *Political Diary* (March, 1970), in S. Cohen (ed.), *An End to Silence* (New York, 1982), p. 318.

[30]The debate is discussed by Susan Solomon in her contribution to the essays in honour of H. Gordon Skilling which she edited under the title *Pluralism in the Soviet Union* (New York and Cambridge, 1983).

[31]Among the many re-statements of the view, variously modulated, are Moshe Lewin, *The Gorbachev Phenomenon* (1987); Gail W. Lapidus, 'Gorbachev and the Reform of the Soviet System', *Daedalus*, vol. 116, No. 2 (Spring, 1987), especially pp. 6–7; and David Lane, *Soviet Society Under Perestroika* (Boston, 1990).

so political change was indicated. Khrushchev and Kosygin were the harbingers of this change, Andropov the grandfather of perestroika. Chernenko was merely a figurehead, appointed to maintain the appearance of continuity while Gorbachev eased himself into power behind the scenes.[32]

There was obviously a good deal of sense in this. The increasing complexity of society had created new constituencies and demands, and the social pressures generated under Brezhnev would probably have found an outlet of some kind sooner or later. Evidence collected in the last twenty years suggested, moreover, that the better educated Soviet citizens became, the more likely they were to be dissatisfied with the regime.[33] Social change was also a precondition for much of Gorbachev's reform. Glasnost' could not work without mass literacy, and indeed widespread secondary education.[34] Multi-party elections required an abundance of candidates, most of whom have so far been drawn from among better-educated urban-dwellers.[35] But at the same time, this should not be taken to mean that perestroika was inevitable. Gorbachev was not somehow generated by the social context. And figures for urban development, higher education and newspaper circulation did not necessarily indicate that perestroika was destined to succeed. Caution on this issue might have been suggested by the example of countries like Brazil and South Korea, whose economic growth and urban development have neither required nor caused the establishment of western-style democracy.

The main attraction of the idea that economic growth and political pluralism were linked was that it appeared to assure the eventual victory of democracy in the USSR, an outcome which many Western (and indeed Soviet) commentators would still welcome. If the Soviet Union's development could not guarantee the passage from authoritarian rule to democracy, the prospects for perestroika appeared bleaker. But there has never been anything to be gained from insisting that democratisation was moving in synchrony with what we hoped were the progressive forces of Soviet modernisation. The situation has always been more unstable than that. In the first place, the social undercurrents of perestroika have been more complicated than 'modernisation' theory allows. Ethnic and religious conflicts, for example, do not necessarily fit the pattern. Despite

[32]Martin Walker, *The Waking Giant*, (New York, 1986), p. 108.
[33]See Brian D. Silver, 'Political beliefs of the Soviet citizen: Sources of support for regime norms', in James R. Millar, *op. cit.*, especially pp. 116–32.
[34]According to Lakshin, a former member of its editorial board, the circulation of the 'thick' journal *Novyi Mir*, a standard-bearer for glasnost', had increased from 30,000 in the 1920s and 130,000 in the 1960s to 2,600,000 in 1990 Seminar at King's College, Cambridge, 29 May, 1990.
[35]Of 543 members of the USSR Supreme Soviet in 1990, 384 had higher education and 374 were white-collar workers. 442 were men. *Argumenty i fakty*, 27 January, 1990. See also Dawn Mann, 'The RSFSR Elections: The Congress of People's Deputies', Radio Liberty, *Report on the USSR*, 13 April, 1990, pp. 11–17.

the social and technological changes of the last three decades, democratisation remains only one of a range of possible political outcomes of the Soviet Union's present crisis.

Viewed from this perspective, it is true, the achievements of perestroika come to seem more impressive. For democratisation was neither simply another reform imposed from above, nor a 'natural' outgrowth of social and economic change. Each of its achievements was the subject of intense debate. Significantly, too, this debate was confined neither to the leadership nor even to the better-educated section of the population. The majority of the Soviet people was involved at some level in deciding the country's future. Moreover, the process involved the fundamental re-assessment of political practices and assumptions. Many of the traditional buttresses of one-party rule were destroyed, and in the confusion accompanying the collapse of the old system there were signs that new structures might have a chance to grow.

The weight of political habit and vested interest that had to be shifted was colossal. One feature of the 'era of stagnation' was its apparent stability. Some Western political scientists chose to talk of a 'social contract' between leaders and led, a contract which appeared to be accommodating the social changes of the 1970s successfully.[36] Although people's commitment to Marxism as an ideology and to Communism as a political system was weak,[37] even the emigrés interviewed in the USA in the 1950s and 1980s believed that the Soviet regime offered a better, fairer and more progressive system of social security and a more equitable means of economic distribution than capitalism.[38] It was all the more impressive, then, that only five years after Gorbachev came to power, Communism had become an irrelevance for most Soviet citizens,[39] and the Communist Party was having to struggle in many areas (and had already lost the fight in some) to retain its political supremacy. It was even possible to contemplate the abandonment of some central aspects of the Brezhnevite 'social contract'. In the spring of 1990 the extent of approval for reform of the property laws and an extension of private enterprise was greater even than some of Gorbachev's advisers imagined. According to Tatiana Zaslavskaya, up to 70 per cent of Soviet people favoured small-scale private property in March 1990, while 87 per cent believed that the peasants

---

[36]G. Breslauer, 'On the adaptability of welfare-state authoritarianism in the USSR', in Karl Ryavec (ed.), *Soviet Society and the Communist Party* (New York, 1979), pp. 3–25.

[37]According to Stephen White, 'The Soviet authorities have so far failed to bring about a commitment to Marxist-Leninist values among their population which would be sufficient in itself to legitimate their rule, whatever its constitutional standing, economic performance and so forth', *Political Culture and Soviet Politics* (London, 1979), p. 142.

[38]This was the conclusion offered by Alex Inkeles and Raymond A. Bauer in their emigré survey of the 1950s, *The Soviet Citizen, Daily Life in a Totalitarian Society* (Cambridge, Mass., 1959). For more recent material, see Silver, *op. cit.*

[39]According to a member of the Communist Party's Democratic Platform, a poll conducted by the Institute of Marxism-Leninism and the Moscow Higher Party School showed that only 2.3 per cent of Soviet citizens, and only 4.8 per cent of Communist Party members, linked the future of mankind to Communism, *Pravda*, 3 March, 1990.

should be given land.[40] The other side of these reforms, of course, including higher prices for food and other basic commodities and services, had yet to win support on this scale.[41]

To some extent the divisions in public opinion followed the boundaries between social groups. It was the scientific-technical intelligentsia (and the growing army of small entrepreneurs[42]) which supported the broadly social– or liberal–democratic reform options. Many manual workers in traditional 'rust-belt' industries (exceptions included the Donbass coalminers) held what have been described as 'right-wing populist' opinions, combining an attachment to traditional Soviet forms of social security and price control with a strong hostility to bureaucratism (partly expressed in support for anti-corruption campaigns) and distrust of the intelligentsia.[43] They were also the principal social base of conservative groups like the United Front of Workers, whose sponsors included cautious or even anti-reform politicians such as Ligachev and Gidaspov.[44] But these social generalisations were not always reliable. Nina Andreeva, for example, a leading light in the United Front of Workers and the author of several open letters critical of perestroika, is a representative of the scientific-technical intelligentsia[45]. Mineworkers in the Ukraine and Siberia were not liberal democrats, but they were not supporters of the party conservatives either. Moreover, the pace of change forced even the most radical groups to adjust to new and unpredictable circumstances.

The political process was not only to a significant degree autonomous, by the spring of 1990 it even appeared to be uncontrollable. No-one could claim that multi-party democracy was planned from the outset. Until 1989, indeed, there was little open pressure for the abandonment of one-party rule, and a good deal of opposition to the extension

[40]Zaslavskaya gave a paper on public opinion polling at Trinity College, Cambridge on 2 March, 1990. According to her, economists like Abalkin were so surprised by this finding that they asked for the survey to be repeated as a double check.

[41]*Moscow News*, No. 6, 6–12 July, 1990.

[42]According to the co-operators' own statistics, there were over 4 million people working in co-operatives in the USSR by the beginning of 1990. This figure was quoted by Academician Tikhonov in a letter to Gorbachev, published in the co-operators' paper, *Kommersant*, No. 8, February 1990.

[43]*Argumenty i fakty* 1990, No. 7, 17–23 February (research conducted in December, 1989).

[44]The United Front of Workers held its first national congress in September 1989. It originated several months earlier in Leningrad. Among its early claims was the statement that industrial workers were under-represented in the Congress of People's Deputies (their representation has indeed fallen under the new voting legislation). It wanted changes in the electoral system (election at the workplace rather than by district) to reverse this process. Reports from the summer of 1989 indicated its close links with Leningrad conservative politicians. Radio Liberty, *Report on the USSR*, July 21, 1989, p. 49.

[45]See, in particular, her letter, 'I cannot forego my principles', *Sovetskaya Rossiya*, 13 March 1988.

of democracy.[46] People were not sure how to respond to the first multi-candidate elections. To many, 'democratisation' appeared in 1987–88 to be simply another slogan, like the 'self-criticism' of the 1920s, which would turn out to have a specific meaning in the Soviet context. The conservative press attacked the idea of 'opposition', reviving the argument that it diverted precious energy from the tasks facing the Soviet people.[47] Local party officials awaited instructions. 'Informal' political groups adopted a very cautious line. It was several years before they began to take the initiative. The watershed, in fact, was probably the election of the USSR Congress of People's Deputies in 1989. The increase in popular political activity was apparent from the moment candidates began to offer themselves for selection, and was sustained throughout the televised debates which gripped the Soviet public night after night in the summer of 1989. The rapid adaptation of Soviet voters to pluralistic politics and the rise of a multi-party system represented a genuine break with the past. The absence of democratic traditions in the USSR did not prevent its people from seizing the possibilities offered by perestroika.

The Communist Party's leaders themselves had to adjust very rapidly. It is not clear how many actually changed their minds about multi-party democracy. What appeared to be a change of tack (most spectacularly, Gorbachev's capitulation to the pressure to drop Article Six of the Soviet Constitution), may in fact have been the culmination of a long-nurtured but carefully husbanded policy. More likely, conservatives in the leadership may have hoped that apparent concessions might be counter-acted by careful management of their implementation.[48] The Communist Party leadership has never been eager to relinquish power. Powerful organisations such as the KGB and professional sections of the armed forces were still available to protect its supremacy; these bodies have never appeared to share the reformers' commitment to democracy.[49] But the Party's position was nonetheless eroded. The Politburo was increasingly by-passed by new institutions such as the short-lived Presidential Council,[50] which reported, not to the Party, but to the Congress of People's

[46]'In my experience', Martin Walker wrote in *The Guardian* on 24 December, 1986, 'most ordinary, non-intellectual Russians do not like dissidents.' His view would have been confirmed by the anti-pluralism polemic which appeared under the title 'Komy vygodny sovety bez kommunistov?' in *Moskovskaya Pravda* on 21 October, 1989. Its author, A.A. Nikolaev (a representative of the scientific-technical intelligentsia) concluded his polemic against Yuri Afanasev with a warning that 'the spectre of anti-Communism' was 'haunting the country'.

[47]For an example, see *Sovetskaya Rossiya's* reaction to the foundation of the Inter-Regional Group of Deputies, 5 August, 1989.

[48]This is the suggestion behind Dawn Mann's study of the Congress of People's Deputies' Standing Orders, 'Bringing the Congress of People's Deputies to Order', *Report on the USSR*, 19 January, 1990, pp. 1–5.

[49]The draft law on the KGB appears to maintain many of its controversial powers, including its right to intercept mail, tap telephones and to detain citizens for extended periods without trial. *Moscow News*, No. 15, 7–13 September, 1990.

[50]J. Steele, *The Guardian*, 12 April, 1990.

Deputies. Moreover, the establishment of republican presidencies cut the ground from under the central Party apparatus in many cases. The boundaries between all-Union and republican powers remain unclear, and seem, in January 1991, set to be tested, but, as Yeltsin's record as RSFSR President has demonstrated, the scope for organised opposition to the central apparatus from outside the Party has been considerable.

The Communist Party has also had to face the possibility of its own disintegration. Several more or less organised tendencies within the Communist Party have been fighting for the membership, status and material resources of the old ruling vanguard. In April 1990, one of these, the Democratic Platform, proposed to drop the word 'Communist' and even 'Socialist' from its title altogether.[51] The previous autumn it had been argued that different groups within the Communist Party might substitute for a multi-party system, that the diversity of social and political pressures could be reflected in a more 'democratic' Communist Party. Vadim Medvedev made this point in an interview on Soviet television on 2 October 1989. He explained that a 'profoundly democratic party' and a 'law-governed state' could provide all the flexibility needed for perestroika without the need for a multi-party system. What was not envisaged was an open split within the Party. Medvedev insisted that even a more 'democratic' Communist Party would need to be organised on the principle of 'democratic centralism'.[52] 'Democratic centralism' was included in the draft party statutes issued in March 1990.[53] The fact that a large section of the Party promptly rejected the concept – and could say so openly – showed how fast the picture could change in the space of a few months.[54]

Even more impressive, however, was the growth of popular political activism. In some of the more recently assimilated republics, and especially in the Baltic, this burgeoning of popular activity was to be expected. Autonomous 'horizontal' social and civil groupings in these societies had never entirely disappeared. The Lutheran and Catholic Churches, cultural organisations, and environmental groups (especially active after the Chernobyl' nuclear accident, but also vocally opposed to the over-exploitation of toxic minerals within their borders)[55] in these republics provided a ready-made political network in 1989. In the RSFSR, by contrast, people had little experience until recently of large-scale meetings independent of the Communist Party and its

[51]J. Steele, *The Guardian*, 13 April, 1990.
[52]*BBC Summary of World Broadcasts (USSR)*, 14 October 1981, B7.
[53]*Pravda*, 28 March, 1990.
[54]The Democratic Platform (thought to represent roughly a third of party members in May 1990) rejected the principle in its policy statement. See *Argumenty i fakty*, 17–23 February, 1990, p. 8.
[55]On the Church, see for example, *Radio Liberty Research*, 14 July 1981, 'Estonian Pastor ends up in Psychiatric Hospital for Expressing Nationalist Views'. On the environment, see *ibid.*, 28 September, 1977, 'Scientists Protest the Devastation of Nature in Estonia'; and more generally, Thane Gustafson, *Reform in Soviet Politics: Lessons of recent policies on land and water* (1978).

client organisations (including the Komsomol and official trade unions).[56] And even in 1990 there was still a wide range of different attitudes towards multi-party democracy. Individual political platforms and ideas often attracted venomous criticism in the conservative press.[57] Overall, however, democratisation achieved some spectacular victories.

Not surprisingly, the first Russian attempts at self-generated political activity were small scale and had an amateur air. The 'informal' political groups of 1988 and 1989 were typically restricted to a few dozen members. Some addressed themselves to local issues, others appeared to be reviving the heroic revolutionary traditions of the nineteenth century; their programmes offered little which might relate to the present crisis, but dealt in generalities, such as anarchism or some form of primitive socialism.[58] History figured prominently in most of their publications. The first impulse of many popular movements was to demand the righting of wrongs whose roots could be traced back to the 1930s, the consolidation of the 'partocracy', and even to the Bolshevik Revolution itself.

Given their uncertain legal status, 'informal' groups found it difficult to attract large followings, and few could hope to organise on a national scale. The average Soviet voter found the whole business very confusing, and there was a temptation (as there still is) to dismiss the informal groups as a distraction from the real power politics taking place in the Kremlin. The apparent strength of anti-Semitic organisations like Pamyat' further added to the confusion, raising questions about what might emerge from Pandora's box if the lid were not held firmly down by an enlightened leadership. Russian history was invoked as evidence of the perils of democracy. Valery Legostayev, described as 'a CPSU responsible official', argued that a multi-party system was the root of Russia's immediate post-revolutionary problems. 'The abundance of our political parties didn't do this country any good', he wrote. 'Our country's dramatic past – the February and October Revolutions of 1917 (when Russia had about a hundred political parties), the ruining of centuries-old political and religious structures, the ensuring fratricidal Civil War, etc., didn't come out of the blue but grew up on the prolific soil of Russia's multi-party system of the early twentieth century.'[59]

Despite abundant material of this sort, however, the March 1990 elections saw a victory for the reforming parties in Russian politics. Their

[56]Soviet youth, however, began to break away from the Komsomol's apron strings in the early 1980s. See Jim Riordan, 'Stalin's children', in *Detente*, Nos. 9–10, pp. 13–15.

[57]Notably, for example, *Sovetskaya Rossiya*, and *Molodaya Gvardiya*.

[58]Examples of their publications, purchased on Pushkin Square in 1989, include *Chernoe Znamya*, 'The organ of the Anarcho-Communist Revolutionary Union', which included in its second issue a large number of references to the works of Kropotkin; and *Prizrak Kommunizma*, 'The information leaflet of the Organisational Committee of the Communist-Democratic Fraction of the Democratic Union Party', whose fourth issue, confusingly enough, had a front-page column entitled 'Anarchy: 10 questions, 10 answers', more on anarcho-syndicalism on page two, and also a poem about the last Tsar ('Ah you, son-of-a-bitch Romanov Nikolai').

[59]*Moscow News*, 1990, No. 17.

outcome reflected the degree of commitment, political sobriety and activism of the reformers' numerous supporters. One manifestation of this activism was the organisation of voters' clubs, sparked by the 1989 elections and much invigorated by the 1990 campaigns. In the RSFSR, their members seemed in 1990 to have favoured neither reactionaries nor the more extreme supporters of change. The Democratic Union, the first political party to declare itself (even before the law was changed to allow political parties to exist) suffered as a result of its militant image.[60] Its apparent programmatic confusion was also a problem.[61] In a survey which asked respondents to award points out of five to a number of public organisations, the Democratic Union scored 3.1, less than Pamyat'; and among members of the Communist Party, its score was 2.7, barely higher than the 2.6 awarded to the Social-Democratic Party.[62] In this survey, conducted in the spring of 1990, discredited organisations such as official trade unions and the Komsomol also scored badly (3.3 and 3.0 respectively), the Communist Party did relatively well (3.9 on average), and the top scores went to the democratic organisations which appeared at the time to be the most effective: the Inter-Regional Group of deputies (4.0) and the Moscow Voters' Association (4.0).

The March 1990 elections also demonstrated that the Soviet voter could read more than the first few lines of a candidate's manifesto.[63] In Moscow at least, voters were less concerned with whether or not a candidate was a Party member than they were with his or her political programme. This probably reflected the declining importance of *partiinost'* for its own sake compared with the identification of Communists with one or other Party faction.[64] Surveys of what Soviet electors valued in their parliamentary candidates also suggested that, democratic traditions or not, people were not at this stage gravitating to extremes. According to one pre-election survey conducted in Moscow, the most valued quality in candidates was a 'broad view' (required by 61 per cent of respondents), followed at some distance by 'knowledge of the needs of the electorate' (50 per cent) and 'knowledge of the law and of judicial norms' (49 per cent). Only 7 per cent of respondents wanted evidence of strong leadership qualities.[65]

Information like this, together with warnings about potential 'dirty tricks' and advice about how to present oneself to the electorate, was soon to be available to would-be Soviet politicians from the Postfaktum research service, headed by Nina Belyaeva and supported by the

[60]This conclusion is confirmed by research published in its own journal, *Svobodnoe Slovo*, 31 October, 1989, p. 2.
[61]Its first meeting could not decide whether to oppose the whole 'totalitarian system' or 'just' the CPSU. It did not agree on what to support either. *Svobodnoe Slovo*, 31 October, 1989.
[62]*Argumenty i fakty*, 1990, No. 7.
[63]J. Wishnevsky, *Report on the USSR*, 6 April, 1990.
[64]B. Lysenko, *Argumenty i fakty*, 17–23 March, 1990.
[65]*Vechernyaya Moskva*, 9 January, 1990.

newspaper *Moscow News*.[66] Postfaktum published a weekly bulletin, *Vybory–90*, containing survey material.[67] Its research identified seven broad categories of political opinion in the Russian republic on the eve of the twenty-eighth Party Congress.[68] These were 'westerners', whose orientation was mainly towards the USA as a model for future Soviet reform; 'Left Populists', whose goal was 'socialism with a human face'; 'Right Populists', including the supporters of the United Front of Workers described earlier; the 'State' group, who valued most in Russian history the achievements, such as military success, attributable to a strong state; 'Greens'; 'National-Patriots', including the supporters of Pamyat'; and the 'a-political mass of the population', which *Vybory–90* saw as a basis for (mainly right-wing) populist politicians.

Postfaktum, and public opinion polling institutions like Tatiana Zaslavskaya's, helped to strengthen the democratic process. Both the electorate and the new parties were better informed. Developments like these indicated that, by the spring of 1990, new patterns of political behaviour had been established in the USSR alongside the old. The Communist Party was still there, and many of its representatives still publicly insisted that Communism should remain the guiding ideology for perestroika.[69] And its traditional auxiliaries, such as the KGB and the army, remained in the shadows. Despite the obstacles, however, the mass of the population, and a significant number of politicians, had abandoned the Communist Party, and with it, many of their reservations about opposition politics.

These gains, however, were fragile. The problem was and is that the competing interests of different groups of Soviet citizens (most obviously, the tensions between the different ethnic groups) are not readily reconcilable, and there is little ground for believing that free elections in themselves can resolve the difficulties. Gorbachev has described Russians as intolerant by nature. Their ready acceptance of democratic institutions suggests that this may be a mistaken view. But the problems they face do not encourage liberal give-and-take solutions. In conditions of ethnic violence, food and other shortages, impending unemployment and environmental disaster, it will be impossible to appease the whole of the electorate; more likely is an outcome which satisfies nobody. The legacies of the past are partly to blame for this. Some competing interests could be resolved even under authoritarian government, but the majority were simply repressed. Gorbachev has had to pay a bill run up by generations

---

[66]*Izvestiya*, 11 March, 1990.
[67]Its print-run was 2,000 in March 1990.
[68]*Vybory–90*, 1990, No. 7.
[69]As CC secretary Oleg Baklanov put it,'the wonderful idea of constructing a Communist society has somehow or other conquered the minds of millions and millions of people. I believe in that.' *Rabochaya Tribuna*, 28 March, 1990, cited in *Foreign Broadcast Information Service Daily Report, Soviet Union* (hereafter FBIS), 29 March, 1990, p. 55.

of Soviet and Russian leaders. He was probably correct in his initial belief that open discussion and more or less democratic competition between the different interest groups in Soviet society was the least undesirable way of clearing the slate. The vigorous Soviet reaction to democratisation bore this out; people wanted elections, and most still seem to want to see their differences resolved peacefully. But the new democratic institutions have been on probation, and their time is running out. They will have to deliver something in the near future, or other means will almost certainly be found of satisfying the demands of the most vocal sections of the Soviet population.

To date, one possibility has been that Soviet people might take matters into their own hands. This occurred several times in 1989–90. After all, this was the time when the example of Eastern Europe suggested that if the ballot box could not produce results, more direct means of applying popular pressure could be spectacularly successful. *Pravda* bewailed the increase in the number of street demonstrations in January and February 1990.[70] But admonitions in the official press were probably counter-productive in a society where authority was losing its credibility. According to Zaslavskaya, by March 1990 almost a third of the Soviet population had lost all faith in its political institutions, and believed that the bureaucracy represented only its own interests.[71] She was not the only person to speak of a 'crisis in authority' in the USSR. The party journal, *Kommunist*, devoted its discussion section to the same problem in February 1990.[72] A survey of 662 Muscovites conducted on behalf of *Moscow News* in May 1990 found confidence in the authorities 'falling sharply', especially among the young and middle-aged. In the 18–29 age group, 36 per cent did not trust the current Council of Ministers, compared with 14 per cent who did. The report noted the contrast with Poland, where the level of trust for Tadeusz Mazowiecki's government was as high as 86 per cent.[73] Civic Action, a pressure-group formed in Moscow in March 1990, stated in its programme that the existing institutions would stagnate if they were not forced to act. Civic Action's constituent groups were not extremist (it was composed, among others, of Moscow Tribune, the Memorial Association and the Moscow Federation of Voters). But it called on its supporters to put pressure on the government through 'civic resistance', including (in extreme cases) political strikes, civil disobedience campaigns and 'other non-violent actions'.[74]

Direct action like this sometimes proved effective, at least in the short term. The Baltic republics' independence movements were dramatically successful, although they may now be the first to suffer from the panic that they helped to induce among politicians of the old school. Their initial success was probably owed to the harmony of aims which existed,

[70]*Pravda*, 26 March, 1990.
[71]Seminar in Trinity College, University of Cambridge, 2 March 1990.
[72]*Kommunist*, 1990, No. 2.
[73]*Moscow News*, 1990, No. 19.
[74]FBIS, 21 March 1990, p. 73.

at least at the outset, between the local political élite and the popular movement. In other national republics, frustration and inter-ethnic hostility led to street violence and even pogroms, but it did not bring political concessions for the minorities involved. The extra-parliamentary movements in Russia sometimes proved more powerful. Popular protest forced the resignation of a dozen or more regional party committees, and in many of the areas involved, ad hoc local committees were still supervising party and Soviet administration several months later.[75] More significantly, organised workers' movements began to challenge the whole structure of regional government. During the miners' strike of 1989, the strike committee largely ran the Donbass.[76] At least temporarily it looked as if the miners' demands might be met (as indeed on paper they were). The miners' reaction to the price-rises which reform threatened to bring in its wake in the summer of 1990 was widely feared; they had the ability, if they chose, to bring the Soviet economy to a standstill.[77] These movements were not disorganised or, to use *Vybory–90*'s phrase, a-political, but they did not work within the constitutional structure set up by Gorbachev.

If one were looking for historical parallels, the obvious one here would be 1917, when the Provisional Government was 'a government without a state' and the Petrograd Soviet, local militias and factory committees a 'state without a government'.[78] The Congress of People's Deputies and Supreme Soviet had yet to build the confidence needed to render them a 'government with a state'; local strike committees, recalcitrant Party mafias and popular demonstrations, though not, at this stage, sufficiently organised to constitute an alternative locus of state power, could still ignore their decrees. The tensions between central and local government, and between party and soviets, reduced some areas to virtual anarchy in the summer of 1990.[79] As in 1917, the peripheral nationalities were threatening to leave the empire. And as in 1917, the economic crisis seemed to be setting the limits for further democratisation. The candidate who told the electorate the truth about economic reform would have found it hard to get elected. It was difficult to see who would vote for massive price rises, increasing unemployment and greater inequality. Surveys indicated that voters were prepared to wait three to five years for significant economic improvements, but it was not clear that they would be so patient if the heating were switched off in the winter.[80] The autumn

[75]See Dawn Mann, 'Authority of Regional Party leaders is crumbling', *Report on the USSR*, 1990, No. 8, pp. 1–5.
[76]See E. Teague, 'Embryos of People's Power', *Report on the USSR*, 11 August, 1989.
[77]*The Guardian*, 23 May, 1990.
[78]Marc Ferro, *October 1917: A Social History of the Russian Revolution*, (English trans. 1980), p. 273.
[79]*Moscow News*, No. 15, 7–13 September, 1990, citing the example of Leningrad.
[80]A majority of respondents in a *Moscow News*, survey believed the economic situation would improve in five years (but not before), but the same sort of majority (50.9 per cent) believed that the general situation in the USSR would not stabilise for a long time. *Moscow News*, 1990, No. 19.

of 1990 saw riots over petrol and cigarette shortages. Bread queues were a common sight in Moscow.[81] Anyone who promised quick solutions, an end to violence, a crack-down on profiteering, and prosperity for the average citizen would, like Lenin in 1917, have done very well among the discontented population of Russia's cities in the winter of 1990–91.

The parallel with 1917 should not be stretched too far. The social context was entirely different, the international pressures on the USSR were much less, and there was not yet a consensus that the current regime should be replaced. This time the mass of the population was involved in the electoral process, and could follow the political debates through information in the press, radio and television. But for all that, there could still be no certainty that the new political parties, and the parliament in which they operated, could build enough credibility to defend themselves against a takeover from within or the establishment of some form of authoritarian super-government. By January 1991, whatever may have been happening in the national republics, it was hard to imagine who would take to the streets of Moscow to defend the Congress of People's Deputies.

The diversity and relatively small size of the new political groups has also militated against their success. The small parties have found coalition difficult, and outside the national republics no party has been able to claim a 'heartland' or proven core of supporters. In April 1990 Roy Medvedev predicted that the Communist Party would continue to dominate Russian, if not Soviet, politics for the foreseeable future, and the view was shared by other commentators.[82] Moreover, the new parties' behaviour tended to encourage these predictions. The leader of the new Liberal–Democratic Party, for example, gave an interview to *Moscow News* which included a substantial discussion of his future perks as party leader. 'As far as privileges are concerned', he told his interviewer, 'our party will decide which of them the chairman should have; whether I'll drive a Chaika or a Mercedes.'[83] At the time, the LDP had 4,000 members, and its chairman's prediction that 'by the end of the year, membership is expected to reach half a million' must be taken with a pinch of salt.

The same politician told *Moscow News* that although his party admitted anyone, 'we prefer intellectuals'. Public confidence in the new parties was easily damaged by remarks like this. Politicians were readily viewed as careerists who represented no-one but themselves. Rumours of corruption were rife. *Moscow News*, for example, ran an item entitled 'An Incorruptible Deputy', which featured 43 year-old Vladimir Chernenko from Krasnodar. A Soviet hero in the old style (clean-shaven,

[81]*Moscow News*, No. 15, 7–13 September, 1990.

[82]*The Guardian*, 20 April 1990. The political analyst Segei Plekhanov made broadly the same point to an interviewer on the 'Top Priority' programme in February 1990, citing Russia's lack of democratic traditions as a further barrier to democratisation. FBIS, 12 February 1990, p. 97.

[83]*Moscow News*, No. 17, 1990.

clean-living and a Lenin Komsomol prizewinner), he was 'the first among hundreds of people to write about life behind the scenes in the deputies' corps'. What he claimed was that deputies were offered cash or even 'the latest Volga' in exchange for votes in favour of private ownership.[84] True or not, the suggestion was bound to be widely believed. People resented the growing power of local mafias, and any links between deputies and unpopular lobbies like the co-operators were viewed with concern. It was no surprise to a population reared on the idea that success depended on Party membership that politicians should be corrupt. And there was general knowledge that influential politicians enjoyed access to the scarce goods their policies could not provide for the rest of the electorate.

Politicians of a populist persuasion could easily make political capital out of these suspicions. Many right populist leaders publicly questioned the justice of a market system, and with it, 'bourgeois' democracy. 'We have linked our destiny with a socialist choice and have ruled out the categories of 'capital' and 'hired labour', V. Romanov wrote in *Sovetskaya Rossiya* in March 1990. And he inveighed against 'bourgeois' parties which 'reflect the fundamental interests of businessmen from the shadow economy and the private ownership structure.'[85] Here, mistrust of the intelligentsia combined with a fear of the consequences of market reforms. The United Front of Workers has claimed that the existing voting laws disadvantage the working class, and some of its representatives have argued that the 1990 election results should be overturned.[86] It does not matter that their rhetoric has not always been consistent.[87] Indeed, as we have seen, vague optimism combined with attractive slogans, the stock-in-trade of populists at any time, may have come to seem the only option to a population faced with otherwise unacceptable choices.

Some corruption might have been forgiven if the Congress of People's Deputies and Supreme Soviet were making any headway in their attempts to reform the Soviet system. But here again there have been problems. The electorate may have learned to vote, but the deputies have not yet mastered the art of organising a multi-party parliament. The reformers' programmes have often been vague, and their behaviour in the Congress has so far lacked the concerted seriousness required of organised opposition parties. Shevtsova's view of the Soviet Union's recent record of 'ambition, petty vanity, . . . political infantilism and demagoguery'[88] may sound extreme, but it was shared by commentators of most political hues. Many of the debates in the Congress of People's Deputies have consisted of a sequence of set-piece speeches bearing little relation to each other. British viewers of televised sessions of the House of Commons may say that the Soviets are expecting too much of their

---

[84]*Moscow News*, No. 17, 1990.
[85]*Sovetskaya Rossiya*, 23 March, 1990.
[86]J. Wishnevsky, *Report on the USSR*, 6 April, 1990.
[87]See Jonathan Steele's assessment of Yeltsin in *The Guardian*, 30 May, 1990.
[88]*Izvestiya*, 28 February, 1990.

Congress, but the problem is that alternative political groups in the USSR have yet to prove that they can tackle the daunting problems facing the Soviet Union. They have not even yet established the legitimacy of the new political institutions.

Even recognised coalitions like the Inter-Regional Group of Deputies (the forerunner of 1990's Democratic Russia group) soon discovered that they could not always act effectively. It was true that the IRG included only 400 of the 2,250 USSR People's Deputies, but the rest did not necessarily act together. The Inter-Regional Group's inability to amend the legislation on Gorbachev's presidency in 1990 was seen by its members as a major blow. One of them told *Vybory–90* that the Group's discipline was weak, and that it had no mechanism for taking collective decisions or putting them into action.[89] At a meeting of its members in March 1990 one deputy remarked that on the presidency issue 'The Inter-Regional Group turned out to be completely unprepared . . . . We were not even able to get together in the intervals'. Its leaders were largely blamed for this. Afanas'ev and Popov had left the Congress on the second day, and Yeltsin did not attend at all.[90]

Both the Moscow Soviet and the Russian Parliament quickly demonstrated that radical groups could achieve specific goals.[91] But it was one thing to elect a President or organise a committee, and another altogether to see through a set of complicated reforms, many of which were likely to cause hardship to large numbers of people. Moreover, the election of radicals at the local level brought regional and local government into head-on collision with the centre. The present Congress of People's Deputies has been dominated by party nominees and supporters, and cannot be as flexible as the more recently-elected local organs. And the Congress is too large, and its debating time too limited, for it to act as a serious filter for constitutional change. The Supreme Soviet, which is better suited to preparing legislation, cannot amend the Constitution.[92] In these circumstances, and in view of the indecisive and ill-organised nature of the opposition, it is difficult to see how the Soviet Union's democratic structures can resist determined initiatives aimed at overturning them. And deadlock between the republics and the all-Union government is also unlikely to further the interests of reformers. By the autumn of 1990 it had brought only chaos and a series of squabbles whose principal result was to reduce the new institutions' credibility still further in the eyes of the Soviet population.

The pressures on the new democratic institutions, then, have been building up from all directions. If organs like the Congress and the Supreme Soviet cannot build public trust, if the economic crisis and ethnic conflicts intensify, it is possible that the new democratic structures

[89]*Vybory–90*, No. 4, January 1990.
[90]FBIS, 19 March, 1990, p. 78.
[91]Julia Wishnevsky, *Report on the USSR*, 6 April, 1990, p. 13.
[92]See Dawn Mann, 'Bringing the Congress of People's Deputies to Order', *Report on the USSR*, 19 January, 1990, pp. 1–5.

will be by-passed. A stronger, perhaps unelected, executive might seek to re-impose some kind of order. This was the outcome predicted by the retiring Foreign Minister, Eduard Shevardnadze, in December 1990, and the first month of 1991 saw plenty of evidence to support his suspicions. But the suppression of democracy remains only one of a number of possible outcomes. If it happens, to return to our original discussion of historical continuity, it will not be because Russians are somehow fated to be ruled by authoritarian leaders. The clock cannot simply be turned back. Whatever emerges from the current crisis in the USSR will be the product of a unique set of circumstances, of which the legacy of Russia's authoritarian past is only one.

3
What time is it in Russia's history
Robert C. Tucker

Western sovietology and official Soviet thought have differed greatly in their descriptions of what happened in Soviet history. The standard Soviet texts (now under reconsideration) tell a story of the rise of 'socialism' and then 'developed socialism', on the road to full 'communism', as the substance and drama of the Soviet era, whereas much Western sovietology has it that what arose under Lenin and Stalin was 'Communist totalitarianism'.

These opposing viewpoints have, however, shared an underlying premise – that the October Revolution of 1917, in which Lenin and his fellow Bolsheviks took power, marked a fundamental rupture with earlier Russian history, save for that of the Russian revolutionary movement of which Bolshevism was one current. As a long-time dissenter from this position, I believe that a reversion to the Russian past took place after 1917, that what emerged under Lenin and Stalin was a kind of neo-tsarist order calling itself 'socialist', and, accordingly, that the present-day events in the Soviet Union cannot be understood in any depth without taking Russia's whole history into account.

If a reversion to the Russian past took place in Soviet history, this means that certain earlier Russian historical patterns, cultural and institutional, reappeared, albeit under new names. The new names are not easy to read with understanding by people who are not Russian historically minded, as very many Soviet-educated people are not and numerous Western sovietologists are not.

In espousing a deviant position, it is not my intention to dismiss as outworn such classics of our sovietology as Merle Fainsod's *How Russia Is Ruled*, Leonard Schapiro's *The Communist Party of the Soviet Union*, and John Armstrong's *The Politics of Totalitarianism*. They, and various more specialized studies in Soviet history, have stood the test of time. Moreover, the totalitarian paradigm that made it seem unnecessary to a Fainsod to delve deeply into the tsarist past in telling the Soviet story was serviceable up to a point. The historical approach that I favour aims only to help us to go beyond that point.

How shall we conduct this scholarly debate? One possible way is to consult the thinking of knowledgeable contemporaries in the Soviet side. For *glasnost'*, especially by mid-1990, had given them something bordering on full freedom to voice in print their thoughts on the relation between the Soviet period and the Russian past. And because it is their country and culture whose history is in question, we ought to find, and we do, much of interest and value in what they have to say.

As we would expect, they are divided in their views on this subject. Some go on seeing – although now in an anti-Soviet light – a disjunction between the Soviet period and what went before it in Russia. According to the painter Ilya Glazunov, a 'chasm' lies between old Russia, based on Orthodoxy, autocracy and nationality, and the USSR, based on atheism, proletarian dictatorship, and internationalism.[1]

The philosopher Aleksandr Tsipko considers the Soviet period a kind of hiatus in history:

> We probably deceive ourselves in thinking that we lived in the twentieth century. Maybe history just performed an experiment on us, freezing our brains, thoughts and feelings, compelling us to wander about the world asleep, committing a mass of idiocies, murdering one another, doing no end of atrocious things.

Hence the task now is for Russia to 'return to the movement of historical time'.[2] And some of Tsipko's fellow citizens carry placards nowadays that say: 'Seventy years on the road to nowhere!'

But more widespread among Soviet intellectuals is a different viewpoint. As they see it, the seventy years – and no one disputes the fact that terrible tragedies took place during them – traversed some roads previously trod in Russian history. 'Feudalism' is the term some use to express the idea that history in the Soviet period went forward in a backward way, that tsarist absolutism, and centralized bureaucratic statism, made a comeback in the frame of the Communist party-state. Says Gorbachev's close colleague Aleksandr Yakolev: 'Socialism hasn't really been built in the country. What we have is departmental feudalism.'[3] *Literary Gazette* editor Fyodor Burlatsky calls the Soviet system 'feudal socialism'.[4] The theater director Mark Zakharov calls it 'our feudal-patriarchal way of life'.[5] And the historian Mertsalov refers to the 'feudal traditions' of the Soviet Academy of Science, whose thoroughly bureaucratized historical division might be called an 'administrative echelon for affairs of historical science'.[6]

The revival of old Russian patterns began at the outset of the Soviet period, these thinkers tell us. The nationalisation of the country's resources transformed them into state property, which led to a rebirth of historic Russian statism. The forcible retention by the new regime of

[1]I. Glazunov, 'Kto lyubit Rossiyu menya poimyet', *Sovetskaya kul'tura*, 14 June 1990.

[2]A. Tsipko, 'Neobkhodimo potryasenie mysl'lyu, *Moskovskie novosti*, 1 July 1990.

[3]A. Yakovlev, 'Dlya menia eto posledni s'ezd', *Moskovskie novosti*, 15 July 1990.

[4]F. Burlatsky, 'K sovremennoi tsivilizatsii', *Literaturnaya gazeta*, 5 September 1990.

[5]M. Zakharov, 'Sumburnye zametki k poluchennoi informatsii', *Literaturnaya gazeta*, 15 August 1990.

[6]A. Mertsalov, 'Stanet li nashe prosloe predskazuenym?', *Izvestiya*, 21 August 1990.

the great bulk of the minority-inhabited territories on the periphery of the Russian Empire meant the factual rebirth of empire under the title of 'Union of Soviet Socialist Republics'.[7] And whatever was said about 'Soviet power' having been established by the October Revolution, what *de facto* emerged was a new line of tsars under another name, starting with Lenin.

'Soviet power, from its very first days, showed its autocratic and absolutist character, only under different slogans', writes Yuri Feofanov. 'Rejecting the division of three powers as a bourgeois principle, our state authority took all of them unto itself.'[8] Elsewhere he cites the new mayor of Leningrad, former professor Anatoly Sobchak, as saying that 'In Russia, both in the Soviet period and through the centuries, it was not laws that ruled, but persons'. So it was, says Feofanov, from Lenin through Stalin, Khrushchev and Brezhnev to Gorbachev. And this primacy of 'First Persons' over laws and institutions extends back through 'whole layers' of the history of Russia, whose sixteenth and seventeenth century 'assemblies of the land' (*zemskie sobory*) had less resemblance to actual parliaments than to Soviet party congresses, which have simply 'sanctified the sovereign's will'. So, it was not the party or its apparatus or even a small group of party progressives that inaugurated the *perestroika;* it was a new First Person, Gorbachev.[9]

The declared goal of the perestroika has been to dismantle the 'administrative–command system' handed down from Stalin's time. The writer Anatoly Ananiev argues that this system had a tsarist predecessor that originated in the second half of the sixteenth century under the 'terrible' tsar, Ivan Grozny:

> 'What *is* this administrative-command system, this bane of our life', he asks and asserts that 'at the base of the administrative-command system lies a situation in which the people was estranged from the state. It was Ivan Grozny who began this.'[10]

Another writer, Ya. Gordin, finds in the Soviet order historical patterns going back to the time of Peter I, in the early eighteenth century, and 'Iron Tsar' Nicholas I (1825–55). 'I do not share the widespread opinion that 1917 marked a great rupture in our history', he writes. 'I dare say that what we call the Soviet period has been, in basic features and significance, a restoration of state principles that ruled from Peter I through Nicholas I, principles that were pressed back after the Great Reforms and reforms of 1905.'[11] One such state principle was serfdom. It ruled from the sixteenth and seventeenth centuries down to the Great Reforms of the 1860s, which began with the emancipation of the serfs.

Under serfdom, the serf rendered compulsory service to the landowner

[7]Anatoly Streliany, 'Pesni zapadnykh slavyan', *Literaturnaya gazeta*, 8 August 1990.
[8]Y. Feofanov, 'Fiktsiya 'tret'ei vlasti'', *Moskovskie novosti*, 2 September 1990.
[9]Y. Feofaanov, 'Printsipy i litsa', *Ogonyek*, No. 29, July 1990, pp. 4–5.
[10]A. Ananiev, 'Dokazatel'stvo aksiomy', *Sovetskaya kul'tura*, 30 June 1990.
[11]Ya. Gordin, 'Chto pozadi?', *Literaturnaya gazeta*, 26 September 1990.

either in the form of working time (*barshchina*) or produce (*obrok*). This pattern rose again as a result of the collectivisation of the peasantry in 1929-33. According to the vice chairman of the USSR Supreme Soviet's Committee on Legislation, K. Liubenchenko, 'We returned to what existed before 1861, that is, to serfdom, all the way to such a detail as the attachment of the peasants to the land'.[12] An agricultural specialist, Academician Vladimir Tikhonov, writes of 'serfdom' in the Soviet countryside and describes the contemporary bosses and defenders of that system, men like V. Starodubtsev of the self-styled Peasant Union, as serf-owners (*krepostniki*) and little tsars (*tsar'ki*).[13]

Cultural life was likewise enserfed. The literary scholar Yuri Burtin asserts:

> 'Just as our collective-farm countryside, unlike the serf countryside, where there was either *barshina* or *obrok*, has had to go through both a multi-level preliminary censorship and then a punitive censorship afterwards.'[14]

The theater director Oleg Efremov says that after the shock wave of collectivisation came

> '. . . smaller-scale actions aimed at the complete and total statitication and enserfment of the country's spiritual life. . . .They created a state for officials and a theater for officials. . . . We now stand on the threshold of the abolition of theatrical serfdom, which developed in the depths of the Stalinist regime, where the theatrical setup was part and parcel of the whole system.'[15]

A pillar of the tsarist administrative–command system which reappeared in the Soviet period under a new name, was the rank order of higher officialdom. Tsar Peter I promulgated in 1722 a Table of Ranks which set up a hierarchy of fourteen military and corresponding civilian ranks and made service to the autocratic state a highroad to noble status. Starting on the bottom rung of the ladder, a military officer or civil servant could obtain personal and eventually hereditary nobility on reaching the requisite higher rungs (classes one to four carried hereditary nobility). The Table created an aristocracy of rank (*chin*) and organized the tsarist ruling elite as a corps of uniformed holders of rank (*chinovniki*). A Soviet historian finds that in essence this system rose again in the Soviet period under the name of *nomenklatura*, save that it was not made public in the tsarist way and in numbers became many times larger. The *nomenklatura* comprises the system of party-controlled higher party and governmental ranks and appointments to them. The historian tells us that Stalin's subordinates back in the 1920s even went to old tsarist official records for particulars on how to organise the *nomenklatura*, whose tsarist

[12]K. Liubenchenko, 'Bezrabotnye zakony', *Izvestiya*, 7 July 1990.
[13]V. Tikhonov, 'Golod i urozhai', *Moskovskie novosti*, 26 August 1990.
[14]Y. Burtin, 'Mertvoe i zhivoe', *Literaturnaya gazeta*, 22 August 1990.
[15]O. Efremov, 'Pered otmenoi krepostnogo prava', *Moskovskie novosti*, 17 June 1990.

predecessor was the higher rank-holding class comprised in the top four ranks, subject to appointment by the tsar.[16]

How history turned full circle, and the dark postwar Stalin years came to resemble the repressive 1830s–1840s of Nicholas I, came home to some of us in Moscow's foreign colony. One day in 1948 I picked up in a Moscow secondhand bookshop an out-of-print Russian translation of *Russia in 1839*, by the Marquis de Custine. It was published in 1930 by the Society of Former Political Prisoners and Exiles, which Stalin had disbanded in 1935. Custine, no supporter of the French Revolution, came to Russia in 1839 as a sort of monarchist fellow-traveller and was graciously received in the closed Petersburg court society, as fellow-travelling André Gide would be in Stalin's Moscow of the later 1930s. Even on a four-month visit under close surveillance, he saw enough to disillusion him, as happened later with Gide. In his book, written in the form of letters home to France, he found that Nicholas I's Russia was not the civilized monarchy he had thought it was but a true tyranny, a serf state with a tsar-cult upheld by officialdom. 'The Russian Empire', he wrote in a typical passage, 'is an enormous theatrical hall where, from all the boxes, people try to follow what is happening behind the scenes.' Of the Tsar: 'There is no man on earth with such unlimited power'. Of *chin:* 'A military regime applied to society as a whole.' Of the mode of government: 'Absolute monarchy moderated by murder.'[17]

The book went through many editions in Western Europe but censorship prevented it from being published in Russia. However, some educated Russians read it in French, and one of them, a dissident of that day named Aleksandr Herzen, called it 'the most entertaining and intelligent book on Russia by a foreigner'. Higher Russian circles were indignant. By covert arrangement with Count Benckendorf, chief of the Third Department of His Majesty's Chancellery, the Russian secret police of that time, a semi-official publicist, N.I. Grech, wrote an anti-Custine tract in French for circulation abroad. So strikingly similar in some ways was Custine's Nicholaian Russia to the Stalinist one we foreigners observed in 1948 that the book seemed to us to be *A Journey for Our Time*, the title given it in an English translation made by Phyllis Kohler, wife of our then deputy chief of mission in Moscow Foy Kohler, and published in America in 1953. Walter Bedell Smith, our ambassador in Moscow between 1946 and 1949, wrote in a foreword to it:

> 'I could have taken many pages from his journal and, after substituting present-day names and dates for those of a century ago, have sent them to the State Department as my own official reports.'[18]

The Soviet Nicholaian period extended from Stalin's final years through

[16]V. Sirotkin, 'Nomenklatura v istoricheskom razreza', *Cherez terni* (Moscow, 1990), pp. 292–334; Sirotkin, 'Nomenklatura', *Nedelya*, pp. 21–27, May 1990.

[17]Marquis de Custine, *Nikolaevskaya Rossiya* (Moscow, 1930), pp. 72, 133, 163.

[18]*Journey For Our Time: The Journals of the Marquis de Custine*, ed. and trans. Phyllis P. Kohler, Introduction by W.B. Smith (Portland, Oregon, 1953), p. 13.

the neo-Stalinist administration of Brezhnev. This comes through in a memoir published in 1990 by Soviet film-maker El'dar Riazanov. In 1978 he and a colleague, Grigory Gorin, set out to make a film to which they gave the title 'Say a Word for a Poor Hussar'. Their purpose was to say something by cinematic hints and allusions about Stalin's terror-filled time, but to do it in a film ostensibly about the time of the Iron Tsar, when blue-uniformed gendarmes from the Third Department spied on and tyrannised over Russian society and made life very hard even for a great poet like Lermontov. The Soviet cinema ministry, called Goskino, rejected the script and treated the authors in its usual way as serfs. But Gosteleradio, the ministry of television, decided to take up the project as a way of making a bureaucratic move against Goskino. Then, writes Riazanov, began the process of polishing up by censorship which 'so edits a branchy pine tree that it becomes a telegraph pole'. At one point he and Gorin were informed that their script paid too much attention to the Third Department and portrayed it too negatively. Here Riazanov comments:

'Good lord! Did Benckendorf ever think that a hundred and some years later, his honor would be upheld by Communists at the head of Soviet television! Of course, their solicitude for the Third Department was understandable: they were terribly afraid of distressing the department over on Dzerzhinsky Square. They didn't seem to realise that by equating the Third Department with contemporary State Security they were giving themselves away. In their thoughts they equated these two organisations and they were striving to stand up for the KGB by whitewashing the Nicholaian gendarmerie.'

Later, the two film-makers were forced to drop the idea of having a hero of their film declaim, before being executed, Lermontov's classic quatrain:

> Farewell unwashed Russia,
> land of slaves, land of masters,
> and you in those blue uniforms, and
> you the people that obeys them.

The higher *chinovnik* from Gosteleradio explained: 'No verses needed. Not those anyway.' Riazanov broke in to say: 'But that's Lermontov. That's a classic. We learned those verses in third grade.' 'Nothing doing', replied the *chinovnik*. 'And you understand why.' Such was the tsarist Soviet Russia of 1980, a land from whose airways the Lermontov of 'Farewell unwashed Russia, land of slaves, land of masters' was banished. Riazanov says that the emasculated version of the film finally shown then was 'an indictment of everything on which the Russian social system rested and still rests. For we are the true and faithful heirs of all that was worst in tsarism'.[19]

[19]E. Riazanov, 'Kak raz na zhizn' svoboda opozdala', *Ogonyek*, No. 36, September 1990, pp. 22–25.

Nicholas I was succeeded by Alexander II, whose Great Reforms, starting with the abolition of serfdom, caused him to go down as the 'tsar–liberator'. This reforming tsar was also, however, a tragic one. As he drove in his carriage to the palace in 1881 after signing the draft of the first Russian constitution, he was blown to bits by a bomb hurled by revolutionary extremists from a group calling itself the People's Will, and reaction set in under Alexander III. And if the Soviet Nicholaian period lasted through the early 1980s, what happened in 1985, as various present-day Russians see it, was the accession of a new tsar–liberator in the person of Mikhail Gorbachev. For was it not the earlier one, Alexander II, who in 1861, for the first time in Russia, proclaimed *glasnost'*?[20]

All this may throw light on a notable phenomenon: the keen and positive interest Russians are showing nowadays in tsarism and tsars. Nicholas II, who was executed with members of his family in 1918, is mourned by many as a martyr. Merezhkovsky's play *Paul I*, written in the aftermath of the 1905 Revolution, is running to full houses in Moscow and arouses some sympathy for this non-reforming tsar. Announced for the new season in Moscow's theatres are plays about Ivan Grozny, Tsar Fyodor, Boris Godunov, Peter I, Catherine II, and Nicholas II.[21] And Glinka's opera, revived under Stalin as *Ivan Susanin*, is now playing in the Bolshoi Theatre under its nineteenth century name, *A Life for the Tsar*. What does all this mean? No doubt, many things. The drama critic Andrei Karaulov suggests one of them when he says, in commenting on a current play about a tsar, 'The audience is mainly interested in the parallel with the current reforming tsar, Gorbachev'.[22]

The new reforming tsar soon proclaimed the need for a *perestroika*, a deep-seated reformation of the Soviet political culture. But he could not carry through such a project by his own governing efforts alone. Success in dismantling the administrative–command system and creating a new one would depend on the ability and willingness of society to adopt new ways of thinking and acting, and of a still privileged and powerful governing élite to foster such new ways or at least not to resist them. So, what happened in the later 1980s, according to historian Sirotkin, bears comparison with what happened under reforming tsar Alexander II in the 1860s and 1870s. Then a schism opened up within the tsarist *nomenklatura* between reformers who supported Alexander II's *perestroika* and conservatives who opposed it. Something similar has happened now, within the Soviet *nomenklatura*. Those earlier conservatives were opposed to all talk of a constitution or parliament; the present-day ones oppose all talk of private property.[23]

Now, in the seventh year of the second Soviet *perestroika* (the first,

[20]Y. Korolev,'Grani nashego krizisa', *Moskovskie novosti*, 8 July 1990.
[21]B. Liubimov, 'Imperatorskii teatr', *Literaturnaya gazeta*, 13 June 1990.
[22]Cited by Cynthia H. Whitaker, 'The Reforming Tsar', Paper presented at Fourth World Congress of Soviet and East European Studies, Harrogate, England, July 1990, p. 16.
[23]Sirotkin, 'Nomenklatura v istoricheskom razreze', p. 321.

another Soviet historian tells us, was Lenin's New Economic Policy[24]), the 'serf-owners' still dominate the countryside and the remnants of Stalinist serfdom have yet to be abolished.[25] *Izvestiya*, nowadays a reformist paper, evokes the later nineteenth century with a resounding headline: 'Give the peasant land and freedom'.[26] The writer Boris Mikhailov bids the intelligentsia to 'go to the people'.[27] New Westernisers fend off attack by new Slavophiles of various persuasions. One of the claimants to Slavophile leadership is the Vermont-dwelling Aleksandr Solzhenitsyn, who, in a huge homily printed in twenty-six million copies in the Soviet press, tells Mother Russia how to put her crumbling house in order. And V. Lakshin publishes in *Izvestiya* a lengthy interview with the great nineteenth century Russian satirist Saltykov-Shchedrin, drawn exclusively from the latter's critical writings about tsarist Russia, on the manifold ills and problems of contemporary Soviet life.[28]

The neo-tsarist Soviet order has almost ceased to function, but has not yet been displaced, or has only begun to be, by new political and economic structures that can work. It is a situation that reminds one Soviet writer of something Herzen said in the later nineteenth century about Russia having shed an old skin but not yet having grown a new one. The Soviet era as we have known it is ending, but a post-Soviet culture has only started to appear. And so we come to a concluding question: what time is it now in the Soviet cycle of Russia's history? From our interlocutors over there come two answers, which I will contend are two versions of one.

According to the first, Russia is entering a new Time of Troubles (*smuta*), comparable to the one that afflicted Muscovy between 1598 and 1613. After Ivan Grozny died, an influential courtier, Boris Godunov, became factual ruler during the reign of Ivan's son Fyodor and was elected tsar in his own right in 1598. A famine and plague in 1601–2 were followed by Boris' death, political unrest, breakdown of the state order, a succession of pretenders to the throne, civil war, and Polish intervention; and only with the election of Mikhail Romanov to the throne in 1613 was a new dynasty established and stability restored.

Nowadays, as economic and political turmoil mounts and the Russian empire re-established in the Soviet period disintegrates, we read articles about the present time as a new *smuta* or the start of one. Professor Ruslan Skrynnikov of Leningrad University, who gave a paper on the first *smuta* at the World Congress of Soviet and East European Studies at Harrogate, England in July 1990, mentioned in the discussion period that his audience at public lectures on this subject in Leningrad have grown much larger of late. When asked why, he answered that people have a 'premonition of *smuta*'.

---

[24]V. Volzhsky, 'Dvoevlastie?', *Nedelya*, 23–29 July 1990.
[25]Yu. Chernichenko, 'Slovo kotorogo ia ne prosil', *Izvestiya*, 7 July 1990.
[26]G. Bystrov, 'Dat' krest'ianinu zemliu i voliu', *Izvestiya*, 26 August 1990.
[27]B. Mikhailov, 'Nadeius' na intelligentsiyu', *Knizhnoe obozrenie*, 6 July 1990.
[28]V. Lakshin, 'Ne meshat' zhit'!', *Izvestiya*, 11 August 1990.

Viacheslav Kostikov goes further. He writes that Russia has experienced several times of troubles in her history. Their deeper cause, he suggests, lies always in a state power that deadens society, represses *glasnost'*, and turns citizens into slaves who are easy to rule. Thus it was under Ivan Grozny, and the reasonable leader who came after in the person of Boris Godunov was unable to prevent the collapse at the start of the seventeenth century. The tragedy of Russian history, Kostikov concludes, lies in the fact that 'the times of troubles arise after the deaths of tyrants and dictators. So it was with Ivan Grozny, and so it was with Stalin'.[29] The disturbing implication of this article would have been amply clear to Soviet readers by the time of its publication: August 1990.

According to the other version of the answer to our question, the country is now in the early years of the twentieth century. Some proponents of this position point to the time following Nicholas II's October manifesto of 1905, when the Duma came into being as a Russian parliament and legal political parties emerged. So, now, a semi-elective parliament has appeared in the new Congress of People's Deputies and its Supreme Soviet, and various small parties are emerging, including Social Democrats, Constitutional Democrats, Russian Democrats, anarcho-syndicalists, and monarchists. But the democratic developments of then and now go along with another, ominous parallel: the rise then and again now of arch-nationalist, anti-Semitic movements of the radical right. Then there was the 'Union of the Russian People', to which Nicholas II gave his blessing. Its slogan, 'Beat the Jews and save Russia' found executors in the Black Hundred thugs who perpetrated pogroms against the Jews in 1905–7.[30] And nowadays the threat of pogroms by the fascist *Pamyat'* society, which has the support of some prominent Russian nationalist literary figures, is one of the factors leading Soviet Jews to emigrate in large numbers.

Pyotr Stolypin, the tsarist prime minister who inaugurated in 1906 a land reform which aimed to end communal land tenure and establish peasants as individual farmers, is receiving favourable attention at present from Soviet advocates of a similar land reform that would enable Soviet peasants to leave their collectives and become individual farmers who own the land they till. A Soviet law professor finds the 1906 Stockholm congress of the Russian Marxist party to be very topical. Lenin and Plekhanov clashed there over the land question. Lenin wanted land nationalisation to be in the party's programme. Plekhanov opposed that, warning that it would lead to centralisation and bureaucratisation. His plan was to give peasants property rights to their land and turn over the landlords' estates to municipalities, which would rent them out to peasants. The professor says Plekhanov was right. 'Today, we know who was right in that dispute and it's time to recognise it honestly and not pay

[29]V. Kostikov, 'Vlast' mertvaya i vlast' zhivaya', *Sovetskaya kul'tura*, 11 August 1990.
[30]V. Sirotkin, 'Mrak pogromov', *Nedelya*, No. 40, 1990.

homage to that utopian project of nationalisation.'[31] Out goes Lenin.

The second version of the answer to our concluding question finds expression, further, in the idea that the Soviet period has reached its year 1917. The historian Volobuev finds the present situation, in the fall of 1990, in many ways stunningly similar to 1917, 'the time between February and October'. As then, so now the country is in total crisis. As that earlier systemic crisis was a result of centuries of tsarist absolutism, so the present one is an outgrowth of an even more ferocious adminis- trative–command system. Then, as now, the country was in the midst of a stormy democratisation, with Petrograd and Moscow, then and now, in the lead. Mass-meeting democracy, with all its heated passions, was then and is now going full blast. Then, as now, all sorts of new parties were appearing. Then, as now, politicalised social forces were polarising, depriving the reformists (now called 'centrists') of hope for national con- ciliation. Then some politicalised army generals were moving toward the Kornilov revolt, which paved the way for revolutionary extremists – that is, the Bolsheviks – to take power; and now it would be a good idea for generals to stay out of politics. Never before 1917 was there such responsiveness in Russia to astrologers, magicians, prophets and faith healers, and so again today. Then, to the dismay of conservative forces, the country was moving to the left. And so it is now, and again to the dismay of the main conservative force, which is the Communist Party.[32]

The present situation also reminds the philosopher Nikolai Mikhailov of the post-February one in 1917. The February Revolution and rise of the Provisional Government were, he says, the perestroika of that time, or start of it. The question now is whether the post-February democratic coalition, meaning those on the left today, can forestall the loss of their popularity; whether the new governing structures can avoid the errors of the Provisional Government; and how real is the possibility, today or tomorrow, of an attempted neo-Kornilov generals' revolt? And can a new October be avoided? Here Mikhailov explains that the October 1917 coup was 'the price paid for the opportunism of the fathers of the February 'perestroika', for their inconsistency, their shifting first to the left and then to the right, their fear of radical reform and action'.[33]

In this way of thinking, Gorbachev's regime is the contemporary Pro- visional Government, perestroika is the course toward an evolutionary, democratic development of the country, and the danger is that *this* Provisional Government will go the way of its predecessor by failing to pursue, consistently and firmly, a line toward radical systemic change. And, again in this way of thinking, the threat looming up is that of either a new attempted military putsch like the Kornilov rising in 1917 or a new October, that is, a new takeover by today's Bolsheviks.

And who might they be? They are the ultra-radicals, the extremists, the intolerant and impatient ones, those prepared to fight for human

[31]Bystrov, *loc. cit.*
[32]P. Volobuev, 'Strana leveet, a partiya?', *Sovetskaya kul'tura*, 8 September 1990.
[33]N. Mikhailov, 'Vysokoe napriazhenie', *Izvestiya*, 8 September 1990.

happiness to the last man, those whose 'genetic Bolshevism' takes the form of a fanatical anti-Bolshevism.[34] The 'genetic Bolsheviks' have representatives, says another writer, in the extremist so-called 'Democratic Union', whose organ, *The Free Word*, uses epithets like 'political prostitute' to refer to liberals or centrists of today. It does so, the author observes, in the polemical style of that ultra-left Bolshevik Ulyanov-Lenin, who hated liberals.[35]

I have suggested that the two proffered answers to our concluding question are really one. In other words, that the revolutionary period, with its ending of the Romanov dynasty, disintegration of the Empire, internal collapse, disorder, civil war and foreign intervention, was a new Russian Time of Troubles. This is not the way that we in the West have generally thought of it. We have been influenced, perhaps over-influenced, by Crane Brinton's book *The Anatomy of Revolution* (first published in 1938), in which Russia's twentieth century revolution was analyzed along with England's of the seventeenth century and America's and France's of the eighteenth as a paradigmatically modern, hence modernising, one. Some Russians who lived through their revolutionary years are of different mind. To them it was another Russian breakdown, another dynastic interregnum, another *smuta*. That is how P.B. Struve characterised it in 1918 and how Yurii Got'e saw it in his diary of 1917-22, so much so that Terence Emmons has given the title *Time of Troubles* to his English-language edition of Got'e's diary.[36] And another American scholar, Lars Lih, finds paradigmatic significance in that view of the revolutionary years in his pathfinding new book, *Bread and Authority in Russia, 1914–1921*.

If we see the Revolution as a second Russian Time of Troubles, and hence the rise of the Soviet regime as the emergence of a new dynasty (the *Bol'sheviki*), it ceases to seem so strange that a new cycle of Russia's history unfolded in our century, and that a new *smuta* threatens now. Such a reading of the Soviet era might have two strengths from a scholarly standpoint. By showing that tsarism rose again in what seemed, somewhat illusorily, an epoch of modernisation through urbanisation and industrial development, this reading can render the present systemic breakdown more comprehensible to us. It is a predominantly *archaic* system that has nearly ceased to function. Second, this way of thinking may help us comprehend the tenacity of the still partly extant old order. For in Russia this system that we glibly call 'Communism' is one with roots that go deep into the centuries and hence are not so easy to pull up.

The question becomes: Can Russia at long last escape from the cycle of administrative–command systems followed by times of troubles? Our history-minded contemporaries over there are asking it in their own

[34]A. Uliukaev, 'Priglashaiu k promedleniyu', *Moskovskie novosti*, 26 August 1990.
[35]L. Saraskina, 'Kainova pechat' revoliutsil'', *Vek XX i mir*, No. 7, 1990, p. 25.
[36]*Time of Troubles: The Diary of Iurii Vladimirovich Got'e*, ed. and trans. Terence Emmons (Princeton, 1988).

manner. One of them writes: 'If you take a close look, all our Russian and Soviet perestroikas came exclusively from above and were just as easily withdrawn by the next oncoming authority. And the whole question is: why? Why have they never come from below in any other form than that of an all-destroying tornado?'[37]

And here is Viktor Erofeev's formulation: 'Can it be that this sixth part of the globe has its own special relationship to time and social development, so that stagnation and misfortune are the constant elements not only of the regimes of Brezhnev and Nicholas I but of Russian national history in general, a history that moves in circles? If so, what historical swamp will eventually swallow up perestroika and all the hopes connected with it. How can we break out of the vicious circle?'[38]

I cannot answer, save to say that it will take much time and effort, no little good fortune, and, possibly, substantial assistance from this country, which came to Russia's aid with Lend–Lease in World War II and has as much reason to want her to come out of this time of trial democratically victorious as we had for wanting her to come out of that one militarily so.

If fortune smiles, this reforming tsar will go down as the founder of a presidency. This Provisional Government will stop wavering and seek systemic change that can stabilize the national situation. This Duma will stand. The incipient law-governed state will evolve further, and Benckendorf's agency will become a normal intelligence service. The imperial structure will be replaced by that of a commonwealth of nations or confederation. Liberals will come to the fore in a multi-party polity in which the party long known as 'Bolshevik' may become Menshevik in both senses of the word. Russian generals will respect the supremacy of civil authority. Peasants will become proprietors of the land they till if they wish, and the Starodubtsevs will go into retirement. A destatified economy will emerge and, with it, a modicum of prosperity for the people. Russian culture will prosper in freedom. The government will continue co-operating with others to establish an orderly world under international law, in which the demographic, technological, economic and cultural forces now making for universal human catastrophe can be checked before it is too late.

And if fortune frowns, we pretty well know from history what that will mean. Another round of the cycle, after another full-scale Russian *smuta* climaxed by civil war. When asked at Harrogate whether he thought the latter outcome likely, Ruslan Skrynnikov just said: 'May God forbid!' Let those words of his be mine as well.

[37] A. Sabov, 'Obmorok ot svobody: tri revolyutsii bez nas', *Literaturnaya gazeta*, 28 September 1990.
[38] V. Erofeev, 'Neither Salvation nor Sausage', *New York Review of Books*, 14 June 1990.

4
Reforming the party: Organisation and structure 1917–1990

Francesco Benvenuti
(Translated by C. Woodhall and edited by C. Ward)

Introduction

In February 1990 the central committee ratified the draft resolutions for debate at the twenty-eighth congress. The most significant stated that the party must renounce its political monopoly. The party's leading role, guaranteed by the 1977 Soviet Constitution, now had to be fought for, possibly in competition with rival political forces: henceforth communists would have to 'struggle to maintain their position as the party of government within the framework of a democratic process by winning the votes of the electors'.[1]

Despite a number of puzzling passages, the document marked a considerable weakening of the principle of one-party rule which emerged *de facto* after 1917. Defined as 'an autonomous politico-social organisation' and 'a voluntary union of the membership', emphasis was placed on the party's political nature. The former definition, confirmed at the twenty-seventh congress of February–March 1988, first appeared in the party statutes at the October 1961 twenty-second congress. The second originated in a statute approved by the nineteenth congress in October 1952. If the former can be traced to the Khrushchevian thaw, the latter's antecedents are more surprising; in 1952, for the first time since 1934, no mention was made of the party's 'vanguard' role in Soviet society.[2]

This new outline of the party's role paves the way for some form of multi-party system, but is also the case that it invalidates much of the thinking developed by the leadership since 1985. In summer 1988, for instance, the nineteenth conference confirmed that the one-party system would be maintained, albeit within the framework of political perestroika. In exploring these apparent contradictions I shall attempt to illustrate some of the implications of the plan for political perestroika conceived by the party leaders around Gorbachev prior to February 1990. I shall also touch on the reforms to the party apparatus which were discussed at that time. I have taken the view that the problem can be illuminated most effectively by reference to the historical background.

[1] *Izvestiya* (13 February 1990).
[2] *XXVII S''ezd KPSS. Sten. Otchet* (vol. 4, Moscow, 1988); *KPSS* (vol. 8, Moscow, 1985), p. 285; (vol. 10, Moscow, 1986), p. 186.

History

In his speech to the nineteenth conference, and especially in his concluding remarks, Gorbachev stressed the need for a profound change in party–state relations. The final conference resolutions spelt out two essential tasks: 'to delimit the functions of the party and the state', and to carry out 'a profound democratisation of the internal life of the party'. These tasks were intimately connected. From 1918 onwards the authoritarian and bureaucratic degeneration of the party – its depoliticisation – paralleled the increasing interpenetration of party and state. Indeed, the latter was one of the main causes of the former. From the historical perspective, therefore, the line taken at the nineteenth conference was correct. The conference made plain its opposition to the traditional 'formal approach' inspired by *nomenklatura* – the selection and posting of cadres. In this vital area of party activity 'democratic procedures', based on elections, were essential.[3]

In July 1988, immediately after the conclusion of the conference, a central committee plenum declared that the party apparatus was to be reorganised.[4] Next month Gorbachev addressed a *zapiska* to the Politburo. The General Secretary's proposals were approved by the Politburo and the central committee in September. At the end of October G. P. Razumovskii and N. E. Kruchin presented the central committee with the findings of a survey of party committees at *okrug* level and above, and unveiled proposals for the reorganisation of the local apparatus similar to those advanced by Gorbachev and the Politburo. These were the first steps in the drafting of a new party statute, to be submitted to the twenty-eighth congress. Public discussion of the drafts began towards the end of 1989.[5]

Gorbachev proposed to simplify drastically the central committee apparatus, at that time subdivided into twenty sections. In his opinion only nine should remain. Many sections specialising in administration and economic management should be abolished. The *zapiska* stated that 'it is necessary to proceed resolutely towards handing over the functions of economic management from the central committee's sections to the government and its organs'. The retention of two administrative/management sections ('Economic and Social Issues' and 'Agriculture'), was justified by reference to 'the enormous importance of these matters at this stage'. However, declared Gorbachev, 'their functions, and consequently their structures, must be modified'. They would deal only with 'the most important questions' without 'interfering in detail with the practical work of the state's organs'.[6] Gorbachev insisted that, to avoid the danger of interference, the sections should not be split up

[3]*XIX Vsesoyuznaya Konferentsiya KPSS. Sten. Otchet (28 iuniya – 1 iuliya 1988)* (vol. 2, Moscow, 1988), pp. 36, 143.
[4]*Partiinaya zhizn'* (16, 1988), pp. 29-30.
[5]*Izvestiya TsK* (1, 1989), pp. 8–10.
[6]*Ibid.*, pp. 84–5; *Partiinaya zhizn'*, (16, 1988), pp. 29-30.

into sub-departments specialising in various economic and administrative matters, as had been the rule previously. His insistence on this point is politically significant: in July 1988 the central committee recommended, not the abolition, but the 'strengthening' of the sub-departments.[7] In September 1988 the Politburo decided to introduce analogous changes into the party committee apparatus at republican and regional level.[8] Here the reforms were less ambitious. Since 1978 it had been permissible for local parties to elaborate a plethora of sections; what was envisaged was a sharp reduction of personnel coupled with big salary increases for those who remained at their posts. The Politburo declared that:

> '. . . the reorganisation of the apparatus presupposes a radical change in the functions, content and methods of work of all organs. Command methods, parallelism, the duplication and substitution of state and economic organs [by the party], and methods of a technocratic character, must be thoroughly rooted out.'

In fact the initial and revised drafts of the new party statutes were elusive on the exact structure of the apparatus. While sections were renamed 'permanent commissions', and whilst in the first draft the 'productive and territorial' principle was advanced in relation to the permanent commissions, in the revised draft this was replaced by the phrase 'territorial-productive'. The difference between these two formulations will be explored below. It is clear, however, that the revision had been influenced, not only by contemporary political factors, but also by historical precedents.[9]

II

The 1988 reorganisation was only the latest in a long line of reforms stretching back to 1917. Its political significance can best be understood

---

[7]According to Hough's reconstruction of the central committee apparatus, in 1978 there were at least twenty-one sections, each sub-divided between three and fifteen times, making a total of more than 150 sub-departments. In June 1990 Razumovskii revealed in *Pravda* that the sub-departments had actually been abolished in autumn 1988. J. F. Hough and M. Fainsod, *How the Soviet Union is Governed* (Cambridge, Mass., 1980), pp.412–17, 420; S. White, et al., *Communist Political Systems: An Introduction* (London, 1982), p. 126. For the mid-1960s see: J. A. Armstrong, *Politics and Government in the Soviet Union* (New York, 1967), p. 67. The structure of ministries and state committees in the early 1970s is described in W. J. Conyngham, *The Modernization of Soviet Industrial Management* (Cambridge, 1982), pp. 5, 9. The structure of the sections did not correspond exactly to the sub-divisions of the state administration: *Pravda* (26 June 1990).

[8]*Izvestiya TsK* (1, 1989), p. 87;*Lektsii po partiinomu stroitel'stvu* (vol. 1, Moscow, 1978), pp. 192ff.

[9]*Izvestiya TsK* (1, 1989), p. 88; *Pravda* (28 March 1990; 28 June 1990). See the essay by F. M. Borodkin in *Postizhenie* (Moscow, 1989), pp. 252, 254, 261; G. K. Kriuchkov, in *Stranitsy istorii sovetskogo obshchestva* (Moscow, 1989), pp. 420–22. See also the essay by V. N. Lysenko, in *Postizhenie, op. cit.*, pp. 337–9.

from this perspective, since it will become apparent that reorganisation was the product of an evolving Bolshevik organisational culture. Successive organisational structures reflect a logic peculiar to the one-party system – the 'laws', one might say, that have helped to fashion and regulate Bolshevik government throughout its history. I am in agreement with those historians who identify the process of the formation of the one-party system (and the economic and social conditions in which this process developed) as the key to the understanding of the history of the party.[10]

The fundamental principle of the party's organisation was given its first formal definition in the statute ratified by the eighth conference of December 1919:

'The party is structured on the basis of democratic centralism, following the territorial principle. The organisation which serves a given area is deemed superior to all other organisations serving single parts of the said area.'[11]

Democratic centralism regulated the internal life of the party as a whole whilst the territorial principle defined the relations between party organisations and framed a hierarchy of leading organs structured along territorial lines. From the outset, therefore, 'democratic centralism' and the 'territorial principle' represented two coherent and complementary organisational criteria, two faces of the same organizational model. This was a structure common to all major political parties of the contemporary age.[12]

During the Civil War party structure underwent a series of major alterations. Of these, the most important related to the Red Army. It was here the first specialised section of the central committee was created. After the eighth congress of March 1919 the *Politicheskoe Upravlenie Revolyutsionnogo Voennogo Soveta Respubliki* (PUR) developed in

---

[10]There are, of course, those who take the view that it was the doctrines elicited in *What is to be Done?*, and in 'Leninism' generally, which exerted a decisive influence on the party's organizational structure, before and after the October Revolution. See R. Schlesinger, *Il Partito Comunista nell'URSS* (Milan, 1962); L. Schapiro, *The Communist Party of the Soviet Union* (London, 1975). For a thoroughly scholarly discussion of the influence of *What is to be Done?* on Bolshevism see V. I. Lenin, *Che fare?* ed. V. Strada, (Turin, 1971), introduction; V. I. Lenin, *What is to be Done?* ed. R. Service, (London, 1988), introduction.

[11]*KPSS* (vol. 2, Moscow, 1983), p. 202.

[12]I am aware that many scholars would not accept this statement. J. Keep and G. Swain have developed the thesis – which, I believe, was first advanced seriously by R. Pipes – that the conspiratorial circle grouped around Lenin between 1903 and 1917 had very little in common with a modern political party, such as the German Social Democratic Party, and that after 1908 there existed in Russia the possibility of constructing a party of a Western (German or Belgian) type; i.e., a more modern and less arbitrary alternative to the Bolsheviks. See: R. Pipes, *Social Democracy and the St Petersburg Labor Movement 1885–1887* (Irvim, 1984); J. L. H. Keep, *The Rise of Social Democracy in Russia* (Oxford, 1983); G. Swain, *Russian Social Democracy and the Legal Labour Movement 1907–14* (London 1983). For a substantially different view see: R. C. Elwood, *Russian Social Democracy in the Underground* (Assen, 1974).

the military. The PUR directed the work of communist cells, of their bureaux, and the political commissars in regiments and units through new special party organs, 'political departments' located at the front and in the army.[13] The PUR survived the Civil War, but its peculiar organisational structure (vertical rather than territorial) and functions (appointment from above rather than election from below) were not incorporated into party statutes until the fourteenth congress of October 1925. The existence of a central committee section specialising in a particular field and directly linked to the primary party organisations in that field remained, for several years, a striking anomaly. Although the central committee had eight other sections, they were organised on entirely different principles[14]. They were 'functional' sections: each performed a *single* political function within *all* the branches of economic and social work carried out by the territorial party organisations. In contrast, the PUR was the prototype of the 'production-branch' sections of the 1930s: the PUR performed *all* the political functions of party work within a *single* branch.

Industrialisation exerted considerable strains on the party apparatus. The result, from as early as 1930, was the elaboration of specialised economic sections. The section dealing with party and state cadres was divided into a sub-department directing the work of the territorial party organisations and an 'Assignment Section' which controlled the posting of party and state cadres to various branches of the economy and administration.[15] L. M. Kaganovich, speaking to the sixteenth congress (June-July 1930), defined the objective of the reorganisation as 'a greater differentiation of functions', adding that:

'. . . the reorganisation of the party apparatus must not be considered from a narrow and technical point of view. The party apparatus must be more flexible, more sensitive than any other apparatus of the dictatorship of the proletariat, because it is only thanks to its flexibility and sensitivity that the party, as a party of government, is able to set in motion the whole system, all the levers and transmission belts of the proletarian dictatorship'.[16]

At the same time the process of severely curtailing democracy within the party was already well underway. It was not only technical–economic factors that underpinned reorganisation on the production-

---

[13]F. Benvenuti, *The Bolsheviks and the Red Army 1918–22* (Cambridge, 1988); J. Erickson, *The Soviet High Command. A Military-Political History* (London, 1962). The appearance of political departments was one of the main causes of the 'Military Opposition' of 1918–19. The reactions of party members to the more general phenomenon of the party's absorbtion into the state during the Civil War have been studied by R. Service, *The Bolshevik Party in Revolution 1917–1923. A Study in Organizational Change* (London, 1979).

[14]Schapiro, *Communist Party* p. 652.

[15]*Loc. cit.*

[16]I. Stalin and L. Kaganovich, *Otchet TsK XVI s"ezdu VKP(b)* (Moscow–Leningrad, 1930), pp. 150–1.

branch principle, there was a genuine political imperative as well: the compartmentalisation of the life of the party, the end of the political dimension of the party's life, and the triumph of that basic depoliticisation which Stalin had pursued from the outset of his career as General Secretary.[17]

Within a few years, due primarily to the efforts of Kaganovich, specialisation by production-branch had almost completely replaced the old functional principle. In 1933 new political departments, modelled on the PUR, took over many powers previously held by ordinary party committees in rural areas. The same obtained and in rail and river transport.[18] It was probably at this time that the agriculture and transport sub-departments of the central committee's 'Assignment Section' took responsibility for political departments and primary party organisations in their respective branches. 'Party organisers', appointed by the central committee, or by regional committees, were introduced into the factories[19] and secured the right to direct party cells previously exercised by factory party committees. Simultaneously a fully-fledged 'Industrial Section', in charge of all party work in industry, began to take shape in the central apparatus. The structure of these central sections, conforming to the production-branch principle, found its counterpart in a closer relationship between the central committee and primary party organisations. The new production-branch principle, with its 'efficiency-first' and executive spirit, developed in parallel with a more centralist, disciplinarian and authoritarian internal party regime than was envisaged when the rules of 'democratic centralism' were originally framed.

The statute approved at the seventeenth congress (January–February 1934) projected the fragmentation of the old 'Assignment Section' into a series of production-branch sections, each responsible for the selection of party and state cadres, for mass agitation, and for organisation in the main sectors of the country's economy. Bowing to the principle of specialisation, a section devoted to the education of party cadres, and to the staffing of 'leading party organs' (the territorial committees), was created. The only section to retain a functional structure was that dealing with the 'Culture and Propaganda of Leninism'.[20] Republican and regional party committee sections were reorganised on a similar pattern. They had a triple responsibility: to the committee to which they belonged, to the corresponding section

---

[17]As early as the twelfth congress (April 1923), Stalin had opposed the 'delimitation' between party and state, a principle defended by some economic cadres and the Left Opposition. J. R. Azrael, *Managerial Power and Soviet Politics* (Cambridge, Mass., 1966), pp. 69ff; A. Di Biagio, 'Stalin e Trotskii: dopo la rivoluzione', in *Problemi del socialismo* (17, 1980), pp. 142–8.

[18]*KPSS* (vol. 6, Moscow, 1985), pp. 21ff, 80. On political departments in agriculture see: D. Thorniley, *The Rise and Fall of the Rural Communist Party 1927–1939* (London, 1988).

[19]*KPSS* (vol. 6), p. 51.

[20]*Ibid.*, p. 138; Schapiro, *Communist Party* p. 653.

of the superior territorial committee, and to the central committee. It is very likely that this structure deprived regional party
organisations of their autonomy, and of the powers they previously
enjoyed.

The 1934 statute also introduced a new organisational structure. The
territorial principle was displaced by the 'territorial–productive' principle:

'. . . that organisation which serves a given area is deemed superior
to all other organisations serving single parts of the said area, *or* the
organisation which serves an entire production branch or an administrative branch is deemed superior to all organisations serving parts of
the said branch'.[21]

After autumn 1935 the 'Leading Party Organs' section was run by G. M.
Malenkov and, for a time, by N. I. Yezhov. The internal structure of the
section changed. Sub-departments were formed for the main branches of
the economy, as had been the case in the pre-1933 section for 'Organisation and Instruction'.[22] These were further specialised by territorial area.
This marked the start of a trend leading to the abandonment – or at least
to the weakening – of the production-branch principle.

During the Great Purges of 1936–38 the movement to restore the functional principle and to concentrate all work with cadres into a single section gathered pace. The Purges, however, were unleashed with particular
violence on territorial organisations and the system of local power in
general, especially at regional level. At the central committee plenum of
February–March 1937 Stalin accounted for the ubiquitous presence of the
'enemy within' by arguing that organisations and leading party cadres –
particularly the territorial ones – had allowed themselves to be distracted
from economic work and had failed to stimulate 'vigilance' and the 'political' qualities required of the membership.[23] If Stalin's line of argument
possessed any logic (which cannot be taken for granted), it probably
arose from a perverted and malicious use of the criticisms, levelled by
many leading cadres in the regions, against the territorial–production-
branch model, a model fully developed by 1933–34.[24]

On the basis of an address delivered by A. A. Zhdanov, the eighteenth congress of March 1939 broadly re-established the old functional
and territorial principle of party organisation, at least in formal terms.
The 'Agricultural Section', however, was retained. Moreover, the new
party statute approved by the congress accorded primary organisations
the 'right of control' over their corresponding administrations.[25] There
is no consensus amongst historians on the political significance of this

[21]*KPSS* (vol. 6), p. 137.
[22]F. Benvenuti and S. Pons, *Il sistema di potere dello stalinismo. Partito e Stato in URSS 1933–1953* (Milan, 1988), pp.103–4.
[23]J. A. Getty, *Origins of the Great Purges. The Soviet Communist Party Reconsidered 1933–1938* (Cambridge, 1985), ch. 3, pp. 138–40.
[24]Benvenuti, Pons, *Il sistema* pp.172–8.
[25]*KPSS* (vol. 7, Moscow, 1985), pp. 99, 105; Schapiro, *Communist Party* p. 653.

measure.[26] In my view it was intended to emphasise the autonomy of the party's primary and territorial organisations vis-à-vis the economic and administrative bureaucracies of the state. In other words, it was a reaction against the principle of 'verification of execution' which had gained the powerful status of a 'rule' in the early years of industrialisation. The 'right of control' could be characterised as symptomatic of an attempt by the leadership to breathe new life into the party – a party at once half-destroyed by the Purges and modelled on an administrative and economic bureaucracy. It should, I believe, be understood as a corollary of the functional principle of organisation.

As in 1934, the 1939 statute continued to define the newly envisaged structure as 'territorial–productive'. In reality a clause, approved at the seventeenth congress, which conferred on the central committee the right to set up political departments and to appoint party organisers 'in backward sectors of socialist construction which are acquiring particular importance for the economy and the country', was retained. If Zhdanov had meant to lend more weight to the functional principle of organisation, his attempt proved incomplete and incoherent: we now learn from a Soviet scholar that Malenkov's 'Cadres Directorate' was subdivided into forty-five smaller economic sections. In fact the semi-functional structure envisaged by the 1939 statute again underwent modification due to the vigorous revival of the production-branch principle. In November 1939 special 'Industrial Sections' were re-introduced at republican, regional and city level.[27] The eighteenth conference of February 1941 stressed that the party needed to make more effort to boost production and efficiency in industry and transport and created specialised regional secretaries for these sectors.[28]

The war reinforced the productivist principle. The political departments of rural districts, abolished in December 1934, were re-established in November 1941.[29] Immediately after the end of hostilities many, especially Zhdanov, complained that the economic policies of the preceding years had resulted in a rigid productivist and military approach, resulting the domination of the party over the administrative apparatus.[30] In Schapiro's words:

'. . . the keynote of wartime administration was rationalisation . . . and the complete fusion of the government and party machines, which

[26]D. Granick, *Management on the Industrial Firm in the USSR* (New York, 1954), assimilates 'control' within 'checking and execution', which I consider to be incorrect. The interpretation advanced by J. F. Hough in *The Soviet Prefects* (Cambridge, Mass., 1969), pp. 87, 98, 102, is more complex and closer to the truth.
[27]*KPSS* (vol. 6), pp. 139-40; (vol. 7), pp. 101, 145. See also: V. G. Kolychev, in *Stranitsy istorii KPSS* (Moscow, 1989), p. 30; id., in *30–e gody* (Moscow, 1990), pp.24–5.
[28]Benvenuti, Pons, *Il sistema*, pp. 218–9.
[29]They were abolished once more in May 1943: *KPSS* (vol. 6), p. 186; (vol. 7), pp. 260, 412.
[30]Benvenuti, Pons, *Il sistema*, pp. 288–96.

until the war Stalin had maintained as separate and competing administrations'.[31]

There seems, in the early post-war years, to have been an attempt to delimit the functions of party and state.[32] Zhdanov and Stalin apparently considered that the functionalist course, approved by the 18th congress and subsequently reversed by the 18th conference and the imperatives of war, should now be thoroughly implemented. But in summer 1948, about the time of Zhdanov's death, the party apparatus began to move in the opposite direction – the production-branch principle began to increase in importance. The Leningrad party, headed by Zhdanov since Kirov's death, expressed serious reservations on the wisdom of this policy, just as it had at the time of the 18th conference,[33] but there was no clear resolution of the problem, no restoration of the structure envisaged in the 1934 statute. Instead, a combination of the functional–territorial and territorial–production branch-principles emerged, dubbed by A. Avtorkhanov 'a mixed functional-branch system.'[34]

The central committee 'Cadres Section', first created in 1934 and reorganised in 1939, became, in 1948, the 'Party, Trades Union and Komsomol Section'.[35] Western historians have deduced the existence of nine other sections, but no mention of the central committee's structure was made in the statutes approved by the 19th and the 22nd congresses. The 1952 statute merely reiterated the definitions of the 1934 and 1939 statues when describing the 'territorial–production-branch' principle. Only in 1961 was there some change; the new statute, whilst confirming the same principle, omitted the sentence explaining the nature of the productivist principle.[36]

In May 1956, according to W. J. Conyngham, the number of central committee sections was increased to thirty. It is also likely than an effort was made to group them in a manner that strengthened the territorial principle.[37] This seems to have been part of Khrushchev's 1957–58 attempt to restructure the state's economic administration on territorial lines by breaking up the vertical–ministerial structures established between 1934 and 1953. As is well-known, Khrushchev then launched a recruitment drive for new party members and granted the

[31]Schapiro, *Communist Party* pp. 498–9.
[32]*Partiinoe stroitel'stvo* (Moscow, 1976), p. 375.
[33]Benvenuti, Pons, *Il sistema*, pp. 322–4.
[34]A. Avtorkhanov, *The Communist Party Apparatus* (Chicago, 1966), pp. 200ff.
[35]M. Fainsod, *How Russia is Ruled* (Cambridge, Mass., 1953), p. 175; Schapiro, *Communist Party* p. 653.
[36]*KPSS* (vol. 8), p. 291; (vol. 10), p. 191. The stability of the apparatus after 1948 has also been commented upon by W. B. Simons and S. White, *The Party Statutes of the Communist Party* (The Hague, 1984), p. 405; T. H. Rigby, 'Staffing USSR incorporated: the origins of the nomenklatura system', *Soviet Studies* (4, 1988), p. 534.
[37]W. J. Conyngham, *Industrial Management in the Soviet Union. The Rœle of the CPSU in Industrial Decision-Making 1917–1970* (Stanford, 1973), p.82.

territorial committees greater prerogatives.[38] A few years later, however, Khrushchev moved in the opposite direction when reorganising the entire party apparatus. He characterised the 'bifurcation' of the party into an 'industrial party' and an 'agricultural party' in November 1962 as the abandonment of the territorial–production-branch principle in favour of the production-branch principle:

> 'Primary party organisations shall be formed in accordance with the productive rather than with the territorial principle. This principle will be supported rigidly . . . . The production principle shall form the basis of the direction of the primary party organisations and of the district, regional and republican organisations . . . . In the upper party organs too there will be a specialisation, and sounder organisational methods will be elaborated. This will lead to an even greater increase in the number of cadres, and in their skills'.[39]

Historians are divided on the significance of party bifurcation. Some have argued that it was designed to strengthen the power of the apparatus over the economy, others the opposite.[40] A few have suggested that, by fragmenting the party's organisation, Khrushchev was trying to restore a form of 'autocratic' government.[41] Recent Soviet commentators, however, lay exclusive emphasis on the eccentric and chaotic character of bifurcation.[42]

B. A. Chotiner's researches, taken together with a close study of Khrushchev's 1962 speeches and writings, allow us to come to a precise judgement on one matter at least: the historical and political origins of the bifurcation plan. It was inspired by the Machine Tractor Stations (MTS), created in 1929 and abolished by Khrushchev in 1958. As early

[38]P. D. Stewart, *Political Power in the Soviet Union. A Study of Decision Making in Stalingrad* (Indianapolis–New York, 1968), p. 43.

[39]N. S. Khrushchev, *Stroitel'stvo kommunizma v SSSR i razvitie sel'skogo khozyaistva* (vol. 7, Moscow, 1963), p. 169.

[40]See: Azrael, *Managerial Power*, p. 145; Y. Bilinsky, in J. W. Strong, ed., *The Soviet Union Under Brezhnev and Kosygin* (New York, 1971), p. 28; B. A. Chotiner, *Khrushchev's Party Reform* (Westport, 1984); J. W. Cleary, 'The parts of the party', *Problems of Communism* (4, 1964); J. F. Hough, 'A harebrained scheme in retrospect', ibid., (4, 1965); id., *Soviet Prefects*, pp. 123, fn. 76; M. McAuley, *Khrushchev and the Development of Soviet Agriculture: the Virgin Lands Programme 1953–1964* (London, 1976), pp. 116–7; J. C. Moses, *Regional Party Leadership and Policy Making in the USSR* (New York, 1974), p. 170; M. Tatu, *Power in the Kremlin* (London, 1969), pp. 252ff. C. S. Kaplan, *The Party and Agricultural Crisis Management in the USSR* (Ithica–London, 1987), emphasizes the emergency character of state and party intervention in agriculture down to 1984.

[41]S. Bialer, *The Soviet Paradox* (London, 1986), p. 11; id., *Stalin's Successors* (Cambridge, 1980), p. 112; Conyngham, *Industrial Management*, p. 275; S. P. Huntington, C. H. Moore, eds., *Authoritarian Power in Modern Societies. The Dynamics of Established One-Party Systems* (New York–London, 1970), p. 275; R. McNeal, *The Bolshevik Tradition* (Englewood Cliffs, 1975), pp. 157, 162–3.

[42]Iu. V. Aksiutin, ed., *Nikita Sergeevich Khrushchev. Materialy k biografii* (Moscow, 1989), pp. 96–7, 108, 110; R. Medvedev, *Ascesa e caduta di Nikita Chruscev* (Rome, 1982), pp. 260–2.

as March 1962 district level administration in rural areas changed significantly. 'Agricultural Productive Administrations' were created, grouping together several districts. In November 1962 Khrushchev proposed that the residual territory of the various regions should be reorganised into analogous 'Industrial Productive Administrations', although M. McAuley – correctly, to my mind – prefers to call these new units 'Non-Agricultural Administrations'.

Bifurcation had the effect of altering the party's regional organisations to match this new administrative sub-division. The reorganisation was accompanied by the re-emergence of another old idea; 'political departments' in agriculture.[43] I am inclined to agree with S. Pons' view that bifurcation was an attempt – one far more radical than anything tried by either Stalin or Kaganovich – to restructure the party on the production-branch principle.[44] Khrushchev sought to give the reform a kind of 'marxist' gloss: given the immanent advent of communism in the Soviet Union, the purely administrative and political functions of the state (and the party) would 'wither away'. It was therefore in the party's interest, if it intended to survive as a leading force, to identify itself with genuinely economic functions and organs, because economic organs, unlike administrative ones, were not destined to 'wither away'.[45] One might ask why Khrushchev did not directly propose a return to MTS and political departments in order to tackle the difficult agricultural situation evident by the early 1960s. The fact is that both solutions were too closely identified with Stalinism and collectivisation. Furthermore, just a year previously, at the twenty-second congress, the right to form political departments in 'backward' sectors of the economy, departments that replaced ordinary party committees, had at last been removed from the statutes.[46]

Bifurcation, in Conyngham's opinion, also entailed a number of alterations to the organisation of central committee sections. They were now divided into six groups, each headed by a member of the Secretariat. These 'super-sections' operated on the principles laid down in 1934. Moreover, consistent with the principle of specialisation, the number of sections was further increased.[47] According to Khrushchev's plan, the structures of territorial party committees below regional level (those corresponding to the new 'administrations'), were to undergo drastic simplification: only two sections would remain – 'Organisation' and 'Ideology'.[48] This is probably what misled J. F. Hough into believing that the purpose of bifurcation was to reinforce the political functions of party organisation and propaganda, but it is apparent that the functional principle was subordinated to the production-branch principle.

In November 1964, one month after removing Khrushchev from the

---

[43]Specifically mentioned in Khrushchev, *Stroitel'stvo* (vol. 6, Moscow, 1963), pp. 414–5.
[44]F. Gori, ed., *Il XX Congresso del PCUS* (Milan, 1988), pp. 208–9.
[45]*Plenum TsK KPSS 19–23 noiabriya 1962. Sten. otchet* (Moscow, 1963), p. 65.
[46]L. Schapiro, ed., *The USSR and the Future* (London–New York, 1963), p. 193.
[47]Conyngham, *Industrial Management* p. 161.
[48]*Plenum TsK KPSS* pp. 20–1.

office of General Secretary, the central committee abolished party bifur-cation and the accompanying administrative reform and returned to the territorial–productive principle.[49] The 1962 reorganisation was thus the last attempt to alter the structure of the apparatus after 1948. It was also the last time that the leadership tried, as it had in the 1930s, to address sudden economic difficulties by primarily administrative means. This, I believe, explains the accusations of 'voluntarism' levelled at Khrushchev by his successors. A. Brown has suggested that Brezhnev (and others, who, like him, kept silent at the November 1962 plenum) might initially have favoured bifurcation before switching to the opposition. Indeed, in November 1964, an article in *Partiinaya zhizn'* acknowledged, with some embarrassment, that 'the reform proposed [by Khrushchev] also contained ideas to which it was difficult to object.' However, the same editorial also asserted that many negative features of the style of party work ('rhetoric . . . , interference in the details of economic work, and, above all, administrative and command methods') could not be regarded as defects inherent in any particular organisational model.[50]

It is possible to argue that Khrushchev's successors had outgrown that characteristically Bolshevik style of thinking which held that party struc-ture had some inherent political and economic significance. Looked at in another way, one might say that the organisational restoration of 1964 was, among other things, a symptom of the stability attained by the appa-ratus and the governmental machine, and that the process of the forma-tion of the Soviet political and economic system had been completed. Conyngham has expressed a similar view:

> 'The mixture of political pressure, centralised bureaucratic controls and coercive mobilisation had become functionally irrelevant at a more complex and differentiated state of industrial development'.[51]

According to P. Cocks, an 'incremental bargaining model' of govern-ment replaced methods based on direct party intervention in society and the economy:

> 'The restoration of the administrative system [under Brezhnev] and the retreat from Khrushchev's policy of excessive party involvement and influence in economic management . . . permitted the growth of autonomy and departmentalism in the economic bureaucracy'.[52]

The old 'laws' of operation had made way for new laws. Brezhnev and his collaborators turned their energies, not towards fresh experiments in organisational engineering, but towards economic reform. Even when the idea of economic reform was abandoned in the late 1960s, they at least

---

[49]*KPSS* (vol. 10), p. 419.
[50]In the Stalin years 'administrative methods' were considered an unfortunate consequence of the production-branch principle: *Partiinaya zhizn*, (23, 1964), pp. 5, 7.
[51]Conyngham, *Industrial Management*, p. 254.
[52]P. Cocks, et al., eds., *The Dynamics of Soviet Politics* (London-Cambridge, Mass., 1976), pp. 160–1.

promoted a massive redistribution of resources between the various sectors of the economy.[53] In Brezhnev's lexicon, the 'voluntaristic' approach had been replaced by the 'scientific' approach.

III

One strand of studies in Soviet history regards the organisational changes detailed here as matters of a purely technical nature, as historically and politically marginal. According to this view, the main goals of the system, and the role played by the apparatus, have remained essentially unchanged over the years. S. M. Schwarz has declared that, after the war at least, 'the problems of relations between the plant administration and the party bodies loses . . . its sociological complexity and becomes merely a problem of administrative technique.'[54] According to R. Conquest, 'the totalitarian apparatus [is] a means for imposing the decisions of the leading figure or figures in many political and economic matters, on an often refractory social structure.'[55] For A. Unger the fundamental conclusion to be drawn from the history of the party is merely that it has extended its control over individuals and society at large. The instruments of government are always essentially the same: 'tyranny seldom invents the means to consolidate itself.'[56] R. J. Hill dismisses the issue of the various relationships established between party and state over the years as 'irrelevant': only an end to the party's supervision of the economy and society would constitute a genuinely radical reform.[57] But Hill's view rests on the widespread notion that the implementation of an authentic economic reform would automatically render the leading role of the party superfluous.[58] Many authors have even expressed profound doubts as to the possibility of distinguishing between party and state in the Soviet Union; between, in Weberian terms, a fully political principle and a fully administrative and bureaucratic principle.[59]

L. Schapiro concludes his major work on the history of the party by

[53]G.W. Breslauer, *Khrushchev and Brezhnev as Leaders: Building Authority in Soviet Politics* (London–Boston, 1982), pp. 147, 163. See also: Kaplan, *Party,* p. 163.
[54]G. Bienstock *et al.*, *Management in Russian Industry and Agriculture* (London, 1944), p. 31.
[55]R. Conquest, *Power and Policy in the USSR* (New York, 1961), p. 9.
[56]A. Unger, *The Totalitarian Party* (Cambridge, 1974), pp. 270–1.
[57]M. McAuley, ed., *The Soviet Union Under Gorbachev* (London, 1987), p. 57.
[58]Conyngham, *Industrial Management,* p. 131; T. H. Rigby and R. F. Miller, *Political and Economic Aspects of the Scientific and Technical Revolution in the USSR* (Canberra, 1976), p. 16; Tatu, *Power,* p. 453. This view is not shared by Hough, *Soviet Prefects* pp. 194–5.
[59]See: D. A. Loeber, 'On the status of the CPSU within the Soviet legal system', in Simons, White, *Statutes,* p. 8; T. H. Rigby, 'Stalinism and the mono-organizational society', in R. C. Tucker, ed., *Stalinism. Essays in Historical Interpretation* (New York, 1977); Schapiro, *Communist Party,* pp. 621–4; M. Waller, *Democratic Centralism* (Manchester, 1981), p. 51. According to Hough one can observe a tendency for the CPSU to conform to the Weberian model of modern bureaucracy: Hough, *Soviet Prefects,* p.275.

effectively denying its status as a modern political party. The party, he argues, is essentially:

'. . . a powerful network of influence and control, but to a large extent and always dependent for its influence and authority on the personal links which its individuals, leading officials or members can forge to the dominant wielders of influence at the top.'

Schapiro, nonetheless, closely detailed the evolution of the apparatus. He realised that the adoption of the territorial–production-branch model in 1934 was 'a bold attempt to concentrate control of the entire national economy in the central apparatus, to an extent which had not hitherto been attempted.' In contrast, the purpose of the 1939 reorganisation was 'to encourage greater responsibility on the part of the managers of industry.' It is strange therefore that he should – regardless of the important changes he describes – conclude that in the 1930s 'the territorial model of party organisation remained in substance unchanged from what it was in the 1920s.'[60] From a different vantage point Hough has cautioned against exaggerating the importance of the contradictory changes in the structure of the party apparatus. The fundamental trend of the Soviet one-party system, he argues, has been continuous and consistent: 'the increasing specialisation in administrative and Party structure and personnel.'[61] Other historians, however, have linked alterations to the apparatus to important institutional and political changes. M. Fainsod noted that the functional model was adopted during periods of party 'reconstruction' – the NEP, the first few years following the Purges, the early post-war years. The production-branch model, on the other hand, was a natural consequence of the 'dispersion' of party functions brought about by industrialisation.[62]

Many political scientists have defined the system of government of mature Stalinism – especially in the period 1945–48 – as a 'ministerial system.' According to this line of argument the party's role was largely 'political–generalist' and ideological. By contrast, after 1948 the production branch system (predicated on the party's day-to-day control of the economy) was definitively entrenched.[63] According to J. Azrael the period 1941–48 was characterised by:

'. . . a transfer of many policy-making functions from the Party Secretariat to the Council of Ministers, an unprecedented expansion of managerial representation on the Præsidium, and a marked curtailment of Party participation in enterprise management'.[64]

In a similar vein R. F. Miller has written that, following the Purges

---

[60]Schapiro, *Communist Party*, pp. 447, 435, 455, 626–7.
[61]Hough, *Soviet Prefects*, p. 274.
[62]Fainsod, *How Russia is Ruled*, pp. 175–7.
[63]Conyngham, *Industrial Management*, p. 56.
[64]Azrael, *Managerial Power*, p. 56.

of the mid-1930s, 'the authority of the Party apparatus was greatly circumscribed.'[65] Finally, historians are generally agreed that the rivalry between Zhdanov and Malenkov was about two opposing conceptions of the party's role: on the one hand a concept of political and ideological mobilisation limited to exercising control over party cadres; on the other a notion of direct party intervention in administration and the economy.[66]

Any overestimation of the political significance of the conflict between the functional–territorial model (corresponding, needless to say, to the 'ministerial system') and the territorial–production-branch model under mature Stalinism is obviously liable to confuse – or even distort – our understanding of the history of the party. S. Bialer points out that the ministerial system took root in a party that had largely been destroyed by the Purges and personal dictatorship.[67] The conflict between two organisational models might thus appear to be of secondary importance to any understanding of the main political issues of the time. It strikes me as significant, however, that notwithstanding the Terror, the Cult of Personality, and the militarisation of the war years, some concern to ensure that the party maintained at least a trace of its *political* nature evidently survived.

G. Procacci has placed more emphasis than any other scholar on the historical and political significance of the two models of party organisation. For him the introduction of the territorial–production-branch structure in 1934 entailed 'a radical transformation, through which the structure of the party leadership was modelled on that of the State and adapted to productivist objectives.' According to Procacci the 1934 statute was a fully-fledged and internally consistent 'Magna Carta of Stalinism', comprising:

'. . . the downgrading of political work as compared to organisational and operational work, a new productivist and efficiency-first drive and the consequent narrow interpenetration between the party apparatus and the State, and the limitation of the mass character of the Party.'[68]

In part this analysis reflects a suggestion made by R. Schlesinger who, like Fainsod, discerned the cyclic nature of the party's history:

'During the two wars that the country had to face, the State to a considerable extent absorbed the Party. On the other hand, the Party assumed direct control of the functions of the State during the 'second revolution [i.e. industrialisation and collectivisation], which rejected the established routine. During calmer periods, the Party maintained a certain detachment from the state apparatus. . . .'[69]

[65] Cocks, *Dynamics*, p. 142.
[66] Conyngham, *Industrial Management*, p. 131; Hough, *Soviet Prefects*, p. 123; Schapiro, *Communist Party*, p. 514.
[67] Bialer, *Stalin's Successors* p. 34.
[68] G. Procacci, *Il partito nell'Unione Soietica 1917–1945* (Bari, 1974), pp. 149, 154.
[69] Schlesinger, *Il partito*, p. 390.

In any event organisational developments undoubtedly pointed towards the adaptation of the party apparatus to economic, security and administrative imperatives. The burgeoning patriotic spirit amongst party members during the 'patriotic war' brought the 'nationalisation' of the party – a process initiated with the doctrine of 'socialism in one country' in 1923–24 – to its conclusion. The statute ratified by the nineteenth congress signalled this crucial change in the nature of the party, making it obligatory for members, not only to 'strengthen the active defence of the Soviet Fatherland', but also to maintain 'state security.'[70]

Throughout its history, therefore, the party has undergone a process of 'statisation' and bureaucratisation – even, as I believe, if this has been neither unilinear nor irreversible. Of the various different parties which constitute the CPSU, it is the party as 'public administrator which has prevailed.[71] As a consequence the party has become indispensable to the government of Soviet society and the functioning of the planned economy. After the dramatic period of 'socialist construction' and industrialisation had drawn to a close, and following Stalin's death, the party's claim to power rested largely on stressing its role as manager, innovator and moderniser of the economy.[72] As is well known, the *political* price cost of achieving this goal has been enormous, and Soviet communists have continued to pay it long after the demise of Stalin. It is probable that the legitimation crisis of the one-party system started when Khrushchev had to fall back on a paraphrase of a notorious Stalinist formulation: 'in the process of the construction of communism, the leading role of the *party* must grow and not weaken'.[73]

IV

The stabilisation of the structure of the party apparatus during the Brezhnev years naturally dampened scholarly interest in this aspect

---

[70]*KPSS* (vol. 8), pp. 286–7.
[71]Bialer, *Stalin's Successors*, p. 201.
[72]Bialer, *Soviet Paradox*, pp. 53–4; Cocks, *Dynamics*, p. 142; G. Grossman, 'The party as manager and entrepreneur', in G. Guroff and F. V. Carstensen, eds., *Entrepreneurship in Imperial Russia and the Soviet Union* (Princeton, 1983), p. 697; D. R. Kelly, *Soviet Politics from Brezhnev to Gorbachev* (New York, 1987), p. 5; id., ed., *Soviet Politics in the Brezhnev Era* (New York, 1980), pp. 27–8; D. W. Treadgold, ed., *Soviet and Chinese Communism* (London–Seattle, 1967), p. 185. The challenges to the role of the party represented by the growth of the economic system are emphasized in S. Bialer and T. Gustafson, eds., *Russia at the Crossroads* (London, 1982), p. 5; J. F. Conyngham, *The Modernization of Soviet Industrial Management* (Cambridge, 1982), p. 39; A. Evans, 'The decline of developed socialism? Some recent trends in Soviet ideology', *Soviet Studies* (1, 1986); Hough, *Soviet Prefects*, p. 39.
[73]*XXI s"ezd KPSS. Sten. otchet* (vol. 2, Moscow, 1959), p. 117. On the debate in the Soviet Union in the early 1960s on the 'withering away' of the state see: Kelly, *Soviet Politics*, pp. 194ff.

of the system of Soviet government.[74] Many historians took the view that other matters were more important – the growth, composition and age profile of the membership and the leadership, for instance, or the level of saturation of different social, professional and ethnic groups.[75] In my view, however, these lines of research continue to point to the persistence of an unresolved conflict between divergent principles of party organisation, one similar to the conflict highlighted by a study of the history of the party's structure. I am thinking here of the dilemma which, according to T. H. Rigby and others, confronted the leadership's recruitment policy after Stalin's death. We might call this dilemma the 'Rigby–Unger effect'.[76]

The 'Rigby–Unger effect' notes that from 1953 to the present the rise in party membership has consistently outstripped population growth. This phenomenon cannot be explained by simply assuming that the party is adapting itself to growing economic, social or administrative complexities; recruits have been drawn simply not only from the technical intelligentsia and the bureaucracy, but also from the less privileged strata of society. The massive increase in membership entails a potential for democratisation, because it renders the party more representative of society at large. The dilemma is that if membership increases the enhanced indentification of the party with society might undermine the very concept of a 'leading role'; if on the other hand recruitment is checked, it is difficult to maintain adequate representation from within the various strata of society.

The history of recruitment from 1917 to 1952 shows that in normal political periods the party has sought to recruit administrative cadres and leading technicians in order to reinforce its hold over the state. Moreover, membership has often been accompanied by rapid promotion, detaching new members from their original social environment. The slump in recruitment in the 1970s and 1980s threatened to widen the gap between the party and the less educated and less privileged strata of society. Indeed, in the early Brezhnev years

---

[74]For less far-reaching alterations to primary party organizations during the early Brezhnev years see: T. Dunmore, 'Local party organs in industrial administrations', *Soviet Studies* (2, 1980); S. Fortescue, 'Research institute party organizations and the right of party control', *Soviet Studies* (2, 1983); P. R. Gregory, 'Soviet bureaucratic behaviour: *khozyaistvenniki* and *apparatchiki*', *Soviet Studies* (4, 1989); E. Hoskey, 'Specialists in the Soviet Communist Party apparatus: legal professionals as party functionaries', *Soviet Studies* (4, 1988); R. F. Miller, ' The Role of the Communist Party in Soviet research and development', *Soviet Studies* (1, 1985). Unlike the 1935 efficiency drive in the iron and steel industry, Shchekino's 1967 economic experiment was not accompanied by organizational changes to the party at factory level: KPSS (vol. 11, Mowcow, 1986), p. 426. See also; J. Delamotte, *Shchekino, entreprise sovietique pilote* (Paris, 1973), pp. 119–46; *KPSS* (vol. 6), p. 260

[75]See: B. Harasymiw, *Political Élite Recruitment in the Soviet Union* (London, 1984); T. H. Rigby, *Communist Party Membership in the USSR* (Princeton 1968), and the author's updates.

[76]Kelly, *Soviet Politics*, p. 49; T. H. Rigby, *Il partito comunista sovietico 1917–1976* (Milan, 1977), pp. 340–3. For Hough's views on the 'Rigby-Unger effect' see: Cocks, *Dynamics*, p. 132.

awareness of the 'Rigby–Unger effect' was more or less openly admitted:

> 'Bourgeois ideologues and renegades from Marxism assert that . . . the leadership of society will concentrate itself exclusively in the hands of specialist professionals, the "intellectual élite", whereas the role of the labouring classes and of the Marxist-Leninist parties will shrink to nothing. It is typical that the authors of these "technocratic" theories should seek to set the educated cadres against the political vanguard of the workers. . . .'[77]

Conversely, it was asserted that 'an indiscriminate broadening of party ranks' might have the dangerous consequence of diminishing the role of party in socialist society.[78]

The 'Rigby–Unger effect' lays bare a contradiction similar to that which, as we have seen, was evident in the historical evolution of the party apparatus. This contradiction reflects the dual nature of the party in the one-party system: mass political party versus ruling party; ideal and social functions versus administrative, operational and executive functions.

It only remains to note that in the last few months the party has emphasised the need to speed up the recruitment of ordinary people ('workers') and to change, at long last, the statistical method used to record the social position of its members. The method used since the 1920s – 'according to social origin' – conceals any social mobility occurring *after* admission to the party. Social historians can only be grateful for a return to the more democratic practice of classifying members 'according to current job'.[79]

Conclusion

Since 1917 there have been a succession of models for party organisation: 'territorial' (or rather 'territorial–functional') until 1933–34; 'territorial–production-branch' from 1934 to 1939; 'territorial' from 1939 to 1945 (with an accentuation of the production-branch principle); a return to the 'territorial–production-branch' model from 1945 to 1948 (with a greater influence exerted by the functional principle); and finally a mixed 'functional–production branch' model left in operation until the end of 1988 (still defined in the statutes as 'territorial–production-branch'). In addition, between 1962 and 1964, there was a brief experiment with a thoroughgoing production-branch model, a policy which led to the temporary 'bifurcation' of regional party organisations.

I have taken the view that the historical oscillation between, on the one hand the functional principle, and on the other the production-branch principle, reflects two different imperatives: in the first instance an

---

[77]A. P. Kirilenko, *Politika sozidaniia i mira* (Moscow, 1980), pp. 221–2.
[78]I. V. Kapitonov, *Izbrannie rechi i stati* (Moscow, 1985), p. 91.
[79]*Izvestiya TsK* (8, 1989), pp. 8, 13; (2, 1990), p. 61; (3, 1990), p. 116.

attempt to promote the party as a mass *political* organisation, in the second an attempt to accentuate the role of the party as a *governing* organisation. The reorganisation of the central and local apparatus at the end of 1988 was inspired by the functional–territorial model, to an extent probably even greater than was the case in the 1920s. This appears to be consistent with the broad policy of perestroika in the Soviet political system, a policy supported by Gorbachev until the end of 1989 and approved by the nineteenth party conference. Here perestroika meant the construction of an ideal one-party society based on the rule of law, the revitalisation and democratisation of the soviets, and a clear demarcation between the party and the administration. The project also included a reform plan intended to introduce economic methods into the management of the economy, partial marketisation, and more flexible planning.

II Society

5
Gender and reform*
Mary Buckley

Many of the policies, priorities and prescriptions of Soviet leaderships since 1917 have carried implications, whether explicit or implicit, intended or unintended, for women's social, economic and political roles.[1] In addition, the images of women projected by ideology in different historical periods have been shaped by these policy priorities, themselves linked to broader political, economic and demographic concerns, as defined by leaders 'from above'.[2] Since perestroika was conceived from the start as a dynamic process of interrelated changes in economy, politics and society, it, too, could not by-pass women who, in 1985, made up 53 per cent of the population, 51 per cent of the labour force and 32.8 per cent of the deputies to the Supreme Soviet; nor was perestroika likely to leave debates about female roles untouched. The central question here is not whether perestroika affects gender but **how** it does so, and whether current reforms influence women's working lives, political behaviour, social roles, and discussions of all three, in significantly different ways from policies of the past.

Official CPSU policy statements since 1985 on motherhood, female labour, promotion and women's organisations have shown continuities with the past rather than radical departures.[3] However, four 'new' potential consequences of broader policies have emerged: first, female unemployment, due to a rationalisation of labour and streamlining, themselves integral to perestroika in the economy; second, fewer women's deputies on the soviets resulting from the abandonment of fixed quotas of female representation; third, emergent female political activism stemming from

[1]Gail Warshofsky Lapidus, *Women in Soviet Society: Equality, Development and Social Change* (Berkeley, University of California Press, 1978).
[2]Mary Buckley, *Women and Ideology in the Soviet Union* (Hemel Hempstead, Harvester/Wheatsheaf; Ann Arbor, University of Michigan Press, 1989).
[3]*Ibid.*, pp. 196–200. See also, Mary Buckley, 'What does perestroika mean for women?', in Jon Bloomfield (ed.), *The Soviet Revolution: Perestroika and the Remaking of Socialism* (London: Lawrence and Wishart, 1989), pp. 151–75.

* I am grateful to the British Academy and to the Soviet Academy of Sciences for a research trip to Moscow and Leningrad in September 1989. Thanks are also due to the Rockefeller Foundation for a residency in the Spring of 1990 at the Villa Serbelloni, where the first draft of this paper was completed.

the legality of informal groups and, to a much lesser extent, due to the revived and expanded *zhensovety*; and, fourth, more frank discussions of the *zhenskii vopros* because of glasnost', and consideration of a host of 'new' issues such as prostitution, abortion, rape and suicide, which were previously taboo. Not all these consequences of official policy, however, are entirely new. Female unemployment had grown during NEP, and was criticised during the 1920s in women's journals, such as *Kommunistka*, and in the general press, such as *Leningradskii Rabochii*.[4] And debate about gender roles did not begin in the late 1980s, but took place in the early 1920s, albeit among a relatively small group of women, and flourished again in the late 1960s and 1970s, when lively arguments about the significance of the female double burden raged in several journals and newspapers, notwithstanding the limits set by official parameters.[5]

What makes the implications of perestroika for women different from the past is a combination of the content of its policies, the historical context in which they are being put forward, and the reaction to them by Soviet citizens. Most crucially, the evolving logic of perestroika which demands a transformation of Soviet politics and society allows citizenship as a status and as an independent activity to develop. Citizenship is no longer merely a set of social rights (often not implemented anyway) for largely passive and somewhat cynical subjects who are permitted a tiny political space for activity; citizenship is becoming an active pursuit, a more *political* activity.[6]

A case can be made that although the 'cultural filter'[7] of society from the early days after the revolution often reacted against, distorted, or redefined the policies and messages conveyed to it 'from above', society until recently lacked legitimate political space to exert pressure, to negotiate and openly to contest policies and their results and to

---

[4]E. Lerner, 'Zhenskii trud i novaya ekonomicheskaya politika', *Kommunistka*, No. 16–17, September-October, 1921, pp. 12–16; A. Anikst, 'Bezrabotnitsa i zhenskii trud v Rossii', *Kommunistka*, No. 2 (19), February 1922, pp. 37–40; Chernysheva, 'Bezrabotitsa sredi zhenshchin i bor'ba s neiu', *Kommunistka*, No. 6, June, 1923, pp. 23–5; M. Khlopl"ankin, 'Zhenskaya bezrabotitsa i mery bor'by s nei', *Kommunistka*, No. 3–5, May, 1922, pp. 13–16; A. Gausman, 'Bezrabotny rabotnitsy i trudovye arteli', *Kommunistka*, No. 10, October, 1923, pp. 8–9; B. Markus, 'Zhenskii trud v SSSR v 1924 gody', *Kommunistka*, No. 4, April 1925, pp. 45–51; E. Tsyrlina, 'Voprosy zhenskogo truda', *Kommunistka*, No. 6, June, 1925, pp. 54–6; G. Pavliuchenko, 'Bezrabotitsa sredi zhenshchin', *Kommunistka*, No. 5, 1925, pp. 39–42; P. Sirotinin, 'Bezrabotitsa i pomoshch' bezrabotnym'. *Leningradskii Rabochii*, No. 2, 1926, p. 7.
[5]Mary Buckley (ed.), *Soviet Social Scientists Talking: An Official Debate About Women* (London: Macmillan, 1986).
[6]Bernard Crick, *In Defence of Politics* (Harmondsworth: Penguin, 1964); T.H. Marshall, *Class, Citizenship and Social Development* (Garden City, New York: Doubleday and Co., 1964).
[7]The concept of 'cultural filter' conveys the notion that social systems have their own specific and complex cultures which respond to policies handed down 'from above'. The cultural filter can be unreceptive to policies, redefine them and turn them into something which was initially never intended by policy markers. See Moshe Lewin, *Soviet Society in the Making* (London: Methuen, 1985).

formulate alternatives. The enthusiasm since 1987 with which journalists and intellectuals have embraced glasnost', coupled with the momentum of *demokratizatsiya*, in particular the emergence of informal groups independent of the CPSU, have resulted in a more belligerent discourse between society and party–state (albeit often a monologue on the part of each) about a range of issues, including the implications for gender of reform. Thus the political and social context is certainly significantly different from the past since issues and debates do not simply follow cues from above, but are also defined by an expanding civil society, whose paranoia, fear and deference is fast evaporating, even if its anxieties remain. Pressure to end the leading and guiding role of the CPSU, and Gorbachev's final acceptance of this in 1990, guaranteed that these trends would intensify. Thus agendas are increasingly set, influenced and contested from below. This contrasts with most of Soviet history, with the exception of the early post-revolutionary years.

Yet despite the escalating ebullience of the years 1987–1990, new agendas for gender were slow to emerge from society. While popular fronts were quick to form, attracted large memberships and made bold, even violent demands, women's groups established themselves slowly, were small in size and refrained from making forceful interventions in politics. Indeed, some female academics who for years had examined women's subordination in the workforce and in the home, and who were personally committed to changes in gender roles, in interviews as late as 1989 reiterated the view that 'it is premature to form a women's movement. Society is not ready for this.'[8] Given that women's groups had formed in Leningrad in 1979, and been sustained in exile in Paris and Frankfurt, observers in the West wondered why new Soviet women's groups were not mushrooming in the rapidly changing political context and why some academics feared the destabilising effect of challenges to traditional gender roles.[9] Not until 1990 did Natasha Filippova and Ol'ga Lipovskaya convene a meeting of representatives of many small women's groups in an attempt to launch a women's movement.[10]

Those Soviet women who were critical of the *status quo* for gender had chosen by 1990 to become active in five main ways:

1. To work within broader political movements not specifically devoted to the *zhenskii vopros* and, at most, to set up or join a women's section within a broader movement, such as the women's group of Sajudis.
2. To be active members of a small women's group devoted to consciousness raising and the dissemination of feminist literature

[8]Interview conducted in Moscow in September 1989.

[9]Alix Holt, 'The first Soviet feminists', in Barbara Holland (ed.), *Soviet Sisterhood* (London: Fourth Estate; Bloomington: Indiana University Press 1985), pp. 237–68; Mary Buckley, 'Soviet religious feminism as a form of dissent', *Topic*, Journal of Washington and Jefferson College, vol. 40, Fall, 1986, pp. 5–12.

[10]*Guardian*, 19 March, 1990.

(whether or not they were active in a broader, and unrelated, political movement), such as the Leningrad women's group which produces *Zhenskoe Chtenie*.
3. To set up women's professional groups linked to particular work concerns rather than to broader social movements, such as the club of women journalists.
4. To publish 'new' feminist arguments, once ideologically taboo, in academic, political and popular publications, such as *Kommunist, Nedelya, Soviet Weekly, Sovetskaya Zhenshchina* and *Rabotnitsa*.
5. To work through more 'establishment' bodies, such as the Soviet Women's Committee, itself becoming slightly radicalised by glasnost', fears of female unemployment and concern about the decreasing percentage of women on the soviets.

Thus *demokratizatsiya* has resulted in a diversity of political action by women, finding expression in official institutions, informal movements and informal groups, some registered and some not. Much of this action relates directly to gender issues and raises questions generally not posed by men, or at best accorded a low priority by them. A plurality of action highlights the diversity of political paths taken by women, and a heterogeneity of views about the relevance of reform to gender.

1. Women's sections within broader political movements: the case of Sajudis

After Sajudis formed, female members organised a women's group within the broader movement because they believed that in daily life women endured particular problems which needed to be discussed separately from men. The information presented here was gathered at a meeting in Vil'nius in March 1989 with five representatives of the women's group.[11]

Female nationalists have a distinctive view of political change. As one put it, 'Men in Lithuania should conduct political struggle, while women should create a beautiful home. There is no point in having an autonomous Lithuania if home life is not improved'. There was unanimous support for a sharper division of labour according to gender between 'public' and 'private' spheres, coupled with backing for an improved status for working women. The main predicament according to an actress was that 'women cannot be complete women in the Soviet Union because home and family are considered insignificant'. Women were perceived as living 'miserable lives in miserable conditions, neglected by men'. Male neglect, it was felt, stemmed from men's attempts to escape reality through 'useless activities'. Unhappy in their jobs 'men can only drink'. Sajudis women argued that men could not develop their full potential as individuals within the Soviet system. However, they believed that women

[11]These five women were employed in the following occupations: acting, factory work, teaching, journalism and cleaning.

enjoyed one essential advantage: 'at least we women can retain dignity through childbirth'.

The clear message was that 'we want women to become women and men to become men. We are not a feminist movement'. There was agreement that mothers should stay at home with children if they so wished, and not have to leave them in kindergartens. As a third put it: 'kindergartens are crowded, do not teach children properly and leave them with atrophied brains. Children struggle, but for what, they do not know.' The difficult task for mothers is 'to normalise' the children later. Soviet power was the main target for blame since it passed on to children 'monstrous information' and 'words with no meanings' in its political education. Another added, 'we are on the brink of an abyss. Our children have no personalities. They are not always human beings. The crime rate shows this. We want to set up our own kindergartens and give children a spiritual education.' A fourth volunteered, 'a bright future will come through family life. We want to change the world by changing individuals.'

Sajudis women acknowledge that Russians do not always share their hopes, nor understand them. When they met Raisa Gorbacheva and explained that they opposed crèches, she was allegedly dumbfounded. Perceived control by Russians of various aspects of their lives is resented. Crèches and kindergartens are seen as imposed by Russian rule. Inadequate care of deaf children is blamed upon an inhumane system. The way in which the Lithuanian magazine *Soviet Woman* is run is negatively affected by decisions made in Moscow. A journalist claimed that 'profit goes to Moscow' and regretted that 'we cannot give the latest news because it takes three months to produce the magazine on our poor equipment'. She believed that financial constraints decided by the centre held the magazine back. 'If we were independent from Moscow, we would know what to do and become more profitable. At the moment, a lot of material is censored and we take orders from above.' Local women also changed the magazine's name to *Lithuanian Woman*, but Moscow objected.

As in most political movements and political parties worldwide, when the female nationalists formed their women-only group, the men were surprised, initially viewed it with derision, made jokes about it and, in this instance, nicknamed it 'skirt'. The Zhenotdel in the 1920s suffered similar wisecracks such as 'Tsentro-Baba' and 'Zhenotdel-Dzhinotdel', but also endured serious opposition from male communists, regular attempts to shut it down and verbal and physical abuse against its female activists.[12] Its goals, however, included a radical transformation of gender roles, especially in rural areas and in Muslim communities, in a largely illiterate society unresponsive to its aims. By contrast, 70

[12]Carol Eubanks Harden, *Feminism and Bolshevism: The Zhenotdel and the Politics of Women's Emancipation in Russia, 1917–1930*, PhD dissertation, University of California at Berkeley, 1979; Mary Buckley, *Women and Ideology in the Soviet Union, op. cit.*, pp. 97–102.

years later, women in Sajudis claim widespread support for their vision of Lithuanian independence, which does not undermine traditional gender roles, but which celebrates *Kinder, Kirche* and *Kucher*. Men in Sajudis apparently overcame their initial objections to a separate women's group. 'Once we showed we were serious, acted independently and went to talk to Raisa Gorbacheva in Moscow, the men respected us', said a mother of four.

Whereas the Zhenotdel seriously challenged the social fabric and set out to undermine social norms and values, women in Sajudis advocate a return to some aspects of the social *status quo ante*. They object to official 'Soviet' values, but not to Catholicism or to traditional patterns of Lithuanian culture. The Zhenotdel sought revolutionary changes in gender roles; women in Sajudis do not. These Lithuanian women represent one example of more conservative contemporary demands, which contrast both with the early revolutionary tradition and with other recently formed organisations, such as SAFO (*Svobodnaya Assotsiatsiya Feministskikh Organizatsii* – the Free Association of Feminist Organisations) and also with the smaller Leningrad group whose main aim is to put out the women's journal *Zhenskoe Chtenie*.[13] Not all nationalist movements, however, have conservative women's groups. Female activists in Rukh who live in Kiev began in 1990 to hold special women-only meetings. These Ukranian women meet to discuss feminist and ecological issues. But like the women in Sajudis, they experienced disapproval from some male nationalists.[14]

2. Small women's groups: Leningrad women and *Zhenskoe Chtenie*

What women in this very loosely structured Leningrad group have in common with the women in Sajudis is the desire to 'raise women's consciousness'. However, how they interpret women's predicament varies, as do their goals and direction. The 'consciousness' they set out to promote is thus radically different. Their central goal is to put out the journal *Zhenskoe Chtenie* under the direction of Ol'ga Lipovskaya.

The journal is oriented towards Western literature and Western feminism and a large part of it is devoted to translations of Western writings. Its fourth edition, for instance, included a translation of Louise Eichenbaum's 'What do women want?' which explores the relations between women and men during pregnancy, focuses on women's emotional needs and discusses the different ways in which men respond to the idea of a child entering their lives. Eichenbaum

[13]Like earlier samizdat materials, *Zhenskoe Chtenie* is typed rather than printed. The bulk of the work is done by Ol'ga Lipovskaya, the group's main organiser. In the near future she hopes to increase the journal's circulation from 30 copies to thousands. It will, therefore, have to take on a more popular style.
[14]Interview conducted in July 1990 with a female member of Rukh.

points out that socialisation processes determine that women will care for children. Women enjoy closeness with their offspring, whereas men who are out at work all day, do not. She holds that 'such a situation is unsatisfactory for everyone: the children lack a father, the father lacks children, the woman lacks a husband'.[15] Like most of the articles in *Zhenskoe Chtenie*, the theme is intensely personal. Its concentration on patterns of intimate relations suggests various ways in which the personal is political. Many of its conclusions are at variance with official Soviet ideology which for decades has held that different 'psycho-physiological characteristics' fit women and men for different, but complementary, tasks.[16] The translation questions the adequacy of constructing 'femininity' as caring, since ultimately it distorts male/female relations.

Other translations in *Zhenskoe Chtenie* break past taboos on sex. The humorous piece, 'Why cucumbers are preferable to men' would not have received approval from censors in any period of Soviet history and would be unlikely to find a place in *Ogonek* or *Moskovskie Novosti*. Firmly in the radical feminist mould, distinct from the socialist feminist or liberal feminist traditions, it begins:

It is not difficult to get to know cucumbers
You can feel a cucumber and know in advance whether or not it is hard

With a cucumber you never discover dirty socks in your washing
A cucumber never gives you a birthday present paid for with your money
A cucumber won't teach you to wash windows, clean fish or prepare beef
A cucumber will never introduce you as 'just an acquaintance'
A cucumber won't reduce you to tears

A cucumber never asks, 'Am I the first?'
A cucumber never tells other cucumbers that he was your 'first'
A cucumber will never tell other cucumbers that he 'was not your first'
With a cucumber there is no need to be innocent more than once.[17]

Hard-hitting radical feminism which isolates men as its main target rather than a particular economic system or a set of discriminating laws is largely unknown in the USSR. *Zhenskoe Chtenie* offers Soviet women the opportunity to acquaint themselves with it and to get to know an eclectic variety of Western literature, generally without editorial comment. It also gives

[15]Louise Eichenbaum, 'Chego khotiat zhenshchiny? Beremennost' i zavisimost'', in *Zhenskoe Chtenie*, No. 4, January–April, 1989, p. 3.
[16]Mary Buckley, 'Soviet interpretations of the woman question', in Barbara Holland (ed.), *Soviet Sisterhood, op. cit.*, pp. 24–53; see also Lynne Attwood, *The New Soviet Man and Woman – Sex Role Socialisation in the Soviet Union*, PhD thesis, University of Birmingham, 1988.
[17]'Pochemu ogurtsy predpochtitel' nee muzhchin', *Zhenskoe Chtenie, op. cit.*, p. 47.

women space to explain their own views about personal experiences. Ol'ga Lipovskaya's description of her visit to the USA fits into the same expressive mould.[18] The thread that holds the journal together is women voicing feelings and thoughts about different aspects of daily life, ranging from sex to pregnancy, housework, childcare, travel and harassment from the Soviet authorities.

One consequence of political reform for gender is the formation of women-only clusters whose members are questioning traditional gender roles and using Western literature to analyse them. Ol'ga Lipovskaya and others, such as the philosopher Ol'ga Voronina, are, at the time of writing, concerned to link some of these embryonic groups and to establish the institutional structures necessary for a women's movement. Most of the organisational work is currently taking place in Moscow.

3. Women's professional groups

Women-only groups organised according to profession are examples of other new initiatives. By the end of 1989 several specialised groups and clubs had formed. These included: the club of women journalists; the union of women cinematographers; the association of women scholars; the federation of women writers within the Writers' Union; 'Woman messenger' (*Vestnitsa*) – a Moscow club of women writers; *Femina* – a women's writers club in Irkutsk; a women's writers association in Petrozavodsk; 'Creativity' (*Tvorchestvo*) – an umbrella association of women from different professions.[19]

As women enter male-dominated professions, there seems to be a tendency for them to hold informal women-only meetings in order to give each other support, share work experiences, pass on information, clarify forms of discrimination against them, and define strategies to protect themselves in professional arenas. Western groups such as women lawyers and female academics suggest that exclusion from informal decision-making processes, sexual harassment and reluctance to recognise women's issues are among the most common problems aired. But whether these issues are the central ones for Soviet professionals awaits empirical research and should not be assumed.

Limited information about the Federation of Women Writers indicates that whilst there is some overlap in goals with Western women's professional groups, there are also quite distinctive aims. Writing in *Literaturnaya Gazeta* about its founding conference, Larisa Vasil'eva listed its four main goals: first, to confirm 'the feminine principle' (*zhenskoe nachalo*) in society and literature; second, 'with the help of women to change the climate of society'; third, 'self-determination of the

[18]O. Lipovskaya, 'Amerikanskii dnevnik', *Zhenskoe Chtenie, ibid.*, pp. 20–31.
[19]Larisa Vasil'eva, 'Zhenshchina. Zhizn'. Literatura', *Literaturnaya Gazeta*, 20 December, 1989, p. 7. I am grateful to Gerry Smith for this reference.

feminine principle' (*samoopredelenie zhenskogo nachala*) in the literary process; and fourth, 'establishment and strengthening of relations among women writers'.[20] The last goal is often the central goal of Western women's groups. The promotion of *zhenskoe nachalo*, however, is more specific to the USSR. It remains undefined by Vasil'eva, but connotes the championing of female difference and all that is feminine – gentleness, sensitivity, caring and dignity. The Federation of Women Writers wants to promote a different way of working and of conducting business within professions and, more generally, to alter the values of broader society; *zhenskoe nachalo* is the means to these ends. The celebration of feminine values also had a place in Russian religious feminism expounded by the Mariia group in 1979 and again in exile in the early 1980s and has recently developed as one strand within Western feminism.

The concern of Soviet professionals to draw upon *zhenskoe nachalo* overlaps with the aim of women in Sajudis for women to develop as women. Professionals, however, seek to incorporate *zhenskoe nachalo* into a broader arena – into their workplaces, into their writings and throughout society; Lithuanian women currently focus more narrowly on *zhenskoe nachalo* in the home and in childrearing.

4. 'New' feminist arguments

Glasnost' has resulted in women making arguments that break out of past ideologically acceptable interpretations of the *zhenskii vopros*. Concepts once taboo, such as 'patriarchy' and 'male dominated bureaucracy' have since 1988 entered articles and been expressed in interviews. Feminist ideas once condemned as counter-revolutionary for being divisive of working-class unity and ridiculed as examples of bourgeois self-indulgence, now find outlets in the press. They are often articulated with the firm conviction, even anger, characteristic of second-wave Western feminism. Professional women, in particular, are venting their outrage that working men not only refrain from participating equally in housework and childcare with working women, but also dominate public life, discriminate against women and treat them as inferior.

As one researcher for the All-Union Central Council of Trade Unions put it in an interview in Moscow in September 1989, 'Our men have been busy in a Command–Administrative system – a male dominated bureaucracy (*muzhekratiya*)'. She views this *muzhekratiya* as a system which celebrates male power, is oriented towards men and perpetuated by male solidarity; women who make it to prominent positions are no more than symbolic tokens. One result is that male policy makers have not systematically addressed what perestroika means for women. She believes that '*khozraschet* is geared to male labour and will entail working from morning to night. *Khozraschet* will mean unemployment for women.' Women, therefore, must become involved in politics:

[20]*Ibid.*

'We need women among our leaders, but where are they? The CPSU does not help. You can compare democratisation today with the 1960s in the West. The New Left ignored women, so women had to organise separately. Perhaps this is what will happen here.'

The interviewee also suggested that women would make significantly different political decisions from men: 'If women were in power, many problems would not have existed, such as Afghanistan'. One strand of Western feminism also holds that women's politics would be peaceful and more humane than the results of male leadership. Of course, conclusive evidence is wanting.

Two important attacks on Soviet patriarchy in print have come from the philosopher Ol'ga Voronina and journalist Larisa Kuznetsova, both of whom argue that Soviet society is a 'man's world' in which 'patriarchal habits' and 'patriarchal ideas' warp male/female relations and destroy humane ties between fathers and children.[21] In politics, patriarchy results in women being 'elbowed out' of top jobs and in 'yes-women' being taken on as 'political extras'. In society, patriarchy means a lack of contraceptives and 'the world's worst abortion system', which treats women as 'biological specimens' not as human beings. In Kuznetsova's view, the nature of the Soviet abortion system is a 'political issue', which men neglect so to define. She asks why a women's movement does not exist and apparently sees one as essential to an understanding of how the 'personal is political'.[22] Issues defined as 'political' by Western feminism in the 1960s and 1970s, such as rape, abortion, hiring, promotion, the subtleties of gender subordination, and more generally, how men speak to women and what they expect from them, are beginning to be conceived by some Soviet women as 'political' too. To expose the stereotyping of gender roles perpetuated by patriarchal society, Voronina, together with other female academics in Moscow, has set up LOTOS, the League for Society's Liberation from stereotypes.[23]

Evidence to suggest that these 'new' ideas 'officially' arrived was the publication in 1989 in an enlivened *Kommunist* of Nataliya Zakharova, Anastasiya Posadskaya and Natal'ya Rimashevskaya on 'How we solve the woman question'.[24] These academics outlined four main approaches to the *zhenskii vopros* – patriarchal, economic, demographic and egalitarian – and provided the first systematic Soviet analysis of methodological approaches to studying the position of women in society. As outgoing Chair of the Soviet Women's Committee, Valentina Tereshkova had called for such an analysis at the All-Union Conference of Women

[21]Ol'ga Voronina, 'Muzhchiny sozdali mir dlia sebya', *Sovetskaya Zhenshchina*, No. 11, 1988, pp. 14–15; Larisa Kuznetsova, 'What every woman wants?', *Soviet Weekly*, 26 November, 1988, p. 15.
[22]Kuznetsova, *ibid.*
[23]Cited in Barbara Heldt, 'Women and Glasnost', working paper, 1989.
[24]H. Zakharova, A. Posadskaya and N. Rimashevskaya, 'Kak my reshaem zhenskii vopros', *Kommunist*, March 1989, No. 4, pp. 56–65.

held in Moscow in January 1987, regretting that 'we do not have profound, fundamental and theoretical research into the position of women in socialist society'.[25] Zakharova and her colleagues provided the first serious response. They point out that advocates of a patriarchal approach see a 'natural' division between gender roles. Those who pursue an economic analysis focus primarily on women as a labour resource, and see female labour as relative to other goals, such as an intensification of economic growth. The demographic approach focuses on women as reproducers, with birthrates as the main reference point. The egalitarian approach, held by these authors, begins with the assumption that society is moving away from traditional patterns of dominance and subordination towards 'relations of complementarity in society and family'. In sum, they advocate the removal of social barriers which prevent individuals from developing their full potential, call for an end to gender role stereotyping, and advocate the adoption in Article 35 of the Constitution of a statement that men, like women, have the opportunity to combine parenthood and career. Like Tereshkova two years earlier, they argue that a discipline of 'social feminology' (*sotsial'naya feminologiya*) is needed to study the position of women in society and a discipline of 'applied feminology' (*prikladnaya feminologiya*) to explore women's issues within the disciplines of economics, demography, ethics and psychology.[26] Rimashevskaya is Director of the Institute of Socio-Economic Problems of the Population in Moscow, where she is currently pioneering a 'new' women's studies, previously taboo in the USSR.[27]

While some female academics believe that glasnost' has helped immensely in making a critical examination of the *zhenskii vopros* possible, and has provided the opportunity for articles to break out of past ideological lines and ask questions such as whether maternity should now be viewed as a 'right' rather than a 'duty', they also regret that the 'new thinking' about women's issues lags far behind 'new thinking' in other spheres, such as foreign policy.

5. 'Establishment' bodies: the case of the Soviet Women's Committee

The Soviet Women's Committee was set up after the Second World War and grew out of the Soviet Women's Anti-Fascist Committee formed in 1941. As an official organisation it has never been an outspoken critic of the system. Until Gorbachev extended its brief in 1986 to oversee the new hierarchical structure of the revived and expanded *zhensovety*, its main purpose was 'developing co-operation with women's organisations abroad in order to promote peace, friendship and mutual understanding'.[28] Its

[25]*Izvestiya*, 1 February, 1987.
[26]*Ibid.*
[27]Interview with Rimashevskaya in Moscow, June 1990.
[28]Soviet Women's Committee, *Soviet Women's Committee* (Moscow, 1983), p. 2.

aim was not to agitate for radical changes in women's lives inside the USSR, but to build links with foreign women and to construct an international image of a peace-loving USSR devoted to equality of the sexes.

The role of the Soviet Women's Committee is slowly undergoing change. Glasnost' has helped its members to speak out against difficulties in women's daily lives and its new function of the apex of the *zhensovety* gives it a more legitimate voice in domestic concerns. According to Zoia Pukhova, the Chair of the Committee from 1987 to 1991, its time is now equally divided between international pursuits and attention to domestic problems.[29] Moreover, pressing fears of female unemployment and concern about falling percentages of women deputies have made criticisms of the disadvantages for women of *khozraschet* and of *demokratizatsiya* compelling.

Disquiet about various aspects of women's lives, such as the double burden, male alcoholism, infant mortality rates and poor working conditions was expressed in January 1987 at the All-Union Conference of Women by Tereshkova.[30] More forceful criticism of the idea that women should leave the labour force at a time of perestroika was made by Pukhova at the nineteenth Party Conference in 1988. Her speech included a sharp attack on appalling conditions in the textile industry and conveyed the message that equality of the sexes did not exist.[31] In a recent interview, Galina Sukhoruchenkova, Secretary of the All-Union Council of Trade Unions and member of the Presidium of the Soviet Women's Committee, echoed the same concerns. In her view the time was ripe for a 'body' (*korpus*) to defend women's interests' because 'we do not have unity in the women's movement', 'nor a clear direction'. Women's positions in the workforce, in particular, needed protection since a decentralisation of decision-making and negotiation of local collective contracts could result in women's rights being ignored.[32]

Political reform is no less worrying for the Soviet Women's Committee than economic reform. Although the new electoral law in effect for the 1989 elections guaranteed seventy-five saved seats for the *zhensovety* as social organisations, female representation at the All-Union level fell from 32.8 per cent to 15.6 per cent.[33] Women candidates were less likely to be nominated than male for contested seats, and less likely to put themselves forward. Critical reaction to the 'undemocratic' nature of reserved seats subsequently led to legislation giving republics the right to abolish them for the 1990 elections to the Supreme Soviets of the republics and to the local soviets. Thirteen of the fifteen republics abandoned them. Anxious that no saved seats for the *zhensovety* would result in an even more drastic fall in the proportion of women deputies (which by the early 1980s averaged 35 per cent at republic level and

---

[29]*Krest'ianka*, No. 7, 1987, p. 6.
[30]*Izvestiya*, 1 February, 1987.
[31]*Izvestiya*, 2 July, 1988, p. 10.
[32]Interview conducted in Moscow in September 1989.
[33]*Rabotnitsa*, No. 1, January 1990, p. 19.

over 50.3 per cent at the local level), the Soviet Women's Committee issued a formal 'Appeal to Women Voters', which in November 1989 was published on the front page of newspapers. The Appeal pointed out that since women made up over half of the population, it was only just that they be present on democratically elected bodies. What had to be overcome was the reluctance to nominate women as candidates. The Committee noted that 'we understand how important it is for women deputies to be competent, wise, intelligent public leaders. They exist. But they need your real support and help.' It then called upon the *zhensovety* to back women candidates 'at all stages of the electoral struggle' and asked radio, television and the press to devote time and space to female candidates and to help destroy old stereotypes.[34]

Members of the *zhensovety*, however, were generally not committed political activists in the 1990 campaigns. Pukhova later regretted that 'they worked badly'.[35] Female representation on the Supreme Soviets of the republics fell by as much as 30 per cent. For example, just 4.8 per cent of the Moldavian Supreme Soviet is now female and 5.4 per cent of the Russian Supreme Soviet. Other republics returned a slightly higher proportion of women deputies – 7.4 per cent in Kazakhstan and 11.4 per cent in Turkmenia. Fewer women were also elected to the local soviets. Representation fell in 1990 from just over an average of 50 per cent to 35 per cent in Latvia, 33 per cent in the RFSFR, 30.2 per cent in Kazakstan, 25.2 per cent in Turkmenia and 23 per cent in Estonia.[36]

The extent to which the Soviet Women's Committee can effect favourable outcomes in the economy and in politics is probably negligible. But the reform process has heightened the sensitivity of its members to the outcomes they would like to see and has alerted them to possible pitfalls for women. Definitive strategies to counter the pitfalls have yet to be defined. The Plenum of the Soviet Women's Committee held in November 1989 began to debate how best to proceed. Among the topics explored were the role of the *zhensovety*, the need for support groups for women deputies, and the relevance of quotas for female representation. The inattention of the Congress of People's Deputies to women's issues was also regretted.[37]

[34]*Bakinskii rabochii*, 30 November, 1989.
[35]Interview with Pukhova in Moscow, June 1990.
[36]I am grateful to Irina Kovrigina of the Soviet Women's Committee for these statistics. Evidence also indicates that women's involvement in the CPSU is falling. The proportion of women among CPSU candidate members in the Moscow city party organisation fell to 24 per cent in 1989 from 34 per cent in 1985. See *Pravda*, 25 June, 1990, p. 5. What this means, however, is unclear. It may be the case that many women are choosing not to be affiliated with the CPSU and should not automatically be interpreted as another example of discrimination against them. I am grateful to Stephen White for this reference.
The election of just one woman to the Politburo of the CPSU – Galina Semenova – at the twenty-eighth Party Congress in 1990, however, is consistent with the tokenism of the recent past. Delegate Tat'yana Merzlyakova criticised the extremely low profile of women at the Congress and bewailed the lighthearted attitude of male delegates to women's issues. See *Moscow News*, July 20–26, 1990, p. 3.
[37]*Rabotnitsa*, No. 1, January 1990, pp. 18–20.

The 1990s are likely to see a more active Women's Committee as unemployment bites and as patterns of women's political representation similar to those of Western liberal democracies emerge. Threats to women's positions in the economy and in politics, coupled with flourishing informal women's groups, topped with the spread of pornography, are likely to put pressure on the Soviet Women's Committee to become a more radical political actor.[38]

Conclusion

Although various forms of women's political activity, informal and official, were slow to develop after 1985, once they sprouted they did so with a heterogeneity one would expect in an emergent civil society. But the highly varied nature of women's groups will make the formation of a cohesive women's movement impossible. Nevertheless, one can conceive of several different sorts of women's movements developing, of varying sizes, spanning different geographical areas, with different goals. Smaller *ad hoc* single-issue women's movements or pressure groups may form too, such as mothers organising against their sons being sent to keep order in dangerous trouble-spots such as Nagorno-Karabakh.

The diverse nature of women's political activity is likely to broaden as a multiparty system blossoms in the 1990s and, as space for independent political activity, and awareness of that space, grows. It is precisely this heterogeneity of women's political behaviour that makes it distinctive from previous periods of reform.

The *Zhenotdel* had broad, but reasonably well-defined goals, albeit not static ones, about how best radically to transform women's lives after the revolution. The *zhensovety* of the late 1950s, 1960s and 1970s had a narrower task of encouraging the appropriate social, economic and political involvement of women. Both, however, were subject to the scrutiny of the party and/or soviets. Their work was often defined and critically assessed by other institutions; it was also subject to external opprobrium, derision, attack and neglect. By contrast, contemporary women's groups are not formed because of party resolutions, but due to the initiative of women themselves. They are thus self-defining. Even officially inspired groups, such as the *zhensovety*, in the current context enjoy increasing possibilities for independently defined actions, should members decide to take advantage of them.[39] More than ever before in Soviet history, the nature of women's political activity and its future, depends upon the women themselves.

---

[38]For fuller discussion of pornography and other 'new' women's issues, refer to Mary Buckley, 'Glasnost' and the Woman Question', paper delivered at the IVth World Congress for Soviet and East European Studies, Harrogate, 21–26 July 1990.
[39]For discussion of the activities of three newly established *zhensovety* in Moscow, refer to Mary Buckley, *Women and Ideology in the Soviet Union*, op. cit., pp. 209–17.

6
The Soviet working class movement in the post-socialist perspective
(The outlook in summer 1990)

Leonid Gordon

The end of state socialism

The independent labour movement in the USSR is in its very earliest stage of development. Nevertheless, even today there are industries and regions where hundreds of people are actively involved in the movement. Soon – tomorrow, the day after – it will number millions, if not tens of millions. The social conditions are ripe, and the fire of independent activity could flare up at any moment. We therefore need to begin thinking now about the general tendencies and prospects for the labour movement. The events of the past year, and the opportunity to compare them with experience from other countries and with the increasingly transparent content of the processes of perestroika, give such reflections particular relevance.

There is now no longer any doubt that, barring a forcible return to the past, the transformations that have been taking place since the late 1980s will lead the Soviet Union on to the path of normal human social development. The triumph of perestroika will lead to the creation of a society with a regulated market economy, a democratic political system and a pluralist ideology. In other words, we are moving from an extreme towards the norm, towards those foundations of contemporary civilisation – the market and democracy – on which the majority of humanity now bases, or strives to base, its activity.

However, different societies take different paths towards this common social structure. The classic development in the West was from primitive capitalism with a wealthy few and a poor majority, an uncontrolled market and a state catering entirely to the interests of the propertied classes, to increasing regulation of the market economy and the growth of social security mechanisms protecting the welfare of the broad mass of the population: formal democracy is converted into social democracy. The Soviet Union, like many others that have been dominated by state-monopoly socialism, will have to take a different path. This is the path away from universal state control, blocking any progress, away from the mechanical, non-market organisation of everyone and everything, which guarantees minimum subsistence for the majority but does not allow that majority any escape from poverty, away from the freedom-stifling state-police supervision, through a dismantling of the state apparatus, privatisation and the growth of political and cultural freedoms, to the same goal of the organised market and social democracy.

While there is not a convergence here in the strict sense of capitalism and socialism simultaneously and symmetrically drawing together, it occurs in the more complex form of historical processes which occurred at different times but nevertheless tend towards the triumph of a single civilisation. In the West there has been a gradual socialisation and democratisation of capitalism over the last hundred years. In the USSR the development of capitalism was interrupted, and a state-monopoly, statist socialism opposed to capitalism arose. Under this system the bases of industrial production and some of the simpler elements of contemporary civilisation were created very rapidly. But inevitably the other face of the system was terror against its own people, the decline of non-industrial spheres of activity, poverty among the people, the dehumanisation of human relations, ecological crisis and, eventually, general stagnation, blocking the arteries of social progress. Now we need to democratise and, in our own way, to capitalise socialism, or more precisely, that variety of socialism that has arisen in the Soviet Union.

Lech Walesa has been quoted as saying that Poland was the first country in history to begin the transition from socialism to capitalism. Such a transition can only be understood as progress if we are talking about present-day capitalism, which is revealing an increasing number of features that match the ideals of civilised socialism. The countries where so-called 'practical socialism' has been the dominant system do not have to repeat the entire Western path of development from primitive to civilised capitalism. There is another path open to us – rather than that of pure capitalist development, we can take the path of what we might call post-socialist development.

This kind of development is not a simple matter. Two dangers await the society on the path of post-socialist development. The first of these is indecision, the inability to dismantle state socialism completely enough and to carry out radical democratisation and privatisation. The other danger is irresponsibility, the thoughtless readiness to abolish all social control and to move from total state control to the unbridled, primitive dominance of private enterprise and total market anarchy. In the first case, there will be no development at all: this is a complete impasse. In the second, post-socialist development will slide back uncontrollably to the level of early capitalism: this will inevitably involve a long, agonising period spent combating the ills of this system (which may also lead to the kind of explosion which occurred in 1917, returning society to its original impasse). It is hard to say which of these dangers is the more frightening.

It is here that consideration of the labour movement becomes particularly relevant. For this movement can become a force capable of breaking down the resistance of the opponents of reform, and at the same time able to compel the reformers to retain some degree of social prudence, ensuring that they combine radical transformations with support for a system of social security.

2. The independent trade unions

The clearest example of the importance of the labour movement is in ensuring the provision of social security. Political discussions on mechanisms for social security usually focus on developing appropriate laws and administrative institutions. Historical experience shows, however, that although legislation is indeed important, the organisation of the workers themselves, their capacity to defend their interests, and in particular to ensure that the laws are implemented, is even more important. This is why the tendency towards the creation of independent trade unions, within the new labour movement or under its influence, has become so evident during 1989–1990.

For many decades the official Soviet trade unions worked not so much to protect the workers, but rather as auxiliary parts, 'levers' or 'transmission belts' in the party-state machinery, within the sphere of labour and production.

Even the final records of the 1989 miners' strike were signed by representatives of the workers' committees 'on the one hand', and of the government and VTsSPS[1] 'on the other' (this is the precise wording in the documents). However, since autumn 1989, and particularly since spring 1990, people have appeared within VTsSPS who are working to change the official trade unions so that they gradually become more like a true trade union organisation, whose central task is to defend the labour interests of its members.

In some respects the transformation of VTsSPS, with strike committees winning it over, as it were, would be the best way forward. If this were to happen the independent trade unions would immediately gain large funds and extensive facilities, a highly developed organisational structure, and experienced administrators. However, decades of existing as an adjunct to the party-state machine have engendered strong ideological, political and social-psychological traditions within the official trade unions. The sincerest aspirations, and even the appearance of new leaders, may not be enough to overcome the influence of these traditions and stereotypes. Under these circumstances, the independent labour movement is just as likely to want to create completely new trade unions as to attempt to reconstruct the old ones.

This tendency is clearest among the miners – the area where the independent labour movement has been most successful. The First Congress of Soviet Miners, held in Donetsk in June 1990, declared unequivocally that it '[considered] it essential to create a genuinely independent miners'

[1]The All-Union Central Council of Trade Unions [*trans.*].

union', since the existing union, despite all efforts to change it, was still 'incapable of carrying out the tasks set for it'. Similar attempts are also being made to create new trade unions in other industries.

The new unions understand and express more clearly than VTsSPS the need to combine the defence of the immediate and continuing interests of the workers with their fundamental interest in the transition to a market economy. The resolutions from the Miners' Congress saw social measures as an integral part of the movement towards a civilised market economy, not an alternative to it. The resolutions contained the following words:

> 'In demanding the creation of a government which will ensure the changeover to a market and guaranteed democracy, we believe that this transition should not be excessively painful for the majority of the people. The transition must include provision for social security mechanisms. It is particularly important that measures regarding employment and unemployment be implemented. We understand that in order to create an efficient economy many workplaces will need to be shut down and reprofiled. But we demand that these decisions be made openly, so that we know in good time which factories, mines and construction sites are to be closed, so that arrangements can be made for the workers in them to learn new trades, and so that those left without work can obtain sufficient state benefit. The closure of unprofitable workplaces will only be permitted if the workers' collective has rejected the opportunity to take the firm into collective ownership free of charge. Free transfer of the means of production should also be implemented widely in other cases of transition to collective, share-owned or individual ownership . . . . We believe that only under these conditions will the workers give the government the trust essential to any reforms.'[2]

I do not presume to predict which of these possible paths of development will prevail. Logically, the most efficient solution would be to combine the newly created unions with the best of the transformed old unions. Life in society, of course, rarely conforms to purely rational considerations. But whatever happens in the future, it is already clear that the capacity of the labour movement to form and restructure trade unions is one of the most important means of maintaining the social balance in the post-socialist transition to a market economy.

[2]Resolution of the First Soviet Miners' Congress on the social and economic situation, the implementation of USSR Council of Ministers' Resolution No. 608, and the prospects for a transition to a market economy (Donetsk, 1990).

3. The moment of equilibrium and the political role of the labour movement

But the role of the labour movement extends beyond defence of workers' immediate interests. The last year has also shown that workers' organisations can play a political role, and can influence the rate and even the orientation of post-socialist development.

The current social-political importance of the labour movement stems from the fact that in the summer of 1990, after several years of perestroika, Soviet society finds itself in that situation of polarisation and unstable equilibrium which so often precedes the decisive stage of revolutionary transformations.

Since the late 1980s state-monopoly socialism has been dismantled at a gradually increasing rate in the Soviet Union. There have already been marked shifts in the political and ideological spheres. But there are key changes, particularly in the economy, which have not been made during the first five years of perestroika. Post-socialist development has begun, but it is not yet irreversible.

Social divisions centred on the attitude of certain groups to the market and democracy have appeared, and these groups have become aware of the divisions. Those for the market and democracy include the most skilled layer of society – the artistic intelligentsia, academics and workers in the science and information sector, which is replacing industrial production as the main structure of the economy. Many socially responsible members of the state-political leadership, who understand the futility of attempting to improve state socialism, have also come to support the market and democracy – particularly those who feel that they will be able to continue active work within the framework of post-socialist relations. And market relations are naturally attractive to the new strata of our society, which are just beginning to arise – the private entrepreneurs, members of co-operatives, managers, etc.

The readiness of the masses of skilled workers, who can rely on their trade, agricultural workers, rank-and-file intellectuals, city-dwellers, young people and the better educated strata of the people to support decisive moves towards the market and democracy is becoming increasingly evident. It was in the major cities and centres of labour that democratic candidates won the greatest support in the elections of 1989 and spring 1990, while the collapse of the conservative bureaucrats and the national-patriotic groups was especially marked in these areas. It seems that the skilled and better educated of the rank-and-file workers are now overcoming the anti-market prejudices of mass consciousness and beginning to recognise the necessity not only for democratisation but also for the market.

Among the delegates to the First Miners' Congress, who were directly elected by work collectives, almost 90 per cent supported some form of market economy, while only 4 per cent supported an economy based on direct planning. Only just over 20 per cent of delegates wanted to continue working in state mines, while 77 per cent said that they would prefer to work in share-owned, leased, co-operative, joint-owned or private mines.[3]

The interests of the opponents of post-socialist development have emerged just as unequivocally. It has become quite clear that democratisation and the introduction of a market will render the main elements of the party–state machinery and the ministerial–industrial bureaucracy unnecessary. There is no place in a market economy for ministries, boards and centralised groups of firms administering different branches of the economy, or for party organisations to supervise the administration of firms. Party committees and public organisations employing hundreds of thousand of paid workers cannot exist under democracy. What is more, the professional skills and experience of this type of executive are unlikely to be required in a democratic country with a market economy. Instead of being respectable and highly-valued specialists, they will become people without profession or skills, who will simply have to fight for their place in society.

Those at the sources of distribution are also opposed to a comprehensive free market. The black market chiefs are not nearly as interested in the establishment of a free market economy as their usual protestations suggest. They are fully aware of the strong position they occupy within the framework of restricted commodity relations, controlling the shortages; in a free market they face competition, to which they are not accustomed, and in which many of them will obviously fail.

Unfortunately, a considerable proportion of the rank-and-file workers also fear that the repudiation of state socialism and the transition to a market will create hardship for them. Ultimately the market will improve the life of the vast majority of the people. But it means that the mass of the people will be required to provide labour of a different kind, with a different level of intensity and responsibility, from that which we are used to.

The changeover will be particularly difficult for unskilled and less well-educated workers, for those who live in remote areas, and for the elderly and those who are not in full health. Retaining state socialism would, of course, be a greater catastrophe than dismantling it even for these groups. But it is they who will feel the difficulties of forming the market economy first, and most fully, while they will be the last to experience the advantages of a free society, and will experience them only partially. And there are millions – tens of millions – of such people.

There is also a category among the strong, skilled workers whose losses in the transition to a market will be greater than the average, and whose attitude towards this change therefore tends to be negative. Under normal market conditions (and even under a democratic political system) the military industry will probably lose most of the advantages it held under the bureaucratic-directive planning system. The necessity for rapid

[3]Data from a survey conducted by a team of sociologists led by the author.

conversion will render the once privileged position of these enterprises even more difficult than that of other industries. It is hardly surprising that the activists at the unofficial congress of Russian communists, who proved to be fierce opponents of market reforms, included many workers and party members from the munitions factories.

Thus, the social interests in Soviet society are now fairly clearly polarised, and polarised in such a way that either option – either the rush to the market and democracy which will make post-socialist development irreversible, or total rejection of post-socialist development, maintaining the system of state socialism indefinitely – could win mass support.

'Could win', of course, does not necessarily mean that they will win such support. We must remember the essential difference in the objective nature of the interests underlying the positions taken by the supporters and opponents of post-socialist development. The movement towards a market and democracy is in the basic, fundamental interests of the artistic intelligentsia, skilled industrial workers and white-collar workers, young people, co-operative members, and also farmers, smallholders and entre-preneurs, if such do in fact appear in the Soviet Union.

The anti-market and anti-democratic tendencies, on the other hand, have a genuinely deep and irremovable base only within the state-party machinery and the groups associated with it, who do not make up a particularly large section of the population (considerably less than 10 per cent). The attitude of the mass of unskilled workers, agricultural workers, intellectuals, elderly and less well-educated people who make up the majority of those who are wary of the market is conditioned only by a few, often relatively unimportant interests. The experience of the long-term development of the market and democracy in other countries shows that where any broad strata of the people do find themselves worse off, this is only in a relative sense, i.e. in comparison with other groups in the population. The absolute majority of workers live better under the market economy and democracy than under state socialism.

In short, the objective position of the main social groups in Soviet society is such that a mass base of mass anti-market and anti-democratic feeling could arise, but this does not mean that widespread expression of these feelings is inevitable, or that if it occurs it will be deep-rooted or long-lived. The numerical equilibrium towards which society tends on the eve of major shifts is not in the least insurmountable.

The instability of the balance is clearly illustrated by the actual pro-portions into which our society was divided over particular events during the first half of 1990, i.e. in the months when the time was (or seemed to be) ripe for a decisive step towards withdrawal from state socialism, but when this step nevertheless failed to be taken. These months provide many examples of society being divided into roughly equal proportions, with representatives of major social groups on each side. In this respect the opinion polls are particularly revealing: they show that mass con-sciousness on many important social and political issues was split roughly down the middle. However, during these months there were also events on which the representatives of almost all the mass social groups were united against the bureaucracy. It is worth noting that in many of the roll-call votes at the First Congress of RSFSR People's Deputies, the votes were usually divided with almost all the party–state, economic and military élite (90–95 per cent of the deputies in this category) and half the middle-level executives (50–55 per cent) on one side, and the vast majority of representatives of the remaining social groups (60–80 per cent) on the other.[4]

4. Does the labour movement need its own political organisation?

Given an unstable balance of interests like that which has developed in the USSR in 1990, the course of events and their results will be determined not so much by the relations between social groups as by the struggle between the political forces existing at that moment in the society. The final result depends on the particular social movements, organisations and institutions which are active in the political arena. In such circumstances the importance of the labour movement is that it is potentially one of the most powerful political forces for democracy.

At the moment the labour movement, or rather the work collectives' movement, forms practically the only means of drawing the masses into active political life over most of the Soviet Union. Of course we know from our own history that a crude class approach to the formation of state-political organisations played a major role in maintaining the authoritarian regime in the USSR. Contemporary public life in the mature democracies also shows that as a rule mass democratic parties and movements are built on a broad and varied social base. We must assume that in our future market-democratic society the separate organisations of industrial, agricultural or white-collar workers will continue to be trade unions and similar organisations.

But that is how things will be later, when and if the transition from a state-controlled, authoritarian society to democracy is complete, or at any rate approaching completion. For the time being, in the early stages of post-socialist development, the situation is different.

Admittedly, even today the essential political orientation of the democratic workers' movements differs little from the political aims of other democratic groups (just as the reactionary–conservative workers' associations are similar in outlook to other conservatives). However, there are additional social–cultural and social–organisational factors which are quite insignificant under the normal conditions of a fully developed democracy, but play an important role during this transitional period.

The Soviet Union, where the transition to democracy follows on seven

[4]See *Argumenty i Fakty*, No. 29, 1990, p. 2.

decades of universal state control, does not have a true civil society; there is no developed system of free contacts between people, and no traditions or habits of political self-organisation within local communities, towns and regions. The lack of such contacts can fairly easily be overcome within small groups of political activists (journalists and academics, for example, particularly given that some fragments of civil society relations remain within these groups). But it is not easy for the mass of ordinary people to do this unless they are influenced by some external unifying circumstances such as conflicts of nationality. The majority of our independently organised social–political organisations, apart from those that have arisen in areas of national conflict, are therefore largely top-heavy formations, armies with many generals and very few soldiers.

In areas where there are no specific national factors, the present conditions are such that work collectives represent practically the only social system within which the majority of ordinary people are likely to become involved in regular mass social–political interaction. Accordingly, it is in these collectives that independent political organisations are likely to develop most successfully – organisations that will belong to and actively involve the people – not only the educated, well-read specialists and working-class intellectuals, and not the conscious working-class citizens of the future, who have yet to appear, but the ordinary people of today.

The special position that the labour movement holds in the social–political life of Soviet society today results from the social role of work collectives. For what we know today as the independent and democratic labour movement is largely a movement of work collectives. It is not simply an association of individuals with views in common, like most of the other democratic organisations, but an association of rank-and-file workers who are united both by their aspirations and by the fact that they work together in the same factories, plants, mines, construction sites and institutions.

Hence, as long as work collectives remain the easiest way to involve the masses in social and political life, there will be a place for independent social–political workers' movements and organisations involving all the workers, even if the programmes of such movements are practically identical to the lines of the democratic parties and broad-based democratic organisations.

There are certain cultural and psychological factors which also contribute to this tendency. We are in the very earliest stages of transformation of a state-monopoly socialist society. This society has a unique social and cultural structure, and in terms of the fundamental social problems the objective interests of the vast majority of its members are the same. Ultimately, the abolition of authoritarian structures and universal state control will improve the life of practically every group in the population.

However, here we come up against one of the social traps of total state control: the administrative system is structured in such a way that in everyday life practically all government workers appear to the ordinary workers as the bearers of alienated power, the representatives of a system that condemns the rest to submission, powerlessness and poverty. The majority of government workers are themselves powerless, and their position is essentially no better than that of the other workers. But in the common consciousness they are seen as agents of an external, oppressing force.

The position over cultural differences is similar in some respects. In terms of education, conceptions of the fundamental life values, long-held traditions and even vices (drunkenness, for example!), the population of most of the USSR is fairly uniform (at least within individual national communities).

However, because the state monopoly in the economy and the authoritarian political regime have denied workers the normal industrial workers' right to defend their interests collectively, as in normal industrial production, their conditions of work have deteriorated sharply. In the Soviet Union the division between mainly mental and mainly physical work has also remained up to now a division between 'clean' and 'dirty' work, between work performed in relatively normal conditions and that carried out in absolutely unacceptable conditions, humiliating to contemporary human beings. The relatively high level of education of many workers, particularly the younger workers, and their general level of culture which is roughly on a par with that of the majority of engineers and technicians, makes them feel this distinction between 'clean' and 'dirty' work particularly keenly.

Thus, the industrial and agricultural workers' feeling of cultural–psychological separation from rank-and-file intellectuals is much stronger than the actual social and economic differences between the two groups. Many workers feel that practically all white-collar workers stink of 'the office', seeing them as a collection of idlers and parasites living on public money.

This area (or rather feeling) has no base in reality. And the most conscious activists in the workers' movement understand that such feelings are without foundation. The programme documents of the Confederation of Labour, set up at a conference of independent workers' movements (Novokuznetsk, May 1990), specifically emphasise that 'worker arrogance is no better than the condescension of the intelligentsia and administrative workers'.

But rational declarations are one thing, emotions and feelings are quite another. That the labour movement is to a certain extent psychologically alienated from the intelligentsia today is an objective fact, one of the features of the present state of mass consciousness. This state means that for a time the mass of workers will watch those who lead and represent the work collectives movement jealously. Thus, from this point of view too it is understandable, and clearly inevitable, that a separate movement – generally democratic in aims and mainly working-class in the make-up of its members and leadership – should exist for a time.

5. Possible scenarios for future development

The fact that the labour movement, in the form of work collectives, forms part of the democratic community in the USSR may give the democratic movement added strength. The work collectives, united, will be powerful enough to break the resistance of the groups and institutions which are opposed to democratic changes. At the same time, they are sufficiently organised that, assuming they understand their tasks correctly, and unite with other democratic groups, they will be able to achieve them without violence. In a country like the Soviet Union work collectives, if they are genuinely united, are too powerful a movement to be resisted for long. The political events of the first year of the labour movement have confirmed the potential of the movement as a force in the political as well as the industrial sphere. Even the very first, virtually unprepared workers' actions – the miners' strikes of summer 1989 – showed a high level of organisation, with order being strictly maintained. They showed none of that senseless, merciless element which Pushkin called 'Russian rebellion, which has played a tragic part in the fate of Russian democracy more than once in the past. Nevertheless, the 1989 strikes were an exceptionally powerful movement, which had a marked influence on the overall process of social-political development. It is no coincidence that a number of legislative acts strengthening elements of the economic freedom of enterprises were passed immediately after the July strikes.

The activity of work collectives during the autumn and winter of 1989–90 was a major factor in the legalisation of the multi-party system in the USSR. One of the demands of the Vorkuta miners in their protracted strike in October–November 1989 was the removal of Article 6 of the Constitution, which provided the legal basis for the CPSU's special relationship to the state. In December 1989 this demand was supported in a number of other regions by tens of thousands of workers, who responded to Andrei Sakharov's call for symbolic strikes and demonstrations on the eve of the Second Congress of USSR People's Deputies. It seems that the abrupt change of position of the Soviet party–state leadership, which moved from opposition to the abolition of Article 6 at the end of 1989 to complete agreement with this change by the beginning of 1990, was related in some way or another to consideration of the position of the labour movement.

Similarly, the link between the political strike of 11 July 1990 and the first serious attempt at interaction between the Soviet state–party leadership, under Mikhail Gorbachev, and the leadership of the Russian Federation, represented by Boris Yeltsin, cannot be seen as coincidental. This strike grew from grass-roots dissatisfaction among the workers about delays in reforms. Workers' committees in various regions (first of all in Vorkuta, it appears) began to translate that unorganised discontent into calls for an organised political strike. The resolutions passed by the First Soviet Miners' Congress in mid-June, and the Council of Representatives of the Confederation of Labour, a few days later, gave the workers' demands a politically conscious form and put them on a nationwide scale.

The resolution of the Confederation of Labour revealed the political essence of the strike quite clearly. It declared:

> 'The country is in deep crisis. The way out of this crisis is through the development of democracy and a market economy, with social security for the workers. We demand the resignation of the Soviet government. We need a government in which the people have confidence – a coalition government made up of representatives of various parties and independent social movements.'

The resolution further declared that it was on this basis that 'We support the intention of the workers in the Kuznetsk and Donetsk basins, Vorkuta and the Rostov region to carry out a political strike on 11 July'.[5]

In fact the strikes were not limited to these regions but occurred in many other regions too. According to official figures, hundreds of thousands of workers went on strike. If we take into account the demonstrations, rallies and other forms of political activity, the number of participants is much higher.

It is not difficult to see that the decision taken by Gorbachev and Yeltsin two weeks after the strike, to work together on a plan for radical acceleration of economic and political reforms, and to create a special committee for this purpose, which included many new names, effectively conforms to the demands of the workers. Of course, the workers were not the only ones to make these demands, and it was not only pressure from the workers which prompted the reformers in the Soviet leadership and the Russian democrats to take steps towards joint action. But it is clear that the power and the democratic orientation of the workers' movement played a very important part in this.

It is worth emphasising again the level of organisation and the peaceful nature of the workers' actions. There was not a single violent incident during the 11 July strike, and nowhere were there any disturbances of public order. In neighbouring regions, however, actions by other, less well-organised social forces in summer 1990 led to outbursts of violence and bloodshed.

The experience of its first year of development suggests that the democratic labour movement can help to ensure that acute social conflicts, if they are inevitable, take civilised rather than violent forms: as in the Baltic republics, rather than as in Fergana, Sumgait or the Osh region.

The capacity of the labour movement to combine strength with organisation will be even more essential in the future than it has been up to now. This feature of the labour movement may turn out to be of central importance to the development of the social struggle in the USSR, whatever form it takes, and particularly if there is any move away from the unstable equilibrium in which the country finds itself in 1990.

[5]Resolution of the Council of Representatives of the Confederation of Labour, 24 June 1990 (Moscow, 1990).

The worst possible scenario, as I see it, would be an attempt to restore the bureaucratic–authoritarian order by force. In this case, work collectives could be a real force of resistance. It is difficult to say whether they would be successful, but the experience of China and Poland suggests that without work collectives it is completely impossible to resist organised force.

The labour movement could also have a central role in what might be seen as the opposite scenario – a forced acceleration of democratisation and market reforms directed from above. At this point in time such a development could not be based on universal consensus. The move to a policy of accelerated reform would require either a definitive split between the reformers and the conservatives in the Soviet political leadership, with the initiators of perestroika joining openly and unequivocally with the elements in the lower echelons of the CPSU who support perestroika and with democratic social movements outside the party, or that the leadership of society pass straight to new forces evolved directly from these movements. It is obvious that in this case the developments would come up against the conscious and unconscious resistance of the conservatives. Since in this case mass use of state forces will be inadmissable both on practical-political grounds and on principle, the accelerated movement to the market and democracy would require powerful social support. The work collectives' movement – joining with the democratically oriented elements in local Soviets and party structures, with other democratic and national-democratic organisations, and with the civilised co-operative members and associations of agricultural workers, farmers and smallholders – could become the most important force in this support.

Finally, the democratic labour movement is perhaps most necessary of all in what we might call the middle-way scenario, involving a not particularly rapid and very inconsistent movement towards the market and democracy. This kind of development arises from attempts to avoid the cataclysms inevitable in rapid reform and the desire to preserve the political unity of the ruling groups throughout the period of change (or the reformers' inability to free themselves from the conservatives, which comes to the same thing).

In this case change will be achieved through continual compromise. This is why the development will be inconsistent, with constant vacillations and retreats. Furthermore, in the 'middle-way' scenario there is always the danger of excessive concessions to the conservatives, the threat of a complete return to the past and a total rejection of perestroika.

Ultimately, in order to maintain the dynamic of perestroika under the compromise scenario, it will be necessary to keep up a constant pressure on the ruling structures, urging them towards democracy and the market – pressure of the kind exerted by the peaceful political strike on 11 July 1990. Whether the overall tendency of the compromises is towards or away from perestroika will depend largely on which of the pressures on the ruling groups – for or against perestroika – is the stronger. It is clear that the movement of organised work collectives would be as important among the various factors in democratic pressure on the vacillating leadership in this case as it would in the accelerated reform scenario described above, where it would be among the forces supporting a decisive leadership carrying out democratisation rapidly and without compromise.

This was in effect the situation in the main Soviet coal basins during the 1989 strikes, and has remained the position in the Kuznetsk basin, and to some extent in Vorkuta. In these areas the population now relies just as readily on the workers' committees (the former strike committees) as it does on the Soviets and official administrative agencies, and the workers' committees are constantly interacting with these agencies.

The democratic community of work collectives is fully aware of its capacity to participate directly in the creation of a new social organisation and a new power structure in the developing new Soviet society. It understands the significance of self-managment and considers the best way to participate in this process. 'We are not hoping for kind-hearted leaders and thoughtful bureaucrats', says the Declaration of the association of independent workers' movements created in 1990, the Confederation of Labour:

> 'We do not want to see personnel replaced while the nature and struc-
> ture of power remains the same, but the replacement of the authori-
> tarian–punitive method of government by democratic government. We
> will defend the rights of the workers to their historic work of creation,
> the quest for and creation of new forms of workers' and people's gov-
> ernment where the old forms are inactive or act against the will and
> interests of the workers . . . . We call for the creation of sovereign
> bodies of self-management at grass-roots level. Parallel (additional)
> power structures are one of the factors in the peaceful development
> of revolution.'[6]

It goes without saying that the scenarios described above are only an outline. The most likely outcome is perhaps not any single one of these, but a combination of elements of all three. It is clear, however, that whatever happens the democratic labour movement, if it is politically organised and linked with other forces in the democratic community, could have a powerful influence on the progress of perestroika.

[6]Declaration of the fundamental principles of the Confederation of Labour, *Nasha gazeta* [Our Paper], Novokuznetsk, 15 May, 1990.

7

The roots of political reform: The changing social structure of the USSR

David Lane

Putting the process of perestroika into 'historical perspective' also involves a sociological perspective through which social change and political control have to be analyzed. The paradigm of totalitarianism dominant in the West interpreted stability in terms of the fusion of state and society. The ubiquitous domination of the state over the citizen was ensured through its exertion of physical and psychological control. The absence of social differentiation, of spontaneous social groups which could influence the political sphere ensured the complete domination of the ruling élite over society. Changes that took place were of personalities, of adaptations by the élite to new threats to its power. Legitimacy and support were concepts that were absent from the vocabulary of totalitarianism. This theoretical approach, however, is open to criticism. One might concede that implementation may be achieved through coercion and manipulation but one is unable to explain transformation or the conditions under which coercion breaks down as an effective mechanism of political control. If political control through the 'partocracy' were totalitarian, how could political change take place? A 'new form' of totalitarianism hardly fits the picture of changes in economy, polity and society taking place under perestroika which have undermined the political, economic and ideological foundations of the system created by Stalin. The totalitarian approach also ignores the ways that the activity of the state was legitimated in ideological terms. Marxism–Leninism (as a peculiar product of Russian culture) provided authority for leadership just as liberal democracy has provided a rationalisation of forms of property, solidarity and markets under capitalism.

State socialism was a comprehensive form of organisation of society with its own distinctive organising principles. Marxism–Leninism provided a set of general goals which legitimated state property, social equality, planning and central control under the hegemony of the Communist Party, a collectivist form of social solidarity and the pursuit of gratification through labour rather than consumption. The definition of 'socialism' implied by the schema has been shared by many Western socialists: the Fabians, for instance, and particularly the Webbs, have espoused the organising principles defined here. But these principles of socialism have been cast in doubt in the past 20 years and in the 1980s there has been an ideological crisis on the nature of socialism both in the USSR and the West. Traditional socialist and communist parties in

Western states have revised some of their previously held fundamental principles.

In seeking a new form of legitimation, the Soviet leadership has moved first slowly and lately with rapidity from the organising principles of state socialism to those of Western capitalist states. Claims for an advance to a communist society are no longer made. Administrative methods of control of the economy, public ownership, the hegemony of the Communist Party have been repudiated and replaced by greater reliance on the market, on the legitimacy of private property, on prices and competition. Personal interest, private property, 'freedom', the market, 'democracy', pluralism, law, privacy and consumer gratification have replaced the organising principles noted earlier. A major shift in the organisation of state socialist society has been taking place: it is interest driven rather than ideologically driven.

In all the state socialist societies, the ideology of Marxism-Leninism has been seriously undermined. A consequence has been a lack of confidence and, following a crisis of legitimacy, a collapse of the traditional communist leadership: the monopoly of power of the party has been relinquished and has led to a political vacuum in the USSR and major structural changes in the East European states. What are the driving forces of the reform movement? How has a policy ostensibly intended to 'reform socialism' led to such major changes in the pattern of organisation and process?

Many of the papers in this collection contribute parts of the answer. Discussion focuses on the conditioning factors of the changed international position of the USSR and the rise of a new leadership cohort. The decline of economic growth is regarded as a factor that has undermined the political leadership in all the countries of Eastern Europe. The malfunctioning of the resource-mobilization subsystem has in turn undermined the processes of the political system and the economy (the legitimacy of the planned economy and party control). Economic decline has exacerbated the tensions within the allocative processes and has led to a widening expectations gap on the part of the population. Many commentators regard Gorbachev personally as the crucial motivating political factor. This 'political position' approach, highlighting the rise of new leaders, must be given a prominent place in any explanation. Ideological criticisms have pointed to contradictions between different interests leading to 'stagnation', to the retardation of economic development, to corruption and a decline of socialist morality and to popular apathy and alienation. Such critiques stemming from the political leadership have had the effect of destroying the myths created about the legitimacy of leadership under socialism and have destabilised the social and political order.

A Social Structural Approach

Sociologists would point to the deep-seated and long-term changes that have taken place in the social structure of state socialism. By the term 'social structure' we mean an array of positions or statuses, the conditions that shape them and a network of relationships between people and groups. Statuses give rise to patterns of behaviour, to norms and expectations; they are *foci* which give people a sense of social and individual identity. Statuses include occupations and social groups which may be divided into many categories – such as by sex and age, urban and rural, ethnic and religious, white collar and blue collar, professionals and collective farmers. The sheer size and differentiation of Soviet society has made it impossible to control 'from the top down'. Rather than modern society providing the means for ubiquitous control as entailed by totalitarianism, the contrary is the case. The diverse forms of administrative organisation, the specialised division of labour, the heterogeneity of urban life give rise to a social pluralism and consciousness of group and sectional interests.

If modern political systems are to operate effectively there must be mechanisms through which the political leadership can set goals and mobilise resources. To secure compliance, diffuse forms of support from the public are necessary. Parsonian sociologists describe the exchange between the leadership's policy options and generalised support from political constituents as the political support system. Only through reciprocity between the political leadership and the public can political power be effectively exercised. Power can also only be discharged effectively if it is legitimate. Such legitimacy is dependent on the leadership acting within the pattern of values of society and through the accepted norms of the political system. This paradigm should not be restricted to describe Western capitalist society but may also be utilized to understand processes at work in the state socialist societies.

I do not claim that social structural factors are the only or even the major determinants of the changes in the regime which have taken place. My own preference would be for a fusion model: this entails that several variables (including ideology, economic decline, external constraints, as described above) act concurrently to promote the development of a new regime. The changing social structure, my subject here, is one of these crucial variables in providing support or opposition to a given political leadership and system of rule. Social structure has multifactorial effects – a change in social structure influences norms, values, institutions and processes.

Changes in Social Structure

The social structure of Soviet society today is of a qualitatively different type to that associated with the regimes of Stalin or Khrushchev. Major changes have occurred in the social formation of the Soviet Union during the past seventy years. These have to be seen as providing the major social and political supports and inputs into the political system which has responded to these demands. Gorbachev should be considered not to be 'changing society' from the top but his ascendancy is an expression of new social groups and interests which have developed in the past 30 years. The élites have a different complexion and social background. The role of the reform leadership is not only to propel change and react to demands, it has in addition a purpose of creating an alternative vision, it offers new ways of doing things. Hence the approach adopted here is not a form of sociological reductionism, the role of a creative political leadership is important – though it is not my brief here.

I shall outline only two major developments in the social structure (women and nationalities are examined in other chapters in this collection). First, differential rates of urbanisation and population growth and, second, changes in the occupational and class structure. These changes, in conjunction with other factors, have led to the growth of groups that have been predisposed to dissatisfaction with the processes of Soviet society and have been responsive to calls for reform.

A study of the urban and occupational composition of the population establishes that by the 1980s the USSR was an urban industrial society comparable in many respects to the advanced Western states. Figure 7.1

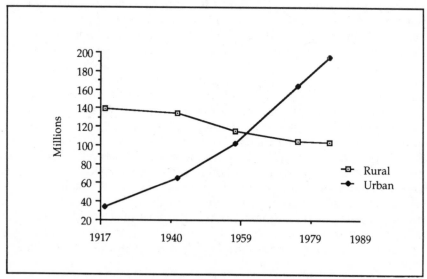

Fig. 7.1 USSR Population: 1917–1989 (Urban – Rural Division)

shows the rise of population for the USSR between 1917 and 1989 (from 163 millions to 286.7 millions); the urban population in 1989 comprised 66 per cent of the population.[1] One must also bear in mind the great regional diversity of the USSR with the Western European republics being more highly urbanised, whereas the Central Asian republics even in 1990 are predominantly rural. In 1989, for example, the Russian Republic had an urban population of 74 per cent, Latvia 71 per cent and the Ukraine 67 per cent, whereas Tadzhikistan had only 33 per cent, and Uzbekistan 41 per cent. The comparative growth of urban populations in selected republics between 1922 and 1989 is shown on Figure 7.2 – the last column in each year block being the total for the USSR.

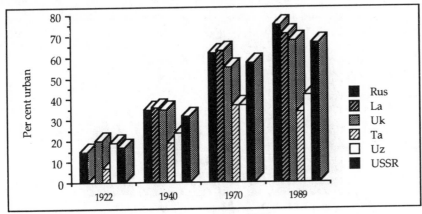

Fig. 7.2 Urbanisation – Republics: 1922 – 1989

Only in the 1960s did the USSR become mainly urban – a condition reached in Britain before the mid-nineteenth century. The rate of growth of the urban population in the past 65 years is remarkable. The total number of urban dwellers rose from some 22 million in 1922 to 186.8 million in 1989 and between 1959 and 1989 the urban population nearly doubled from 100 million to 186.8 million. The greatest share of this increase may be attributed to the European areas of the country. Clearly, this urban population explosion has put great strain on the supply of commodities (especially food) and services. Any government would have been hard pressed to meet the demands on food supply and the provision of social services and housing.

The movement of population from countryside to town has been

[1]Population data are given in the yearly publication: *Naselenie SSSR*, and in *Narodnoe khozyaistvo SSSR*, the volumes for 1988 published in 1989 have been used in this article. Data for the 1989 census appear in *Pravda* 29 April, 1989.

The definition of 'urban' varies between different republics of the USSR. In the Russian Republic, towns are defined as contiguous populations not less than 12,000 with non-manuals and manual workers forming 85 per cent or more of the population, an urban area has to be settled by 3,000 people with at least 85 per cent of the population being composed of manual and non-manual workers.   In the Ukraine, on the other hand, urban areas are defined as 2,000 people with a majority outside of agriculture. *Naselenie SSSR*, 1983, pp.22–3 fn.).

accompanied by important changes in employment, both by economic sector and by occupation. Figure 7.3 illustrates the major changes that have taken place in employment by economic sector: as late as the 1960s agriculture was the major employer, losing its prime place to industry and building in the seventies. The last 20 years have witnessed another major transformation: employment in agriculture in 1988 was only 35 per cent of that of 1940; by 1988, the largest economic sector was services and transport (42 per cent).[2]

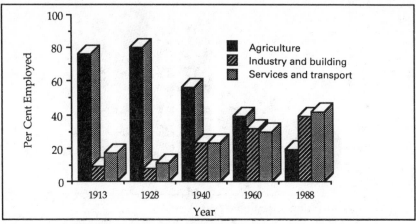

Fig. 7.3 USSR: Employment by Economic Sector

In the past half century the manual working class has grown tremendously: employment was as follows: 1928, 4.628 million; 1940, 12.543 million; 1960, 17.864 million and 1987, 38.259 million.[3] An important change has also taken place in the character of the urban working class. The recruitment of workers in the 1930s involved a very high proportion of young peasants new to the town: the culture of the factory was strongly influenced by peasant mores.[4] These young men and women received their rudimentary training on the shop floor. From about the 1950s, a critical proportion of the manual working class had begun to reproduce itself. For instance, a study of Leningrad workers in the mid-1970s found that 83 per cent hailed from an urban background and 39 per cent were the children of industrial workers; only 28 per cent of the skilled workers came from an agricultural or unskilled manual worker background.[5] With the replenishment of the working class, aspirations have considerably

[2]*Trud v SSSR* 1988, p.14.
[3]*Trud v SSSR* 1988, pp.47, 55.
[4]For further details see: David Lane and Felicity O'Dell, *The Soviet Industrial Worker: Social Class, Education and Control* (Martin Robertson), 1978, Chapters 1 and 2.
[5]N.P. Konstantinova, O.V. Stakanova, O.I. Shkaratan, 'Peremeny v sotsial'nom oblike rabochikh v epokhu razvitogo sotsializma', *Voprosy istorii*, 1978, No. 5, p.11.

changed and the levels of skill and education have significantly improved. For instance, to the workforce between 1960 and 1986 were added 20 million graduates of trade schools (an annual output of 2.6 million in the late 1980s).[6] There is then a development of a significant stratification of the working class, with a younger generation of workers being more skilled and urbanised than their older colleagues. While their education is higher, the actual skill level of the job performed is lower. This is graphically illustrated by the findings of Konstantinova *et al.*[7] which shows the inverse relationship between education and skill when age is taken into account (see Figure 7.4).

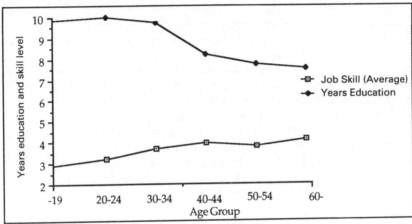

Fig. 7.4 Manual Workers: Age, Education and Job Skill

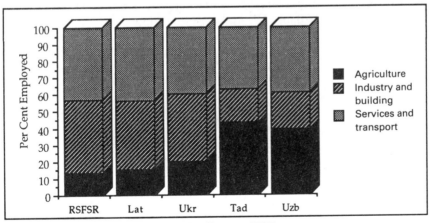

Fig. 7.5 Republics: Employment by Sector, 1987

[6]*Ibid.*: 95.
[7]Konstantinova *et al.*: 14.

There are significant differences between republics: Figure 7.5 shows data representing five republics: the industrially and economically advanced republics of European Russia (Latvia and the Ukraine), the Russian Republic, one of the most backward (Tadzhikistan) and one of the more advanced though unevenly developed Central Asian republics (Uzbekistan).[8] Figure 7.5 shows the different kinds of employment by sector in five Republics: the RSFSR and Latvia have very similar proportions; the Ukraine has somewhat larger industrial and agricultural sectors and the two Central Asian republics have sizeable agricultural ones. Perhaps surprisingly their service sector is relatively substantial. This indicates the presence of a large non-manual class in public fields: teaching, medicine and administration.

Linked to these sectoral changes in employment are developments in cultural levels and a changing occupational structure. Such advancement has led to the growth of a competent and literate citizenship and to the formation of a middle class. One measure of such improvements is the standard of education. In 1926, the Soviet authorities claimed that 51.1 per cent of the population aged over nine years was literate, and by 1939 the figure reached 81.2 per cent.[9] This figure probably errs on the side of charity: according to the census of 1937, of 98 million people aged over nine, 37.3 million (38 per cent) were illiterate.[10] Even by 1959, the census showed that by far the largest group of the population had received only an incomplete secondary education (i.e. *nepolnoe srednee*). The social base on which the Stalinist regime developed was largely composed of poorly educated people. As late as 1937, only 43 per cent of adults (over 15) were self-defined as non-believers and in the census of that year 42 per cent professed allegiance to the Orthodox Church.[11]

Under Brezhnev, as a consequence of the social policies adopted earlier, this social base had changed remarkably. Comparative data for the years 1939, 1959, 1970 and 1979 are given in Figure 7.6.[12] Even in 1959, by far the bulk of the population had no more than an 'incomplete secondary' (mainly primary) education. The figure illustrates the spectacular rise in educational standards during the past thirty years. Some of the major indices are as follows: in 1939, there were only 1.2 million people with a complete higher education (only 911,790 were recorded in the census of 1937),[13] in 1959, there were 8.3 millions and by 1987 the number had risen to nearly 21 millions.[14]

By the 1970s, the density of the professional non-manuals had given them a 'demographic identity'. Figure 7.7 plots the growth of a number of professional groups: engineers and technicians, animal specialists,

[8]Based on statistics from *Trud v SSSR* 1988: 16, 17.
[9]*Nasrodnoe obrazovanie v SSSR* Moscow 1957, p.733.
[10]Calculated on census data published in Yu.A. Polyakov, V.B. Zhuromskaya, I.I. Kiselev, 'Polveka Molchaniya', *Sotsiologicheskie issledovaniya*, No. 7, 1990, p.67.
[11]Data calculated on Table cited in Polyakov *et al.*, p.69.
[12]*Chislennost' i sostav naseleniya SSSR*, 1984, p.23, *Narkhoz v 1987g*,1988, p.476.
[13]See Table in Polyakov *et al.*, *ibid*.
[14]*Trud v SSSR* (1988), p.119.

economists, lawyers, physicians and medical specialists, teachers and other personal services employees.[15] Professionals are here defined as people with a higher or specialist secondary education. Note particularly in each period the growth in the size of the first column of the total number of employees: by 1987 the number had grown to over 35 million people from a mere 2.4 million in 1940. A significant proportion of this skilled non-manual group were women (36 per cent in 1940 rising to 61 per cent in 1987).[16]

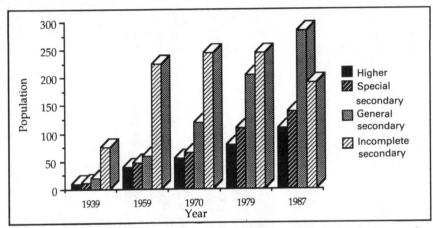

Fig. 7.6 USSR: Educational Level; 1939–1987 (Per 1000 of population aged 10 and above)

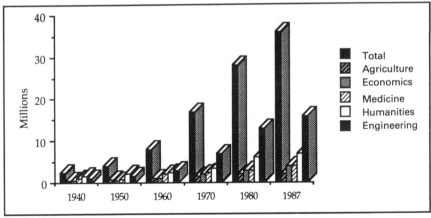

Fig. 7.7 USSR: Growth of Professional Employees 1940–1987

Such developments were not restricted to the Russian Republic but also entailed developments in the republics. Educational achievements

[15]Source *Trud v SSSR* (1988), p.113.
[16]*Ibid.*: 119.

broken down by republic are shown in Table 7.1. These data show the higher levels of tertiary education in the European areas of the country. The strata of upper professionals are to be found in the capital cities of the European areas. But the differences are not as marked as one might have expected. Indeed, the figures for full general secondary education give both Tadzhikistan and Uzbekistan higher ratios than the USSR as a whole (see Figure 7.8). The main reason for this is that the Central Asian republics do not have the large number of older people educated before 1959 when facilities were poor. Nevertheless, levels of higher education in Latvia and the Russian Republic are significantly higher than in the Central Asian republics. Higher education is probably the more important variable to act as a 'push' factor in favour of reform.

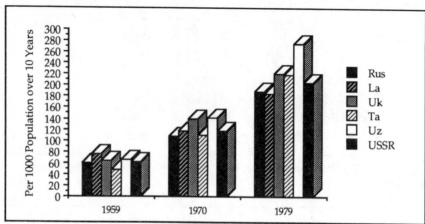

Fig. 7.8 Republics: Secondary Education, 1959, 1970, 1979

These figures suggest a linkage between levels of urbanisation and higher education and political support for a new style of leadership: the Central Asian republics have not been particularly prominent in the drive to establish a new type pluralistic system – rather the contrary. In addition, however, one must add to such predisposing factors those of knowledge and a vision of an alternative political regime. In the European republics, this vision is provided by history of independence and the proximity of the advanced affluent counties of the West. These are lacking in the Central Asian republics. It is possible that in the future the young non-manual groups will be the basis for a heightened national consciousness.

The Social Support of Leadership

On the basis of these data we may make a number of observations. The rapid growth of the urban population, particularly after 1959, has put considerable stress on the resource mobilisation system to supply goods to the towns. Urban dwellers have higher levels of consumer expectations than rural ones: the aggregate demand schedules for goods and services have shifted to the right and the demand for higher qualities of food has strained agricultural production. (In other words, unless prices rise, the shelves will be empty because much more is bought at a given price.)

By the 1980s there was a large educated non-manual urban population. Numerically, the manual working class has replaced the peasant population of the inter-war years and in a qualitative way, the working class has come to possess an urban culture: it is no longer formed of *muzhiks* wearing boiler suits. One might hypothesise that the social base of politics has changed. Under Stalin, the peasant was a social-worker prop of the regime; at the beginning of the Second World War the Soviet Union had a large illiterate peasant population. Even in the towns the typical resident had only a primary education. The white collar middle class was small and undereducated. Under Brezhnev and Khrushchev diffuse political backing was provided by the manual worker. By 1950,

TABLE 7.1: Educational Levels of the Population in the USSR, RSFSR, Latvia, Ukraine, Tadzhikistan, and Uzbekistan. (1959, 1970 and 1979) (Per 1,000 of the population aged 10 and above)

	1959	1970	1979
RSFSR:			
All higher	35	57	86
Full general secondary	58	108	188
Latvia:			
All higher	39	67	95
Full general secondary	75	119	187
Ukraine:			
All higher	31	52	78
Full general secondary	64	139	220
Tadzhikistan:			
All higher	24	41	61
Full general secondary	48	112	220
Uzbekistan:			
All higher	30	52	74
Full general secondary	67	141	275
USSR:			
All higher	34	55	83
Full general secondary	61	119	207

Source: Census data, *Chislennost' i sostav naseleniya SSSR* (1984): 26–41.

employment of manual workers had outstripped that of any other group and by 1980 it was nearly 80 million in size, making it the largest single agglomeration of manual workers in the world.

Under perestroika, the professional non-manuals are ascendant groups and, it may be hypothesised, make a social base which both pushes and is pulled by Gorbachev's policies. Non-manual workers between 1960 and 1987 more than doubled in size to over 36 million employees. These social strata make demands to which the leadership responds. I would thus wish to qualify the widely held and correct view that perestroika is a 'revolution from the top'. It has also been 'pushed' by the demands of these new social forces. In turn, moreover, the reform leadership has 'pulled' to it the non-manual groups with higher education.

Such developments have to be interpreted in the context of the presence of more traditional interests and groupings (the unskilled manual workers still form a very large group). The cultural legacy of previous epochs of Soviet history also makes its particular impact. Furthermore, national identification is a latent force in the Central Asian republics. The growth of a young intelligentsia in the Central Asian republics may indicate a future development of nationalist sentiment. The rise of independence movements in the republics overwhelmingly led by the indigenous intelligentsia has to be analysed in the light of traditional dispositions which give rise to a vision of an alternative political and social order. This is present in the European republics such as the Baltic states in a different guise to that in the Asian, where Islam may prove to yield an alternative mobilising ideology.

Much study of political support in the West has related voting behaviour to social class and in this fashion has depicted the social basis of politics. In the absence of competitive elections, one can only have cruder linkages between the leadership and the population. One may hypothesise that to ensure diffuse supports, the policies of a regime need to be congruent with the interest and culture of salient social groups.

In this sense, I would argue that the social ballast of the political leadership has changed from the manual working class under Brezhnev to the non-manual strata which are a stanchion to the reform leadership. The quantitative data cited here are evidence that this group has a demographic identity.[17] The shift from class positions (in a Weberian sense) to the formation of a class with its own self-consciousness is occurring under the reform leadership.

This may be illustrated by consideration of the social composition of the leading institutions of power. Under Brezhnev, the density of manual workers in the membership of the Communist Party of the Soviet Union rose considerably. In the period 1956 to 1961 (under Khrushchev) workers made up 41.1 per cent *new* Party members, their share rising to 59.4

---

[17]For a comparison with Britain, see J. Goldthorpe, 'On the Service Class, Its Formation and Future', in A. Giddens, G. Mackenzie, *Social Class and the Division of Labour* (Cambridge, 1982), pp.171–2.

per cent in the late Brezhnev period (1981–85).[18] This gave a solid working class membership to the Communist party: manual workers constituted 43.4 per cent of membership in 1981 and 45.4 per cent in 1989.[19]

However, manual workers and collective farmers have been increasingly excluded from positions of power under the Gorbachev leadership which is dependent on the non-manual and professional social groups. Since the mid-fifties there has been a massive increase in the numbers of Party members with higher education: in 1957 only some million members had a higher education; by 1971 it had risen to 2.81 million (19.6 per cent), and to 6.8 million (31.8 per cent) in 1989. Density of people with higher education is even greater at the crucial level of the Party apparat: of the Party's leading cadres (members and candidates of central committees and auditing commissions of Union Republican parties and Province (obkom) and territories (krai) committees), 69.4 had higher education. Even at the level of cities, districts (raykom) and areas (okrug), 56.7 per cent had a complete higher education.[20] These changes in social composition entailed a different world view on the part of the party leadership: authoritative positions in the Party were increasingly occupied by people with higher education and they were respondent to a similar constituency in the Party's membership.

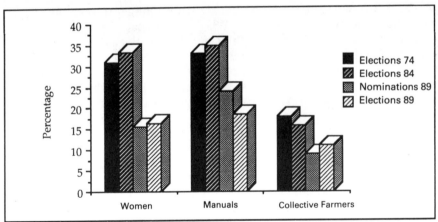

Fig. 7.9 Political Elite 1974, 1984, 1989 (of the Supreme Soviet, Congress of Peoples Deputies of the USSR)

Another measure that indicates the changing political base for the new leadership is the social background of the membership of the Supreme Soviet and the Congress of People's Deputies of the USSR. In 1974, workers constituted 32.8 per cent of the members of the Supreme Soviet

---

18 'KPSS v tsifrakh', *Partiynaya zhizn'*, No. 21, 1987, p.8.
19 'KPSS v tsifrakh', *Izvestiya Ts.K. KPSS*, 1989, No. 2: 140.
20Sources: 'KPSS v tsifrakh', *Partiynaya zhizn'*, No. 4, 1986: 23, 29; 'KPSS v tsifrakh', *Partiynaya zhizn'*, No. 21, 1987: 10; *Iz. TsK. KPSS*, No. 2, 1989: 140.

of the USSR.[21] This figure rose slightly to 35.2 per cent in the Supreme Soviet elected before the reform leadership was in command. Similarly, women constituted 31 per cent of the delegates in 1974 and 33 per cent in 1984. These high figures were secured by notional 'quotas' from various social groups which ensured their representation which was symbolic. The massive decline of working class and female representation may be gauged from the data cited in Figure 7.9 showing the social background of membership of the deputies to the Supreme Soviet in 1974 and 1984 with those nominated and elected to the Congress of People's Deputies in 1989. The share of workers among the deputies in the 1989 election came to 18.6 per cent, collective farmers received only 11.2 per cent (compared to 16.1 per cent) of the seats and the proportion of women fell considerably from 33 per cent to 17.1 per cent.[22] The number of deputies in the professional classes with higher education rose from 7.8 per cent to 15.7 per cent.[23] These data are illustrative not only of a symbolic but also a real shift in the basis of power of the leadership towards the non-manual professional strata.

Allocative Politics

Much, if not most, of Western concern with political support has to do with the allocative process: the 'Who Gets What, When and How', to borrow Lasswell's term. Voting and Party allegiance in the West are explained by reference to individuals and groups which combine to maximize their material interest. With some important exceptions among Western political scientists, such considerations have been little studied in Soviet politics because of the absence of a pluralistic political structure. The representative system has not been constructed to articulate 'interests', but as a form of social representation of different social strata. In my view, however, the reform leadership's appeal to the professional groups may also be cloaked in terms of allocative priorities. This may be examined quantitatively by reference to changes in income differentials and hypothetically by a consideration of the possible gains in status of professionals under perestroika.

Under Brezhnev, the working class has acted as an effective 'veto group' on the political élite. By veto group I mean that the working class as a collectivity has the power to prevent any action by the government or their direct employers unless it is perceived to be in their interests. This has been interpreted by Western commentators such as Echols and Bunce and Hough as a type of corporatist politics. A number of cogent reasons have been put forward in support of this view: the working class had high job security, the worker was cushioned by overfull employment

[21]*Verkhovny Sovet SSSR* (1974).
[22]For election results see: *Izvestiya*, 5 May 1989; *Moscow News*, 16 April 1989.
[23]*Izvestiva*, 6 May 1989.

and low labour productivity. Hence, even if the working class did not have 'independent' political organisations representing its 'interests', it was able to exert pressure on the shop floor by slackening the activity of work. It was also capable of articulating its interests through the Party organisation and also through the unions. An outburst of worker unrest was regarded as a serious failure of local political leadership and hence in various ways manual workers were able to secure significant advantages from the regime.

There had been a slow but constant rise in wages coupled to low price inflation: the index of real income for manual and non-manual workers rose from 100 in 1970 to 155 in 1986; and it rose 17 percentage points between 1980 and 1987.[24] But labour productivity was falling and technological advance required the relocation of personnel. Unlike under capitalism, where unemployment and the price system are levers of change and the working class is relatively weakly organised relative to management and capital, in the Soviet case it has been the other way around. It has been very difficult to legitimate the laying off of workers which is necessary to improve productivity when technology improves. Unlike under capitalism, participation in the increased wealth has accrued disproportionately to the manual working class. This may be illustrated by the changing wage differentials between three main groups (workers, managerial/technical and office workers) in Soviet society.

While these are wide and ambiguous social categories, they show clearly the trends and are corroborated by other qualitative evidence on differentials. Wage relativities for manual workers in industry have improved dramatically during the last 50 years or so: by 1986, they received on average 20 per cent more than office workers (*sluzhashchie*)

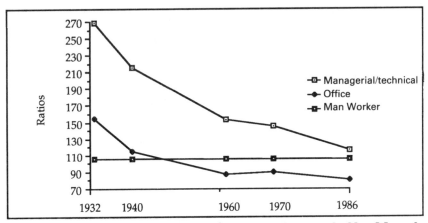

Fig. 7.10 Wage Ratios: Managerial/Technical Personnel, Non-Manual Office, Manual Workers, 1932–1986

[24]*Narkhoz za 70 let:* 441; *Narkhoz v 1987g:* 402.

whose income was 50 per cent greater in 1932, the differential to managerial/technical staff has fallen from 1 : 2.6 to 1 : 1.1 in the same time span. In Figure 7.10 the manual workers' wage is calculated as 100, managerial/technical was 2.1 times greater in 1940, but only 1.1 times in 1986; the office workers' (sluzhashchie) differential fell even more, from 1.09 to only 0.79 times between these two dates.[25]

While these scales apply to wages in industry, they are also true of wage differentials generally. They have led to feelings of injustice by white collar employees in the USSR, not only by upper professionals but also by other lowly paid non-manual workers such as nurses, teachers and clerks. Physicians, teachers, engineers, research personnel usually received salaries less than those of skilled manual workers[26] (though, of course, their forms of consumption and lifestyle are not necessarily inferior). There is a major difference here compared with Western welfare societies where non-manual employees in the public sector tend to support state intervention in the economy. Their salaries and status are linked to active intervention by the government against the market. Under interventionalist left wing governments, significant salary differentials have been secured for the public service professional classes *vis-a-vis* unskilled manual and non-manual workers. In the USSR, differentials have also narrowed among the manual workers; there has been a tendency towards income levelling which has benefitted the relatively unskilled and unmotivated worker. The variation noted earlier between the level of education of the younger and older workers is indicative of different attitudes: the younger also advocating greater use of the market under which they surmise their skills would be more properly rewarded.

The social policy adopted prior to Gorbachev assumed that social strata were and *ought* to be sharing more equal incomes and there developed in the USSR a public consciousness which linked egalitarianism to socialism. Under the traditional administrative system, the workers could use their political influence to prevent layoffs and the speeding up of the tempo of production. The ideology of Marxism–Leninism legitimated the leading role of the working class and it proved impossible to increase levels of unemployment. In this way the working class could 'veto' the management's quest to increase levels of productivity. The political leadership in its desire to 'modernise', to catch up with the West, must extract greater surplus product and must increase levels of productivity. The Soviet leadership has been aware that administrative attempts to discipline the working class have led to resistance in Poland, to the fall of the political élite there, the proclamation of martial law and the collapse of the political system in the late 1980s.

The greater use of the market is a strategy that the leadership has adopted not only to meet such demands but also to use as a means of

[25]*Narkhoz v 1984g.* (1985), p. 417, and *Narkhoz za 70 let.* Later statistical handbooks do not group data in this form.
[26]See the discussion in T. Zaslavskaya, *The Second Socialist Revolution: An Alternative Socialist Strategy* (London, 1990), pp.120–21.

disciplining the workforce to raise productivity and to change the pattern of differentials to the disadvantage of the unskilled manual workers and to the benefit of those with skills and education, particularly the intelligentsia. Ideologically, this has involved the delegitimation of planning and the command system. In more intangible ways, the processes of glasnost' and decentralisation of power will enhance the authority of the intelligentsia.

In his discussion of the 'service class', Goldthorpe has pointed to the autonomy of this group and the advantages of employment in this sector. In the West, it is a class that has consolidated its position.[27] The Soviet equivalent of the service class (the higher and middle intelligentsia), however, lacks autonomy of work situation and salaries are depressed compared to the working class. While it has grown in size and become more homogeneous in social composition, it has lost in status. It is a group which is disgruntled with the 'command system' and is conscious of an alternative in the market societies of the West and its members are often spellbound by Thatcherite and Friedmanesque rhetoric. Curbing the power of the bureaucracy will lead, it is believed, to the fragmentation of power and it is likely that professions will develop as a consequence of 'pluralism'. There are good reasons for the intelligentsia to believe that their work situation and market situation will improve under the conditions of economic and political pluralism. Glasnost', *demokratizatsiya* and *khozraschet* will raise considerably the autonomy of the work situation of the intelligentsia.

Hence the 'support-exchange' theory of allocative politics would suggest that the intelligentsia has much to gain from perestroika, and the manual working class much to lose. One might expect opposition to the Gorbachev reforms to have a material basis among many strata of the manual working class. As in Western market economies, the heaviest burden of redundancy is carried by the unskilled. The large stratum of older unskilled, lowly educated manual workers will be particularly prone to layoffs and welfare support has not been developed in the state socialist societies. It is also likely that the working class will become more stratified with greater differentiation benefitting the skilled manual worker.

Conclusion

This chapter addresses the problem of why and to whom the values and norms of perestroika have appeal in Soviet society. A 'fusion model' of several variables acting concurrently to promote transformation has been advocated. Developments in the social structure (in the sense of the formation of new social groups and strata) have multifactorial effects influencing norms, values and processes. But changes in social structure

[27]Goldthorpe, *ibid.*, p. 178.

have to be considered also in the context of other variables. Relative economic decline of the socialist states has been an important precipitating factor of change and so have changes in the nature of the world economic order.

An 'historical perspective' illuminates the process of change. Contemporary Soviet society is significantly different from that of even 30 years ago. A major feature of social structural development has been the growth of population and the rise in levels of urbanisation. Changes in the social composition of the population have led to diffuse support among the urban population for policies of perestroika. Levels of education have risen considerably and there is a substantial mass of young people with higher education. A 'demographic identity' has developed among the Soviet intelligentsia which has facilitated the rise of a new political consciousness.

Under Gorbachev, the Soviet political culture contains a significant number of individuals and groups having a positive conception of their own interests; this gives rise to a critical mass which may evaluate the government's actions. Soviet society has changed from one with a passive peasantry, as it was under Stalin, to one dependent on the participation of the intelligentsia and on the rising productivity of the skilled manual working class. The current intelligentsia is a stratum receptive to an alternative conception of socialism (which in practice embraces many of the practices of contemporary capitalism), to a vision of the future different from that of their parents.

In the wake of modernisation, the population has come to expect a rising standard of living and a better quality of life. This changing value system has been a 'push' factor for perestroika. 'Moral' incentives and commitment to work as a collective duty are not regarded by the present leadership as being effective and higher differentials linked to greater productivity are favoured. 'Social justice' in the USSR calls for greater earned income differentials rather than, as in the West, lower ones. A contented working class has been at the basis of the political stability of the Soviet system. Until the advent of Andropov, it was cultivated by all Soviet leaders. The cost of stability has been in terms of absenteeism, poor labour discipline and poor quality production: in short, low labour productivity. But in terms of 'allocative politics', the manual working class has benefitted disproportionately from the rising standard of living. It has been a mainstay of the centralised command economy. The falling levels of economic growth and the nonfulfillment of plans have led to widespread consumer dissatisfaction despite the fact that living standards have improved. Policy involves a recalibration of the differentials between various groups and the ways that they are calculated. The working class will become more differentiated, with the skilled and productive being rewarded. The unskilled manual working class is likely to pay a high price under the new policies: it will be subject to greater uncertainty and will increasingly be confronted by redundancy if the quest for greater productivity is successful.

Gorbachev's recognition of 'deficiencies' and 'shortcomings' in policy has been triggered particularly by the lack of fulfilment of the aspirations of groups of intellectuals. The policy of glasnost' is a recognition of a surge of individual and group demands. If one assumes that the political leadership is dependent on the loyal support and creativity of the intelligentsia, it seems likely that as this stratum grows in size and maturity, the opinions of its sub-groups, particularly with respect to their professional expertise, will increasingly be taken into account. To challenge technologically the West, a competent, creative and contented intelligentsia is required. The thrust for reform has come from the professional classes who have become disenchanted with their status under command socialism; they in turn have been cultivated by the reform leadership.

It is undoubtedly the case that the reform leadership has shifted its political fulcrum of diffuse and specific support away from the manual working class and the traditional party and state bureaucracy to an alliance between the more technologically inclined and modernising forces among the political élite and the intelligentsia. This has threatened the traditional alliance between the Party executive, government administrators and their supporters among the manual working class. The maintenance and replication of their own positions will be undermined by the rise of market forces. But the reform leadership under Gorbachev has not only refracted social grievances and aspirations, it has also created them. It has revived old (nationalistic) and stimulated new (market) political ideals.

A social structural analysis alone cannot explain the variation of support for an alternative conception of the Soviet political regime. Proximity to the West and traditional forms of national identity are important variables which give rise to new political ideals and to support for a new regime.

The changes envisioned by the political leadership of Gorbachev require a new ideological shell. Breaking the grip of Marxist–Leninist ideology has been a significant manoeuvre of the reform leadership. It had been a major component of the state socialist system: but the collapse of Marxism–Leninism has entailed the weakening of the regime (particularly the previously dominant role of the Party) to an extent unanticipated by the reformers. The old slogan of 'unity of party and the people' has been replaced by a market plurality of interests which in the transitionary period of 1989/91 has lacked consensus and forms of solidarity have been lacking. In future, the market will deflect criticism away from the administrative leadership which, under the traditional system, was made responsible for society's ills. The market provides no such target: the 'hidden hand' under which it operates is anonymous. This major change was caused both by a 'push' from the more advanced groups in the social structure and by a 'pull' of the ideological promise of perestroika. The major support of the political leadership is to be found among the intelligentsia but also among the younger better educated members of the working class.

III The Economy

III The Rookery

8
Soviet economic reform in historical perspective
R. W. Davies

This chapter surveys the changing Soviet perceptions of Soviet economic experience, from Stalin to Yeltsin, and discusses in a preliminary way the impact of these perceptions on the progress of economic reform.

I: The Stalinist View

The Stalinist textbook of party history, *History of the Communist Party of the Soviet Union (Bolsheviks): Short Course* (1939) distinguished three systems or stages in Soviet development. First, War Communism, 'an attempt to take the fortress of the capitalist elements in town and countryside by assault, by a frontal attack'. Secondly, the New Economic Policy (NEP), which allowed freedom of trade for the peasant and 'a certain revival of capitalism'. Thirdly, from the mid-1930s onwards 'Socialist ownership of the means of production had been established in every branch of national economy as the basis of Soviet society'.

In Soviet textbooks of the 1930s and 1940s there was some analysis of the resemblances and differences between these different stages. In War Communism, all industry was managed by the state; a state monopoly of grain was established, accompanied by arrangements for expropriating surpluses; universal labour service was compulsory; individual peasant households continued, however, to predominate in the countryside. Under the first stage of the New Economic Policy, the 'commanding heights' of the economy, especially industry, remained in state owner-ship, agriculture was largely in the hands of individual peasants, and a market relation existed between them. In the socialist economy from the mid-1930s, state ownership of industry and the agricultural Machine-Tractor Stations was coupled with collective ownership of the collective farms. Much attention was also devoted by Soviet economists in Stalin's time to the role of money in the socialist economy and to the role of economic accounting (*khozraschet*) in state industry. By 1936, money was recognised to be an inherent feature of the socialist economy; this overturned the long-established view that socialism as well as communism would be a moneyless economy.

This traditional Stalinist presentation of the major Soviet economic systems of the inter-war years reflected important aspects of Soviet reality. But it suffered from several major weaknesses. In general, its account of the three systems was one-sided and idealised.

In the case of War Communism, the existence of a free or black market was recognised but it was not treated as an inherent and inescapable element of the system.

The New Economic Policy was defined as coterminous with the whole 'transition period' from War Communism to socialism, and was treated as a single stage and a single economic model. On this view NEP was not primarily the market relation with the peasants; it was the struggle to eliminate capitalism and petty capitalism in the USSR. Therefore it did not come to an end until private trade, private industry and private agriculture had all been eliminated, round about 1936. This extremely broad and somewhat bizarre definition of NEP had little influence in the West, and Soviet economists and historians were always uneasy about it. But it remained the orthodox view until 1987. A Soviet work published in 1982 complained that 'bourgeois authors', including myself, 'date NEP from 1921 to 1928', and explained that 'the objective of this chronological scheme is clearly to distort the true essence of NEP by separating its first years from the period of the decisive offensive against the capitalist elements in town and country, when the socialist nature of NEP disclosed itself more clearly'.[1]

The economy up to about 1936 was thus included in NEP. According to the official account, the crucial features of the socialist economic system which succeeded it were socialist ownership and planning. In fact several markets and quasi-markets continued to exist: a partial market for labour, a fixed-price market for retail consumer goods (involving some consumer choice though not consumer sovereignty), and the 'kolkhoz' market at free prices for part of retail food sales. But these, like the markets of War Communism, were all treated as merely minor aspects of the system. And the unofficial or illegal markets – including barter and other deals within the state sector – were virtually ignored, as was the persistence of repressed inflation. This view of the Stalinist economy influenced – or had common ground with – classical Western writings about the Soviet economy (until the classic view was disrupted by the work of Granick, Berliner and others in the 1950s). The Soviet view was not vastly different as far as the economic mechanism was concerned from the Western model of 'planning under a dictator' (later renamed the 'command economy'), and in Western writings this model of the economy fitted well with the totalitarian model of the Soviet regime.

This Soviet analysis of the history of the Soviet economic system suffered from three major weaknesses. First, the assumption that the Soviet leadership almost always acted entirely in accordance with the requirements dictated by the objective situation; only a few minor exceptions

[1]Yu.A. Polyakov, V.P. Dmitrenko and N.V. Shcherban', *Novaya ekonomicheskaya politika: razrabotka i osushchestvlenie* (1982), pp. 228–9.

were acknowledged. This was not, however, economic determinism. It is true that the theoretical section of the *Short Course* (Chapter 4, part 2), of which Stalin claimed the authorship, insisted that in the socialist economy 'the relations of production completely correspond to the character of the productive forces'.[2] But Stalin strongly insisted that the proletarian state had used its power in an endeavour to pull up the Soviet economy to the level of the advanced capitalist countries: the superstructure transformed the productive forces, rather than being merely determined by them. All this was treated, however, as an ineluctable result of the application of a correct Marxist strategy to objective circumstances. There was no place for analysing the evolution of the Soviet economic system as in part an experiment in the designing of a new and unknown socialist order. The series of fascinating 'false starts' of 1920–22 and 1926–32, for example, from which there is still much to learn today, fell almost entirely out of the picture.

The second weakness of the Soviet analysis was that it assumed straightforward progress from the market economy to a planned economy, and from private ownership via co-operative ownership to state ownership. On this deeply held view, the further development of the socialist economic system involved progress in the general direction of the communist economic order. Under communism, state ownership would prevail universally, collective farms would give way to state farms, and the household plots of collective-farm families would be completely eliminated. The communist economy would be a moneyless economy, and the collective-farm market would give way to planned distribution. This general concept was re-emphasised by Stalin in *Economic Problems of Socialism in the USSR*, a few months before his death.

The third weakness in the traditional Soviet view was its underlying political assumptions. Socialism involved social ownership of the means of production, and distribution of the social product to individuals according to work done. Therefore exploiters and exploitation no longer existed, and, according to the *Short Course*, production was bound to be based on 'comradely co-operation and Socialist mutual assistance'. The analysis did not even consider the proposition that socialist relations of production – whether due to Russian economic backwardness, or to the inherent problems of a certain kind of socialism – could involve the emergence of bureaucratism as a systemic feature or of a bureaucracy as a social phenomenon. And it was taken for granted that 'one-man management', in which managers were appointed and not elected, was not an emergency arrangement due to the shortage of trained politically trustworthy administrators, but a natural feature of socialism as such.

I labour these points about the traditional analysis because its influence has been felt long after Stalin's lifetime, and over areas of the globe far wider than the USSR. In the USSR, even under Stalin, it underwent some modification, and further adjustments were made in the

[2]This formulation was modified substantially by Stalin in 1953.

Khrushchev years.[3] But the basic traditional framework was maintained, and in 1970–85 it was strengthened.

In the West, the assumptions that socialisation meant nationalisation, and that socialist planning meant central control, and the centralised appointment of managerial staff, were also predominant. In the West this view of socialism has complex origins for which the USSR cannot be held entirely or even mainly responsible, but it was undoubtedly reinforced by knowledge of Soviet experience. I recall that when I was a student in the late 1940s the bureaucratic arrangements for the newly nationalised British coal industry and railways seemed to me quite natural in the light of what I knew of Soviet economic history.

II: The Bumpy Road to Reform, 1953–1986

Imperfect understanding of the past circumscribed and slowed down the successive attempts at economic reform after 1953. Powerful ideological and material interests restricted and censored the discussion, and frequently blocked the efforts of Soviet economists to understand how their system worked, especially after the Prague spring of 1968, and the Soviet military intervention which suppressed the reform movement. Brezhnev and his entourage regarded Czech economists such as Ota Šik, who advocated 'market socialism' – far-reaching competition between state enterprises and a more or less free market – as ideological agents for the restoration of capitalism. They also rejected the view of the so-called 'commodity mongers' (*tovarniki*) in the USSR. The Central Mathematical Economics Institute, TsEMI, founded in 1963, at first advocated the use of 'simulated markets' on computers to plan the economy, but by 1968 prominent economists in TsEMI advocated the use of actual market prices in the economy. In an article in the party journal,[4] Academician N.P. Fedorenko, director of TsEMI for the first 20 years after its establishment, bitterly criticised the official rejection of the TsEMI reform proposals. He described how in the 1970s 'the very concept of "self-financing" was treated as almost an enemy concept, contradicting the idea of socialism . . . Twenty years were lost'.

But repression was not the only problem. In the 1950s Soviet economists and economic administrators knew very little about the way in which markets operated. In 1956–57, for example, a vigorous discussion in *Ekonomicheskaya gazeta* about price reform failed to come to grips with the existence of repressed inflation in the USSR; then and later many economists and managers, as in the 1930s, hoped to eliminate centralised supplies, but did not contemplate that this would require prices which equated supply and demand.[5] Even if Khrushchev had

[3] See W. Brus, 'Utopianism and Realism in the Soviet Economic System', *Soviet Studies*, vol. XI (1988), pp. 434–43.
[4] *Kommunist*, No. 9, June 1987, pp. 50–56.
[5] See my survey article in *Soviet Studies*, vol. VIII (1957), pp. 426–36.

passionately wanted to reform the price system, no sound advice would have been available to him on how this could be achieved.

And in 1968, once Czech and some Soviet economists had grasped the price nettle, they understood price formation in the terms of an elementary and unrealistic 'perfect competition' model, and did not seriously discuss how to bring large monopolistic state concerns into a socialist market. Brezhnev was suspicious for the wrong reasons, but he had good grounds for scepticism.

It was different in Hungary. With the development by Kornai and others of their analysis of the planning system, the 1968 Hungarian reform was based on a reasonable analytical foundation. Apart from Yugoslavia, this was the first major case of an integrated fundamental reform. Hungary proceeded further than anywhere else along what one of its economists described as the 'bumpy road to cognition of the economic mechanism'.[6]

In the USSR, the frequent efforts at reform, involving enormous administrative upheavals, were sometimes ingenious and always unsuccessful. In 1955–56, the State Planning Commission was instructed to transfer some of its decisions to industrial Ministries; the Ministries in turn were to transfer some of their powers to the enterprises. Little happened; and, in the absence of serious proposals for price reform, Khrushchev then launched his administrative shake-up of 1957: industrial Ministries were abolished, and replaced by over 100 regional economic councils, each of which was supposed to manage the whole of industry in its area. The initial impact of the reform was not unhealthy; it cleared away some inefficiencies of 30 years' standing. But it brought little if any access of authority to the enterprises.

Within a year or two of 1957, it proved impossible to do without some of the old Ministerial powers. National controls were reimposed step by step, and cut across the new regional administration, to everyone's confusion. Khrushchev's fall in October 1964 was partly brought about by the failure of the 1957 reform, and the hostility of bureaucrats whose lives had been disrupted. In the autumn of 1965 the industrial Ministries were restored and the regional economic councils were abolished.

Like the 1957 reform, the 1965 reform had some positive results. It attempted for the first time to place economic calculation at the centre of the planning system: the profit-motive rather than the administrative instruction would control the behaviour of the individual enterprise. But no radical change took place in the structure of profits and prices; the price reform of July 1967 eliminated some of the worst deficiencies of the industrial price structure, but made no attempt to use prices to adjust supply to demand. Moreover, the 1965 reform did not deal with the most serious weakness of the traditional system, its failure to encourage innovation: it neither provided economic incentives for the production of new products, nor encouraged competition between state enterprises. Three

[6]L. Szamuely, in *Acta Oeconomica* (Budapest), vol. 29 (1982), pp. 1–24.

further attempts were made to remedy these deficiencies, in 1969, 1973 and 1979; these minor upheavals, notable mainly for their complexity and their triviality, hardly deserve the name of 'reform'.

III: From Partial Reform to Socialist Capitalism, 1987–1990

The failure of successive attempts at economic reform over a period of 30 years in the Soviet Union resulted in widespread scepticism about the whole notion of economic reform. Gorbachev was determined to bring about a fundamental improvement in the system; and at the twenty-seventh party Congress in February 1986 he accordingly described his new endeavours as 'radical reform' (*radikal'naya reforma*) in order to indicate the seriousness of his intentions.

At the same time the encouragement of much more open discussion about the past and the present led to fundamental reappraisal of the Soviet economic system. In the course of 1987–90, all the old landmarks and principles were called in question; and by the summer of 1990 it was no longer a question of economic reform, but of how to introduce a fundamentally different system closely resembling Western democratic capitalism.

In Section I above I suggested that there were three characteristic weaknesses in the traditional Soviet view of their own economic history: (1) the policy of the leadership was assumed always to have been more or less correct; (2) state ownership was treated as the highest form of ownership and as the ultimate goal; and (3) it was assumed that in an economy with full state ownership, exploitation and class domination were absent, and politics was no longer a problem.

In the course of 1987–90 the new approaches to the Soviet past swept aside all these assumptions.

Thus in relation to point (1), the policies of the Soviet leadership at every stage in Soviet history have now been called into question. At first Lenin was still handled with some circumspection. But even Soviet historians who regard themselves as Leninists agreed that during the Civil War he went through a learning process, and in 1921 abandoned his earlier conviction that socialism would exclude commodity production. And since the end of 1988 criticism of the Leninist as well as the Stalinist past has been much more far-reaching. In a major series of articles Aleksandr Tsipko, a philosopher who at that time worked in the party central committee, rejected the Utopian elements in Communist thought, and traced the roots of Stalinism to Rousseau's belief in the 'perfectibility of man'. Tsipko strongly criticised what he described as the 'Leftist' trend in the Communist movement: he contemptuously rejected the views of Preobrazhensky as well as Stalin.[7] The 200th Anniversary of the French Revolution in 1989 was celebrated by a number of articles

[7]*Nauka i zhizn'*, Nos. 11 and 12, 1988, and 1 and 2, 1989.

which, in contrast to almost all previous Soviet writing about revolution, condemned the Terror, and pointed out that enthusiasm for Robespierre and the Terror was a major feature of the celebration of the 150th anniversary of the revolution in 1939 at the time of the Great Purges.[8]

Moreover, the policies of all Lenin's successors – Stalin, Khrushchev, Brezhnev, even Andropov (and, with some caution, even Gorbachev) – are continuously criticised. The policies of the Soviet Communist Party between 1925 and 1985 are described at best in terms of trial and error, and often as a succession of disastrous choices of the wrong alternatives.

In relation to point (2), state ownership is no longer treated as coterminous with full socialism. All forms of social ownership tend to be regarded as of equal status. Great emphasis is placed in particular on the important role to be played by co-operatives in an efficient and democratic socialist economy. In 1987 and 1988, the writings of Chayanov, rehabilitated in 1987, received enormous attention. In 1988, the Director of the Institute of Marxism-Leninism, G.L. Smirnov, asked to define socialism in terms of ownership, referred to 'a multi-coloured spectrum of property relations – state and co-operative property, the property of enterprises, and property as a basis for individual labour activity, and the property of various voluntary organisations'.[9] Other writers have frankly argued that private ownership and the right of private capitalists to hire labour should be features of the new model of socialism;[10] I return to this increasingly influential view later in this paper.

The new approaches to the idea of socialism, coupled with the criticism of Stalinism, have led many Soviet economists to refuse to categorise Soviet society between the end of the 1920s and 1985 as socialist or as moving towards socialism. According to V. Kiselev, this was merely 'state socialism with its extra-economic compulsion'.[11] The prominent Soviet political observer Burlatsky claimed that what took place was not the transition to socialism but 'statisation'.[12] And N.A. Popov, from the Institute of the USA and Canada, declared that Stalin *created an ideal totalitarian state, in which his personal power extended to everything – economics and science, literature and art*.[13] Academician Bogomolov, prominent economic reformer, and Director of the Institute of the Economics of the World Socialist System, noted without comment that the Chinese now describe their past system as a 'feudal-bourgeois fascist dictatorship'.[14]

In relation to point (3), a substantial mental revolution has taken place. At a 'round table' in the Institute of Marxism–Leninism in October

---

[8]See N. Molchanov's dispute with the French communist André Stil in *Literaturnaya gazeta*, July 12 1989.

[9]*Kommunist*, No. 11, 1988, pp. 37–38.

[10]See for example G. Shmelev, in *Moscow News*, June 25, 1989.

[11]*Nauka i zhizn'*, No. 9, 1988, p. 42.

[12]*Literaturnaya gazeta*, 20 April 1988.

[13]*Sovetskaya kul'tura*, 26 April 1988.

[14]*Sovetskaya kul'tura*, 12 July 1988.

1987,[15] A.P. Butenko, from Bogomolov's Institute, argued that after Lenin's last writings 'no-one endeavoured to analyse our society from the point of view of the growth and strengthening of the bureaucracy' (Butenko did not mention Trotsky and the Left Opposition).[16] But the bureaucracy was 'a huge danger for socialism':

> 'At a definite stage in the life of the Soviet state it was not the proletariat and the labouring peasantry which were in power but those who usurped power – Stalin and his entourage. Moreover not only the form of rule (*forma vlastvovaniya*) was established, but also the form of administration (*forma upravleniya*) in the shape of a huge stratum of state and party bureaucracy, torn away from the people and not under its control.'

Butenko also asserted that in the 1970s and early 1980s 'the same model of socialism, relying on the state and party bureaucracy', existed as in the 1930s and 1940s.

Butenko's views have been strongly challenged. But they have been widely accepted in a modified form. Thus V.V. Zhuravlev, deputy director of the Institute of Marxism–Leninism, summing up the discussion on the same occasion, while insisting that the working-class and the peasantry remained the social basis of the Soviet system under Stalin, was prepared to concede that Stalin was supported by a bureaucracy, and that Stalin, like Napoleon III, had usurped power.

We have seen that the Soviet analysis of past economic systems is now much more flexible and realistic. How far is it nevertheless one-sided? I shall deal with the new Soviet views of NEP in Section IV below, and will consider here the recent discussions of the command economy under Stalin and after.

In a searching analysis of the Stalinist economic system, Gavriil Popov, using Aleksandr Bek's novel about the management of Soviet industry as his starting point, depicted what he called the 'Administrative System' of the Stalinist economy:[17]

> 'The basis of this system is the centralisation of decisions and punctual, undeviating, over-riding fulfilment of directives from Above and particularly from Stalin – the Boss.

> 'This is a system of specific and detailed management in kind (*in natura*). It is a system of continuous operational management of the forces of production from the centre. This is the Administrative System.'

Popov then argued that the Administrative System had continued till

---

[15]See the report in *Voprosy istorii KPSS*, No. 2, 1988, pp. 110–33.

[16]There is no definite or indefinite article in Russian. *Byurokratiya* could be translated 'bureaucracy', i.e. the phenomenon, or 'the bureaucracy', i.e. the social group. It seems to me that only the latter translation fits with Butenko's argument.

[17]*Nauka i zhizn'*, No. 4, 1987, pp. 54–65.

the present day: terror and fear had gone, but the System in principle remained. This is a distinction similar to Rigby's between the 'mono-organizational society combined with personal dictatorship' of the Stalin period, and the 'mono-organizational society without personal dictatorship' which followed the death of Stalin.[18] Popov drew sweeping lessons for the Soviet future:

> 'N.S. Khrushchev, and all of us, thought that with the elimination of the cult of personality from the system we would solve all the problems of our future. Now, in the light of historical experience, we see that this is not the case. The System has revenged itself on us. The problem is to renounce it, to replace it by a new system, corresponding to the contemporary stage of the development of socialism, relying not on administrative but on economic and democratic methods and forms.

> 'The Administrative System is not at all the synonym of the Socialist System, it never included the whole of our structure (*stroi*), it is an ephemeral stage.'

This analysis was taken up by Gorbachev in his report on the occasion of the 70th Anniversary of the October Revolution. Gorbachev stated that industrialisation and the collectivisation of agriculture had been associated with the emergence of the 'administrative-command system of party-state management of the country'. This system, 'firmly established in the economy, also spread to the superstructure, limiting the development of the democratic potential of socialism, and restraining the progress of socialist democracy'.[19]

In spite of its much greater realism, this treatment of the Stalin system has one feature in common with the 'political economy of socialism' in the past: it treats the market and quasi-market elements of the Stalinist and post-Stalinist systems as too trivial to mention in a general description. This is the mirror-image of the treatment of NEP as a socialist market economy with no elements of administrative planning (see Section IV). In 1990 this one-sidedness still dominates Soviet writing about the Stalin period, though there are important exceptions.[20] It encourages the dangerous view that everything will be solved if only the administrative system is replaced by the market with sufficient determination.

The new attempts to reform the economy took place against this background of a far-reaching reconsideration of Soviet economic experience. It gradually became obvious that the new reform was also intended to be more far-reaching than anything which had preceded it. In the first stages of the preparation of the reform, Gorbachev's most prominent adviser was Academician Aganbegyan, who was extremely familiar with

---

[18]See T.H. Rigby, in R.C. Tucker (ed.), *Stalinism: Essays in Historical Interpretation* (1977), pp. 53–76.
[19]*Pravda*, 3 November, 1987.
[20]See for example O. Khlebnyuk, in *Voprosy istorii KPSS*, No. 8, 1989, pp. 122–26.

and strongly sympathetic to the Hungarian type of 'market socialism'.

The type of reform envisaged for the Soviet Union at the time of the June 1987 plenum of the central committee corresponded in major respects to the reformed Hungarian economic mechanism after 1968: abolition of the fixing of detailed plans from above; replacement of centralised supply by trade between state enterprises; co-existence of state ownership with genuine co-operative ownership and small-scale private ownership. The long series of measures adopted after June 1987 were, however, half-hearted. Significant developments included the law on co-operatives (spring 1988); but the reform as a whole was inconsistent and ambiguous. Hungarian experience showed that even after the removal of major political and ideological obstacles to reform, and the development of a quite sophisticated analysis of the economic mechanism, successful radical reform is inherently difficult to accomplish. The Soviet experience after June 1987 repeated this hard lesson. In consequence of the greater powers acquired by enterprises, inflationary expenditure increased. Yet the authorities were unable to introduce financial controls to prevent the growth of inflation; and postponed currency and price reform as politically unacceptable. The first phase of reform was followed by a very grave financial crisis.

The second phase of economic reform began in 1990, after a further false start at the end of 1989. In the spring of 1990, the reformer Abalkin had for some months been in charge of economic reform, with the even more reformist Petrakov as his deputy. Their influence was supplemented, once Gorbachev had assumed presidential powers, by the appointment of Shatalin as the most influential economist on the Presidential Council. Shatalin is unambiguously in favour of the gradual conversion of the Soviet economy into a mixed market economy in which the capitalist sector is predominant. In an interview in October 1989 he declared that 'progress in England is associated with the conservative Thatcher', and criticised the French and the English for socialising motor-car and aircraft firms.[21]

It is probably true to say that the transformation of the Soviet economy into a managed capitalist economy modelled on Sweden or even West Germany is now seen as desirable by most prominent Moscow intellectuals. Joint-stock ownership of most industry would replace state ownership; there would be capital and labour markets as well as a retail market. But opinion is sharply divided about the way forward to a regulated capitalism. Some economists, such as Vasilii Selyunin, favour a rapid transformation, with 'shock therapy' along Polish lines, involving the stabilisation of the market and the breaking of the power of the party and state bureaucracy: 'to combine the plan and the market', declared Selyunin, 'is just like putting bits of an hour-glass into a watch; all you do is to ruin them both'.[22]

[21]*Literaturnaya gazeta*, 11 October 1989.
[22]*Literaturnaya gazeta*, 2 May 1990.

But Abalkin and Shatalin believe that it is possible to convert the economy by more gradual means. 'One should not be frightened of private ownership, there is nothing terrible in it', Shatalin assured a conference of the central committee in October 1989, 'But it is not appropriate today to propose it as a programmatic task'.[23] A few months later, he again insisted that there was no alternative to 'the main road of civilisation; we shall not switch on the engine of self-development without private property in all its forms, without creating motivation mechanisms which are no weaker than in the West'. But Polish 'shock-therapy' was inappropriate: 'The USSR is not Poland; we are not one nation (and we are certainly not united by the authority of a single church and the colossal authority of the Roman Pope)'.[24]

The economic reform measures announced at the end of May 1990 undoubtedly envisaged the eventual replacement of the present system by a West-European type of mixed economy, and incorporated a serious attempt to stabilise the retail market and public finance through price increases and the abolition of subsidies. But they were inconsistent and ambiguous, offering the certainty of retail price rises combined with vagueness about the likelihood of substantial changes in the economic system. Yet another attempted reform came to nothing.

Nevertheless, in spite of their many differences of view and approach, belief in what might be called 'determined gradualism' is shared by Gorbachev and Yeltsin; and sooner or later a reform is likely to be approved which brings about a substantial move towards a mixed economy; and replaces the existing central planning structure by a far more market-oriented system.

In the meantime, a draft law announced even before the publication of the reform proposals at the end of May attempted to bring to an end an experiment in socialist democracy which received a great deal of attention in the Soviet press in 1987-89, and played an important part in the development of an independent workers' movement. The draft law proposed to remove from workers in state enterprises the right to elect their managers, handing it back to the superior state agencies. The announcement of the draft law appeared next to an article entitled 'How to Help the Unemployed'. . . .[25] In June 1990, the new law 'On Enterprises in the USSR' confirmed this general position, but also left a great deal of room for manoeuvre about the rights of the Councils of the Enterprises, on which elected representatives were normally to occupy 50 per cent of the seats.[26] The fate of socialist self-government in industry remains a matter for future political and social struggle, though technocratic, administrative and even intellectual opinion is biased against it.

[23]*Pravda*, 30 October 1989.
[24]*Literaturnaya gazeta*, 2 May 1990.
[25]*Pravda*, 6 April 1990.
[26]*Izvestiya*, 12 June 1990.

IV: The New Economic Policy and Contemporary Economic Reform

The main intention is to open the way to economic methods of management, to extend considerably the independence of collective farms and state farms, to raise their interest and responsibility for the final results. In essence it is a matter of the creative utilisation of the Leninist idea of a food tax applied to contemporary conditions.

M.S. Gorbachev, Report to the twenty-seventh
Party Congress, February 25, 1986.

Gorbachev's comparison of his new agricultural policy with the food tax (*prodnalog*) introduced by Lenin in March 1921 undoubtedly startled his audience. The food tax replaced the compulsory requisitioning of War Communism and led within a few months to the elaboration of the complete model of NEP, in which state industry and individual agriculture were linked through the market. Gorbachev's statement, almost completely ignored by Western commentators (perhaps because they did not know enough economic history), was a clear signal that the new party leadership intended to bring about major changes in the economic system. Neither Khrushchev, in advocating his economic reforms, nor Kosygin in introducing the 1965 reform, drew analogies with NEP; at that time Soviet politicians saw NEP as remote and irrelevant. Even among intellectuals little was said about NEP. When G.A. Lisichkin, in his pamphlet *Plan and Market*, published in 1968, argued in favour of market prices which balanced supply and demand, and presented this as a continuation of the tradition of NEP, this was an extreme view among economists. But now the view that the present reforms are in an important sense an extension of NEP is almost commonplace. An otherwise conservative article in the party journal in May 1987, while emphasising that NEP differed from present-day Soviet socialism because petty capitalism was very strong in the 1920s, nevertheless conceded that 'there is of course a direct descent and profound resemblance', because both periods were characterised by the 'uncovering, activising and maximum utilisation of material and economic interest'.[27]

A major report on the social sciences on April 17, 1987, by Aleksandr Yakovlev, a secretary of the central committee and close associate of Gorbachev, presented the whole issue of the transition from NEP to centralised planning as an open question; he told the social scientists that they should investigate why the departure from NEP occurred, how 'administrative-bureaucratic methods of administration' became strong, whether there were alternatives, and why they failed.[28]

Most Soviet historians and economists who wrote about these questions during 1987 took the view that the collapse of NEP at the end of the 1920s was due to the extraordinary tasks imposed upon the USSR as

[27]*Kommunist*, No. 7, 1987, p. 63.
[28]*Vestnik Akademii Nauk*, No. 6, 1987, p. 69.

R. W. Davies

a backward socialist country threatened by advanced imperialism; they distinguished this general strategy from the brutal and repressive aspects of the system established in the 1930s, which they attributed to the malign influence of Stalin's personality, and to other special circumstances. Thus L.A. Gordon wrote:

> 'The circumstances of the choice made at the time [the 1930s] – the economic and cultural backwardness of the country, the unavoidable military threat, the absence of democratic experience and democratic traditions – speak in favour of the inevitability of forced industrialisation and rapid collectivisation, and the political arrangements which resulted, rather than of the possibility of a more harmonious development. With a different combination of subjective factors, with a more attentive attitude to Leninist warnings about the political significance of the personal features of I.V. Stalin, no doubt many sacrifices and mistakes could have been avoided.'[29]

Other academics and politicians already stated frankly in 1987 that the departure from NEP at the end of the 1920s was unjustified even in the circumstances of the time. Thus the sociologist V. Shubkin bluntly stated:

> 'Stalin decided to eliminate NEP prematurely, using purely administrative methods and direct compulsion; this led, speaking mildly, to pitiable results.'[30]

By the autumn of 1988 the view that the market relation with the peasants should have been continued in the 1930s, and would have been a viable and superior alternative to the

> 'administrative–command system', overwhelmingly predominated in the Soviet press and media. On the 100th Anniversary of Bukharin's birth in October 1988, the obituaries were full of praise for the 'Bukharinist alternative'.[31]

In conformity with this approach, many economists as well as publicists presented the economy of the 1920s as an unmitigated success. Some even praised the very high rates of economic growth in the early years of NEP without pointing out that these were largely a result of bringing resources back into use after the collapse of the economy during the Civil War. For example, an interviewer in the party theoretical journal, referring to agriculture, wrote that 'in 1920–28 the average rate of growth per year was about 10 per cent – this is really a very high result'.[32]

Most of the radical critics of Stalinism did not distort the record so crudely. But they often considerably overestimated the economic success

[29]*Sotsialisticheskie issledovaniya*, No. 4, July–August 1987, p. 8.
[30]*Znamya*, No. 4, 1987, p. 183.
[31]See, for example, *Nedelya*, No. 39, 1988, *Pravda, Pravda Ukrainy, Sotsialisticheskaya industriya*, all October 9 1988.
[32]*Kommunist*, No. 1, 1988, p. 55.

129

of NEP. Thus they exaggerated the speed of recovery of the economy after the Civil War. Vasilii Selyunin enthusiastically declared:

> 'Within four or five years [i.e. by 1925 or 1926] the pre-war level in industry and agriculture was reached. In 1928 it was exceeded in industry by 32 per cent, and in the countryside by 14 per cent.'[33]

Otto Latsis, first deputy editor of *Kommunist*, claimed that 'the post-war reconstruction of industrial production was in the main completed by 1925'.[34] And Lisichkin even stated that 'the national income reached the pre-war indicator in four years'.[35] The same assessment was made by S.P. Pervushin.[36]

Now the economic achievements of NEP were considerable. But all Western specialists agree that neither agriculture nor industry recovered to their pre-war level until 1927; economists such as Paul Gregory suggest that recovery was far from complete even then. This more sceptical view of progress under NEP was also held by many Soviet economists in the 1920s, including Al'bert Vainshtein. In contrast, the Soviet writers I have cited all accept without question the present-day official statistics about the economic recovery during the 1920s, even though they are extremely critical of official statistics in most other respects!

Optimistic statistics were accompanied by an idealisation of the social and economic conditions of NEP. Thus the playwright Viktor Rozov described how NEP transformed life in his provincial town when he was a schoolboy, so that 'everything began to glisten and laugh'.[37] Vladimir Dudintsev similarly recalled his boyhood observation of the full barns and general prosperity of the individual peasants.[38] This theme was also very strongly emphasised by economists, such as Academician Tikhonov, who advocate the return to individual peasant farming. Agriculture succeeded so well, Tikhonov insisted, because no-one had the right to interfere in the economic activity of the peasant.[39]

Against this background, major economic problems hardly seemed to exist. Thus Latsis praised the resolution on the five-year plan of the fifteenth Party Congress in December 1927 for its judicious support for balanced growth, suggesting that this offered a crisis-free road to economic development within the framework of NEP. Some outstanding historians, who do not accept these rather naïve assessments of NEP, nevertheless share the enthusiasm for the fifteenth Congress resolution. V.S. Lel'chuk, in an article written jointly with L.P. Kosheleva, declared that 'the fifteenth Congress proposed a kind of optimum variant, from

[33]*Novyi mir*, No. 5, 1988, p. 171.
[34]*Kommunist*, No. 18, 1987, p. 18.
[35]*Novyi mir*, No. 11, 1988, p. 164.
[36]*EKO*, No. 10, 1988, p. 132.
[37]*Yunost'*, No. 4, 1987, pp. 6–11.
[38]*Nedelya*, No. 22, 1989.
[39]*Literaturnaya gazeta*, August 5, 1988.

which we can learn even today . . . . *How can one fail to enthuse about those who formulated such proposals, and voted for their realization'*.[40] Viktor Danilov praised the first five-year plan adopted in the spring of 1929 as a viable non-Bukharinist third alternative to the Stalinist course.[41]

While many Western historians accept the view that the Bukharinist alternative provided viable policies for Soviet economic development within the framework of NEP, very few would accept these positive assessments of the viability of the Soviet plans of the late 1920s. The fifteenth Congress resolution was adopted in the midst of great battles about rival drafts of the five-year plan. But to the indignation of the Left Opposition and of many of those on the side of the party majority it failed to contain a single figure, or to offer a specific judgement on any of the major economic problems which were worrying the politicians and the planners. It was strong on noble principles, but avoided the difficult practical issues. And the 'optimum variant' of the five-year plan actually adopted in the spring of 1929, and even its more cautious 'initial variant', were both based on extremely unrealistic proposals for increases in the productivity of labour and capital, and for the reduction of industrial costs. The plan also assumed that a financial balance would be maintained in the economy; but by the time it had been drawn up and approved in the winter and spring of 1928–29 public finance – and the market generally – had already been thoroughly disrupted, rendering all the financial targets of the plan unrealistic.

The writings of professional historians, however, were on the whole more critical about NEP. Thus V.P. Dmitrenko criticised 'publicists, writers and economists' who presented a 'rainbow picture' of NEP, and failed to show that the economic successes of agriculture were accompanied by the 'economic weakness of the state', which proved unable to supply loans and industrial goods to peasants and private traders in adequate quantities.[42] Academician Koval'chenko complained that 'NEP is depicted almost as an era of general prosperity and well-being, although at that time the general level of economic development and the standard of living of the broad mass of the population was low, mass unemployment remained in the country, etc.'[43] The assessment of the state of agriculture during NEP by Danilov and N.A. Ivnitskii contrasted sharply with that by Academician Tikhonov. They argued:

'By the end of the 1920s the objective course of social-economic development, and particularly the development of the industrialisation of the country, sharply posed the problem of the development of agricultural production and its reorganisation . . . . The low level of agricultural production was holding back the general economic development of the country, placed serious obstacles in the way of

[40]*Pravda*, 21 October 1988.
[41]*Gorizont*, No. 5, 1988, pp. 28–38.
[42]*Sotsialisticheskaya industriya*, 27 September 1987.
[43]*Kommunist*, No. 2, 1989, p. 89.

the industrialisation which was beginning, and of the construction of socialism as a whole'[44]

They also hold, against the strong and even bitter opposition of Chernichenko and Tikhonov, that during NEP a kulak stratum continued to exist as one section of the peasantry, and that 'the system of kulak exploitation was primitive, but also crude and without limits'.[45]

Other historians, including an active and well-informed group in the Institute of Marxism–Leninism, claimed that the economic and social crisis of NEP was profound, and that its roots were far deeper than Stalin's departure from Bukharinist policies in 1928. G. Bordyugov and V. Kozlov correctly argued that NEP cannot be understood simply in terms of a simple model of a market relation between the state sector and the rest of the economy. 'From the moment of the introduction of NEP', they wrote, 'the party seriously limited the operation of the market in the relation between heavy and light industry'.[46] The young historian N.S. Simonov, in the most detailed account so far published by an historian from this group, presented the crisis of NEP as due fundamentally to the conflict between two economic formations: 'the traditional semi-patriarchal semi-commodity peasant economy; and the modern industrial economy'.[47]

These historians do not insist that the collapse of NEP was inevitable. But they hold that Bukharin's policies would not have coped with the crisis of 1927–28; by that time it was already too late to save NEP. The turn to a more flexible policy should have taken place, at the latest, by the mid-1920s. According to Bordyugov and Kozlov, the great opportunity was missed in 1925, when the party should have begun to strengthen the co-operative elements in NEP, rather than embarking on the road of transferring resources from the peasantry to the needs of industry.[48] Simonov claims that the state was too generous to state industry after the currency reform of 1924. Instead, in 1925 it should have given priority not to heavy but to light industry; it should have acted against rural differentiation, encouraging co-operation in the countryside (how this would have helped is not clear); and it should have pursued a more flexible foreign policy so that the Western powers were willing to advance loans for economic development. But Simonov remains sceptical about the viability of NEP, arguing that even these policies might not have solved the dilemma, because Soviet military needs required huge expenditures on transport, engineering and chemicals.[49]

Another young historian, M.M. Gorinov of the Institute of the History of the USSR, argues even more strongly in relation to NEP as a system

[44]*Dokumenty svidetel'stvuyut*, Danilov and Ivnitskii (eds.), (1989), pp. 17–18.
[45]*Ibid.*, p. 13; and see the 'round table' reported in *Istoriya SSSR*, No. 3, 1989, pp. 3–62.
[46]*Pravda*, 30 September 1988.
[47]*Voprosy istorii KPSS*, No. 3, 1990, p. 72.
[48]*Pravda*, 30 September 1988.
[49]*Voprosy istorii KPSS*, No. 3, 1990.

based on market equilibrium that 'the threat of technical backwardness, the permanent danger of war, and the instability of the market cast very grave doubt on the effectiveness of this variant'. According to Gorinov, 'a synthesis of the "Stalinist model" and "Bukharinist methods" would, it seems, have provided the optimum variant', but this was prevented by Stalin and his entourage, who stepped over the 'narrow boundary between self-defence and crime'.[50]

Another viewpoint on NEP was at first only expressed by a small minority of writers, but has recently become much more influential. They argue, with increasing frankness, that the whole course of economic policy since October 1917 was doomed to failure; only a capitalist economy could have been successful. Grigorii Khanin diagnoses the economic difficulties of the mid-1920s as profound. According to Khanin, even by 1928 national income per head was 17 per cent below the 1913 level, while the stock of capital was 13 per cent above that level; a 'catastrophic decline' had taken place in the efficiency with which capital was used. These failures were due to the power of the bureaucracy, to the domination of industrial management by ex-workers with low qualifications, and to the elimination of efficient farmers. And the feasible level of capital investment within the framework of NEP was too low to avoid economic stagnation and military weakness. With extreme scepticism Khanin argues that 'the last chance for alternative solutions, it seems to me, was lost at the beginning of the 1920s; and even then it was small'.[51] L. Piyasheva takes a similar approach. An enthusiast for the free-market views of von Hayek, she rejects all schools of Bolshevik thought, and strongly advocates Kondratiev's and Yurovsky's strategy of eliminating price and other direct controls and strengthening the market.[52] V. Evstigneev also claims that the collapse of NEP was inevitable in view of the political and social environment in which it was established:

> 'In the conditions of a totalitarian social system even the more liberal, and especially market (or rather quasi-market) economic forms will inevitably, and sooner rather than later, "grow into" the general totalitarian system and serve it, or will be eliminated as unacceptable.[53]

The rival assessments of NEP are highly relevant to the rival schemes for present-day economic reform. Should the Soviet Union move towards a free-market economy loosely controlled by the state, and including a substantial element of private capitalism in industry as well as agriculture? This roughly corresponds to the alternative course under NEP supported by Kondratiev and Yurovsky in the 1920s, and by Tikhonov,

---

[50]M.M. Gorinov, *NEP: poiski putei razvitiya* (1990) - *Znamya, Istoriya* Series, No. 2, 1990.
[51]*Rodina*, No. 7, 1989, pp. 80–84.
[52]See, for example, *Sotsialisticheskaya industriya*, 14 January 1988, and *Druzhba narodov*, No. 7, 1988, pp. 179–97.
[53]*Voprosy ekonomiki*, No. 3, 1990, p. 33; Evstigneev is a senior member of IMEMO, the Institute of World Economics and International Relations.

Khanin and Piyasheva today. Or should it rather seek to develop genuine co-operatives, and the management of socialised industry by those who work in it, within the framework of a state-managed socialist market? This roughly corresponds to the alternative course under NEP supported, for all their differences, by Chayanov and the Gosplan economists such as Groman and Bazarov in the 1920s, and by Danilov, Kozlov and Bordyugov at the present day.

The 'radical' pro-capitalist economists are influential in Gorbachev's Presidential Council, predominate among Yeltsin's advisers in the Supreme Soviet of the Russian Republic, and control the soviets in Moscow, Leningrad and elsewhere. In their thinking these reformers have moved out of the framework of Soviet socialism. They now look back before the 1917 revolution for their historical precedents. Thus the influential economist Nikolai Shmelev declared about Stolypin, Prime Minister after the 1905 Revolution who attempted to establish peasant capitalist agriculture in Russia: 'I have an extremely positive attitude to Stolypin . . . Stolypin was the hope of the country and he began a very fruitful process. Today the situation is to some extent similar'.[54] And Gavriil Popov, elected head of the Moscow Soviet following the election victory of the 'Democratic platform', has proclaimed that in agriculture 'we must do what was done by the unforgettable Stolypin; we must introduce *otrubs* and *khutors*', peasant family farms separated from the village commune.[55]

V: The Politics of Economic Reform

In one major respect economic reform under Gorbachev differs fundamentally from the New Economic Policy. The introduction of NEP in 1921–22 was accompanied by eliminating other parties, by tightening up discipline within the Communist party, and by the consolidation of the censorship. It is true that in NEP Russia there was a considerable amount of intellectual freedom, and open conflicts and debates in decision-making – a kind of pluralism within a one-party system. But throughout the first half of the 1920s, even during the period of 'high NEP' in 1924–26, the power of the party machine was greatly increasing, and the bounds of discussion were narrowing.

In contrast, Gorbachev's reform, to the complete surprise of almost every Western Soviet specialist, has been accompanied by, or more accurately preceded by, attempts at far-reaching political reform. By the beginning of 1990 a multi-party system was recognised in law, and existed in practice in several Soviet national republics, and in the major towns of the Russian Republic.

The political developments were paradoxical. The formal emergence of a multi-party system was accompanied by the appointment of Gorbachev

[54]*Literaturnaya gazeta*, 26 July 1989.
[55]*Pozitsiya* (Tartu), No. 1, October 1989.

as President of the USSR, with ambiguous but far-reaching powers. Gorbachev hopes to use these powers to push through a radical economic reform and simultaneously to stabilise the political situation. But his opponents, strangely known as 'left radicals', in fact liberals in favour of introducing a capitalist economy, are convinced that Gorbachev is too timid to carry out thoroughgoing marketisation, and is unwilling to break the power of the party bureaucracy which is standing in the way of economic reform. Selyunin recently posed the issues with startling frankness:

> 'Let us discuss how power can be transferred to a new government. In the first instance we agree to a coalition . . . . We are forming a brains trust for economic transformation.'

> '. . . We are beginning to form a shadow cabinet, which will try to seize power when it drops out of your hands, before it has fallen into the dirt. If we do not seize it, it will be seized by the . . . mafia, in a bloc with the right.'[56]

National and democratic fronts sharing Selyunin's economic and political views, if not entirely supporting his tactics, have been victorious in the elections in Moscow, Leningrad, the Baltic Republics and Ukraine. The relatively gradualist Shatalin responded with yet another historical precedent:

> 'The ideology of our radical democrats is right in principle . . . . But it is insufficiently thought out and balanced, one could say it lacks Milyukovshchina.'

As Milyukov, the leader of the pre-revolutionary Constitutional Democrats, shared the fate of all the other non-Bolshevik opponents of the old regime, the precedent is somewhat ambiguous.

VI: Conclusions

This chapter has suggested that, in spite of the immense progress in the frank analysis of the Soviet economic system since 1985, Soviet interpretations of the past cannot be described as objective. In particular, many 'radical' economists seek to demonstrate on the basis of the Soviet past that there can be no such thing as a regulated market, or a combination of plan and market. This argument has understandable political motives: there are good reasons to fear that the conservatives who dominate the administration will seize on every opportunity to resist changes in the system. But as an economic historian I find this claim absurd.

Much of the practice of capitalist economies involves the regulation of the market; a substantial sector in many contemporary capitalist economies is administratively planned or managed. And in pre-revolutionary

[56]*Literaturnaya gazeta*, 2 May 1990.

Russia as well as in the Soviet Union both the state and the market have played a major role in the economy. It is not an accident that the term 'Reform' is used to a much greater extent in Russian history than in the history of most other European countries. We have – in reverse chronological order – the post-revolutionary Reforms or attempted Reforms of 1987, 1965 and 1957 (and of 1921), and also the pre-revolutionary Stolypin reform, the Serf Reform and the Great Reforms of the 1860s, the Petrine Reforms, and even the Reforms of Ivan the Terrible. It was the state as a major economic and political actor that pushed all these reforms through.

Moreover, ever since the 1890s, both before and after the Bolshevik Revolution not only the State, but also its Administrative Economy, were of major economic significance. Before 1914 the state-managed railways and the military exercised a major influence on industrial development. In the 1920s the state directly managed and allocated resources to most industrial investment; state orders, as before the Revolution, exercised a major influence on the shape of industry; and there was no period in the 1920s in which the state did not physically allocate at least a few major producer goods. On the other hand, though markets were in important senses extremely weak during the Civil War and in the Stalin period, they continued to play a significant role in the economy.

Stalinist and Brezhnevist ideologists underestimated the role of the market in these primarily administrative economies, and so also, for entirely different ideological reasons, have many of the present-day economic reformers; and this has hindered understanding of the Soviet economic system and the paths to reform.

This is not to deny the obvious point that the transition from a predominantly administrative economy to a predominantly market economy is an extraordinarily difficult task, and would have been difficult to accomplish even with perfect understanding of the Soviet-type economic system. This point is reinforced not only by the experience of both the Soviet Union and of the whole of Eastern Europe in the 37 years since 1953, but also by the experience of NEP. Judith Shapiro's discussion of the first years of NEP shows that the attempt in the 1920s to combine plan and market was rather unstable, in spite of the remarkably good understanding by Soviet economists of the principles of the operation of the NEP economy.

It should be added, however, that these attempts at economic reform were made in societies in which the one-party state and its immense bureaucracy were still in power. The Hungarian economy achieved remarkable successes in the first decade after the reform of 1968 in spite of this major obstacle. Now that Communist political power is breaking down, perhaps there are greater prospects for an economic reform which does not amount merely to the introduction of a Western-style capitalism.

A serious weakness of this chapter so far is that it has not discussed

Soviet economic reform in the context of the economic development of the world as a whole. The struggle to introduce market economies in Communist countries has been taking place at a time when the thinking of Western economists and politicians, and to a lesser extent Western government policy, has been dominated by enthusiasm for the unrestrained free market. There is no doubt that the contemporary technological revolution requires a major adaptation of all economic institutions throughout the world. The old state monopolies and the old state controls no longer work in the West.

But I would suggest that this very strong emphasis on the free market is a temporary phase in Western development. The international financial markets, with their take-overs for short-term profit, and the multinational corporation, are failing to cope satisfactorily with the economic and human needs of the world in transformation. And several further major factors will impinge on Western capitalism in the coming decades:

1. The population of the newly industrialised countries will no longer be prepared to tolerate the conditions in which they normally work.
2. Much of the Third World, with its huge populations, is already in social and economic crisis; the non-industrialised areas of the world urgently require new international policies to manage this crisis.
3. The growing dangers to the environment will also require the enforcement of international decisions – of some kind of supranational economic planning or administration.

All this will mean that a new relation between international institutions and society will emerge. Planning and the market, or if you like the administrative economy and the market economy, will still be in tension and co-operation, this time on a world scale.

The history of the Soviet economy will eventually look quite different from this new vantage-point.

9

The costs of economic reform:[1]
Lessons of the past for the future?

Judith Shapiro

'Reform is a notion widely used by many parties and political movements all over the world. The present article will apply a narrow
definition designed especially for this discussion. The term *reform*
indicates the change in a socialist economic system, provided that it
diminishes the role of bureaucratic co-ordination and increases the role
of the market.'[2]

This recent purpose-built definition by the well-known Hungarian economist Janos Kornai will serve very well here. The definition is persuasive
rather than neutral. I would not contemplate proposing its universal
applicability. It simply narrows the aperture of this discussion considerably: this is necessary for a sharp focus over a long expanse of time.

I chose to concentrate on two major potential costs of reform: unemployment, especially mass and prolonged unemployment; inflation, especially very large inflation and even hyperinflation. These are not necessarily the only costs that agitate the man on the Sokol'niki trolleybus
today. Crime rates, for example, seem to rise in reform periods, and are a

---

[1]Thanks are due here to the King's College, Cambridge group on Soviet reform in an historical perspective for encouraging me to look beyond unemployment to other costs of
economic reform, and in particular to Catherine Merridale; to Jacek Rostowski for
concentrating my attention on the Soviet hyperinflation, and to Bob Davies for entrapp-
ing me into it all in the first place and much more. The King's International Workshop in
July 1990, and especially the discussant of my paper, Gertrude Schroeder, helped in the
refinement of my argument. Even more importantly it suggested new avenues for
future inquiry.

[2]Janos Kornai, 'The Hungarian Reform Process: Vision, Hopes and Reality', in Victor
Nee and David Stark (eds.), *Remaking the Economic Institutions of Socialism: China and
Eastern Europe*, (Palo Alto, 1989), p. 36.

[3]In 1989 the incidence of reported crime in the USSR shot up 32 per cent, with violent
crime and robbery notably up. Thus the murder rate is up 31 per cent, that of thefts
and robberies involving violence even more (*Izvestiya*, 28 January 1990). D.J. Peterson
('Much Ado About Crime', Radio Liberty, *Report on the USSR*, 15 September 1989)
reports an increase of 130 per cent for premeditated murder, 120 per cent for rape,
for the first half of 1989; I think this may be in some error. Note that the crime rate
fell in the first years of the Gorbachev era and began rising in 1988 [*Sotsial'noe razvitie
i uroven' zhizni naseleniya SSR: Statisticheskii sbornik*, (Moscow, 1989), pp. 315–17].
Sharply rising crime is reported in both Czechoslovakia and the GDR [e.g. *Sunday Times*
(London), 3 June 1990] but without solid figures.

138

source of intense public anxiety.[3] Growing inequality in itself (prosperity for some and not others, as opposed to a decline in living standards) challenges long-standing Soviet values.

I set out to see what a fresh look at the costs of NEP might contribute to the present already morose discussion about the prospects for Soviet marketisation. In many ways NEP Russia is light years from the contemporary Soviet Union. Yet it remains the very model of a modern economic reform. Consider a leading American specialist on unsuccessful Soviet economic reforms[4] challenging the Soviet political leadership to:

'. . . have the nerve to launch an economic reform that is really 'radical', as was Lenin's NEP in the 1920s – a reform that put the wager on marketization and privatization.'

Or the discouraged sigh of the Polish-born economist:[5]

'Except perhaps for agriculture in China and some areas close to it, there is hardly anything in the evolution of the communist system so far that would warrant putting it in one league with the Russian New Economic Policy (NEP) of the early 1920s.'

An additional motivating factor is that Soviet considerations of the lessons of NEP have now begun to move beyond the ideological search for legitimacy to a serious search for practical lessons.[6] In that spirit I wish to turn directly to the debit side of the NEP balance sheet.

'The chapter on the Fall of the Rupee you may omit. It is somewhat too sensational.'[7]

The Soviet hyperinflation of 1921–24 was one of the largest and longest in world history. At the very end, between 7 March and 1 June 1924,

[3](continued)   A May 2 opinion poll of Muscovites with telephones shows this section of the population is far more worried about crime rising with the transition to a market economy than with unemployment! (*Moskovskie Novosti*, No. 19, 13 May, 1990). Only fears of potential inflation exceed worries about likely increases of crime.
   It is not obvious that increases in inequality and market relations have been more important than increased leniency in the criminal justice system. Custodial sentences in the USSR were halved from 1986 to 1988 (Peterson, *op. cit.*). The important thing is that the public sees a tie with the rise of the market. This area urgently calls for skilled social investigation.
[4]Gertrude Schroeder, *The System Versus Progress* (London, 1986), p.95. I am sure Schroeder is aware of the limitations of NEP in practice and is referring to the conception. See, for example, Alan Ball, 'NEP's Second Wind: The "New Trade Practice"', in *Soviet Studies*, vol. XXXVII, No. 3, July 1985, 371–85, for the 'extreme instability and complete uncertainty created in the activity of private capital by the fluctuation of state trade policy' (a quote from a 1927 Soviet study).
[5]W. Brus, 'Evolution of the Communist Economic System: Scope and Limits', in Nee and Stark, *op. cit.*, p. 258.
[6]*Ekonomika i matematicheskie metodi*, V.E. Manevich, 'Denezhnaya reforma 1922-24 gg i valyutno-denezhnaya sistema nepa', vol. XXV, Vyp. 4, July–August, 1989, pp. 599–610, is the best example of a growing list.
[7]Miss Prism, in Oscar Wilde, *The Importance of Being Earnest*, in *The Works of Oscar Wilde* (London, 1987), p. 340.

citizens could turn in 50 billion[8] rubles of Soviet monetary tokens[9] (sovznaki) to receive *one* new ruble. This new ruble treasury note was the equivalent of just one pre-war (1913) ruble.[10]

50 billion to one is an inflationary ratio so far surpassed only four times: in Germany in 1923, Greece after World War II, China from 1945 until the fall of Shanghai, and Hungary in 1945–46.

What is a hyperinflation?

We are much more familiar with common or garden inflation, a mild, moderate, or at most 25 per cent rise annually in the average level of prices, which means a fall in the value of money. The great inflations of world history are qualitatively different phenomena.

Such true hyperinflations used to be rather rare. We have only just run out of fingers to count them on. In the last few years they have become somewhat more commonplace.[11] Conventionally economists have used Phillip Cagan's (1956)[12] criterion: for an inflation to be genuinely hyper, prices should rise by more than 50 per cent a month. This rate is deceptively mild looking: it compounds to over 12,000 per cent a year.

[8]That is a milliard, or 1000 million.

[9]More precisely, 50,000 rubles of the 1923 vintage. 1923 rubles in turn were equal to 1 million pre-1921 rubles, skipping a few steps in the 'cancelling of zeros'. This redemption announcement, Sovnarkom Decree 433 of 1924, implemented one of the measures adopted earlier in the year which are known collectively as the '1924 Monetary Reform'. These stipulated, among other things, that a new treasury note was to be introduced into circulation, and new silver coins, after which the redemption rate of the sovznak would be announced.

[10]According to its new pegged international exchange rate. The monetary reform of 1924 that authorised the exchange and achieved the stabilisation was not a confiscatory monetary reform of the sort Soviets normally contemplate when they think of the dread '*denezhnaya reforma*', no doubt because of the reform of 1947, which aimed at liquidating peasant hoardings accumulated during the war. (See R.W. Davies, *The Development of the Soviet Budgetary System* (Cambridge, 1958), pp. 315–16.

More precisely, inflation itself had already accomplished most of the confiscation. On 1 March, just before the official redemption rate was announced, 61.92 billion sovznaks could purchase the same basket of retail goods as one 1913 ruble, according to one of the common price indices of the time, the budget index of VTsSPS, the All-Russian Central Council of Trade Unions. (While much of value can be learned of the merits and demerits of the various price indices which Soviet statistical pluralism produced, it does not seem valuable to do so here.)

[11]See Michael Bruno et al. (eds.), *Inflation Stabilization: The Experience of Israel, Argentina, Brazil, Bolivia and Mexico* (Cambridge, Mass., 1988), for a survey with a spectrum of opinion; Rudiger Dornbusch and Stanley Fischer, 'Stopping hyperinflations: past and present', in *Weltwirtschaftliches Archiv*, 122, 1986, pp. 1–47; Jeffrey Sachs, *The Bolivian Hyperinflation and Stabilization*, NBER Working Paper 2073, Cambridge, Mass: National Bureau of Economic Research, for discussion of one by the author of its stabilisation plan, now turning his attention to Poland.

[12]Phillip Cagan, 'The monetary dynamics of hyperinflation', in Milton Friedman (ed.), *Studies in the Quantity Theory of Money* (Chicago, 1956). As inflation can be socially, economically and politically paralysing at a much lower rate than this, one of several hundred per cent a year, it is now just as popular to agree that there is no well-defined threshold.

The precise tangle of underlying causes of each of the rare cases of hyperinflation is still disputed. One thing is certain: in every case the government in question covered a massive budget deficit by the printing of money. Modern governments can do for a time what we usually cannot: print money to make up the difference between what they feel they have to spend and what they can raise in income or loans.

This method of financing a government through an 'inflation tax'[13] is exactly preferred in conditions where the government sees no better way to get funds, and it is obviously a sign of grave weakness of economic control.

Even governments cannot do this indefinitely. The nastiest aspect of this process is that it tends to accelerate. As people become aware of, and expect, increasing inflation, they take steps to protect themselves. They get rid of their money quickly, keeping their cash balances to a minimum. They try to arrange contracts in terms of some stable or indexed unit of account, or they avoid anything but short-term contracts. There is a 'flight from the ruble', or the mark or the forint, and into anything else that seems a better store of value. Since World War II the dollar has increasingly played this role internationally, where once it was gold coins. (This phenomenon is known as dollarisation.) The government, just to stay even in terms of expenses, has to print more and more money. When the acceleration reaches a certain level the government loses from trying to increase the 'inflation tax' by emitting more money: the rest of the money it holds declines in value. The entire process has serious disruptive consequences long before that level. NEP hyperinflation was a classic case.

Inflation before NEP

Of course not all of the catastrophic fall in the value of the ruble from 1913 was the product of NEP. But most of it was. At the time of the February Revolution the finance of war by the printing press had driven prices to three times the 1913 level. The Provisional Government managed to accomplish slightly more than this in the eight short months given to it.[14] On the eve of the October Revolution prices were thus about ten times the pre-war level.

---

[13]The 'inflation tax' is the loss in the real value of money held by the public when the government issues an inflationary quantity of money. The government, or its agents, gain by acquiring real goods and services from the paper money issue. One must subtract from this the loss to the government itself from this additional emission. This was likely to be especially high in Soviet NEP conditions where the state was heavily involved in economic activity. Particularly large losses were sustained regularly by the railways and telegraphs because of the currency they had to hold.

[14]The most authoritative source for figures on money and prices is L.N. Yurovskii (ed.), *Nashe denezhnoe obrashchenie: Sbornik materialov po istorii denezhnogo obrashchenia v 1914–1925* (Moscow, 1926). It is obvious that this is a paper addressed to the non-economist who will be grateful that the author has been gently persuaded to remove even the last vestiges of her beloved tables and charts. For those who wish otherwise, tables from the original paper are available on request.

War Communism carried the process considerably further: in January 1921 the level of prices was 16,000 times its pre-war (1913) magnitude. In the first months of 1921, on the eve of the first NEP measures, price rises were running at a very high level just short of the more rigid 50 per cent per month definition of hyperinflation. In 1921 the government ran a deficit of 22 trillion rubles, 84.1 per cent of its total expenditure.[15] NEP was bequeathed the dangerous legacy of a trillion depreciated rubles[16] circulating nearly as fast as people could carry them.

As we know, NEP did not arise from a single blueprint. During 1921 it evolved and extended from the tax-in-kind to a real return of markets and money. And the inflation gathered steam. 1921 price changes were highly uneven from month to month and they were fairly high. No one was in much doubt about the cause of this feverish price rise. The establishment of something resembling a money economy called for expenditure on the part of the government. Not only did it possess virtually no revenue, but it also had no revenue-collecting apparatus.[17] Raising large loans – from home or abroad – was not a serious proposition. So the printing presses were put to work overtime again.

Of course some inflation 'repressed' during the naturalised (demonetised) economy of War Communism could now make itself felt as well. But in early NEP the critical factor was the disproportion between the felt needs for spending and the revenue-gathering possibilities of the government.

NEP Russia behaved remarkably like the other countries that have passed through the fire of hyperinflation. Indeed the financial experts, the bankers and party leaders expected it to. For a moment in the summer, when the start of economic recovery and a traditional seasonal influence caused a halt to price rises, there was a moment when there might have been a bit of hope. Another horseman of the apocalypse, the Volga famine, put paid to that. The miserable harvest drastically reduced the goods that the money available could buy, and it similarly increased the demands on the government's resources. In the month of December 1921 prices more than doubled. An undeniable hyperinflation ruled.

'The year 1922, however, brought with it such a plethora of paper money that the issue of 1921 was dwarfed by comparison and soon appeared a mere bagatelle', remarked the main Western scholar of pre-war Soviet banking. Arthur Arnold,[18] driven to a certain degree of acerbic wit in contemplating the issue of two quadrillion rubles, 'an amount which has sixteen places and that under brighter economic skies is associated with astronomy rather than with finance'. This had its pre-

[15]S.S. Katzenellenbaum, *Russian Currency and Banking 1914–1924* (London, 1925), p. 69. R.W. Davies, who provides a valuable account of the essential monetary events for the whole period, reports very slightly lower figures (*The Development of the Soviet Budgetary System* (Cambridge, 1958), p. 42.
[16]Yurovskii, *Nashe denezhnoe obrashchenie*, p. 153.
[17]See R.W. Davies, *op. cit.*, p. 51.
[18]Arthur Z. Arnold, *Banks, Credit and Money in Soviet Russia* (New York, 1937), p. 126.

dictable consequences upon the price level, and upon the inconvenience of staggering around under the weight of notes.

There were annual attempts to alleviate the physical burden by 'striking off the zeros' but the real burden of inflation on the economy was more difficult to handle. In the earliest NEP difficulties money was depreciating over night at a rate that was important to the enterprises, but human inventiveness had not yet created real alternatives. This was described vividly by Yurovsky,[19] the head of the foreign currency division of Narkomfin:

'The enterprises which had been placed on *khozraschet* . . . as a temporary means of escaping from the situation ceased to draw up balance sheets or to calculate the real cost of production. They endeavoured as far as possible not to keep any money in their cashboxes, converting them quickly into goods . . . .'

As Yurovsky noted, they might not make anything this way, but at least they knew they wouldn't be making losses.

From the end of 1921 there were attempts to deal with the problem by a method we now call 'indexation'. Agreements were arranged in terms of a presumably stable unit of account, the 'commodity ruble'.[20] This notational ruble 'exchanged' at a floating rate with actually existing rubles of the monetary token genus. If you were going to be due 10 rubles, this was translated into today's commodity rubles. When the time came to be paid that number of commodity rubles were translated back into real life rubles. By then you almost always got more. This, as we observe nowadays, soothes the pain of inflation, but accelerates the inflationary process automatically. Contracts can be agreed. Workers, for example, do not suffer so much from price rises as their wages are index-linked. But all this in turn feeds further price rises. This was no doubt recognised in due course by the Soviet authorities. The monetary reform of 1924, with a rigour also classic for successful stablisation attempts, banned such index-linking.

Enter the chervonets

But in 1922 a successful reform did not seem to be on the agenda, because a balanced budget was still a future goal. The first wave of exceptional price rises continued for five months. In May of 1922 came something of a breathing spell, most likely because real production was starting to rise somewhat faster as NEP neared the end of *its* first 500 days. It is in this halcyon interval that the idea of creating a new more stable

[19]L. Yurovsky, *Na Putyakh k Denezhnoi Reforme* (Moscow, 1924), p. 55.
[20]*Ibid.*, especially pp. 61–65.

currency partially backed by gold, issued by the State Bank rather than the Treasury, took hold.[21]

Such a currency, the chervonets, would meet the urgent need of the Bank to grant credit to state industry for investment in something which would be worth something when it was paid back. Later officials of Narkomfin insisted that they had never thought the chervonets was anything but a short term crutch. At the time this was not so clear.

The period between conception and gestation of the chervonets was, however, drawn out. Even when the enabling Sovnarkom decree[22] was signed in July, the actual issue of the new money was, according to all the apparent law-governed processes of reform, postponed. The authorities were afraid of failure in a situation of low public confidence. Such a failure might, they thought, doom future attempts at monetary stabilisation. They resolved to use dramatic ways only if muddling through failed. When the inflation rate in October again spiked above 50 per cent it was clear that all else had failed. The first chervontsy were then introduced on 28 November 1922, into a situation much less favourable than in July.

This strange phenomenon, a parallel currency without a fixed 'rate of exchange' with the state's paper ruble, was only backed (and thus limited in supply) in comparison with the miserable sovznak. Indeed, in retrospect it lost value slowly over 1923 only in comparison with that poor money.

Chervonets romanticism is common in the Soviet Union today.[23] Its mirror image is often found abroad: the assumption that the chervonets promptly destroyed the last uses of the treasury's paper money and was in some sense responsible for the death agony of the sovznak.[24] *The Economist*, evincing scepticism about a Yeltsin advisers' plan for an effective parallel currency[25] actually accuses the chervonets of being 'the gold-backed rouble that caused hyperinflation in Lenin's New Economic Policy.'

This is somewhat unfair to the chervonets. It was the child of hyperinflation rather than the father. If it was the instrument of the flight from the ruble it was not the basic cause. The treasury continued to emit sovznaki generously to paper over the gap in the budget. Indeed

[21]The chervonets had to be backed by no less than 25 per cent of precious metals and stable foreign currency, and the rest of the amount in easily marketable goods and short-term bills. That is, the State Bank had to possess this as a notional guarantee for the notes it issued. But the decree did not actually make the chervonets convertible to this backing by citizens, so it remained a *fiat* currency.

[22]Decree 578 of 1922.

[23]Petrakov's 'Zolotoi chervonets vchera i zavtra', *Novyi Mir*, No. 8, 1987, suffers from this to a degree.

[24]See L. Yeager and associates, *Experiences With Stopping Inflation*. (Washington DC, 1981), who wrongly suggest that the price level took off again immediately after the issue of the chervonets. This error is based on what they themselves call 'scrappy' data, p. 74.

[25]*Economist*, 9 June 1990, p. 51.

the appearance of the chervonets was followed by a renewal, not a curtailment, of the breathing spell.

Why was the effect of the chernovets not at first malign? Simply because chernovtsy were at first few in number and could not possibly replace all the sovznaki. They were unavailable in large areas of the country. They did not amount to half of the value of the money supply until the following year. Moreover, a chervonets was nominally equal to *ten* tsarist gold rubles. Thus the smallest unit of this currency was too large for many purposes.

Further, the chervonets made a place for itself not just by edging out the sovznak, but by competing with the other money substitutes in abundance at this point anyway. Tsarist gold coins circulated in border areas, yen in the far eastern parts, the Turkish lira in Tiflis. Even state industry resorted to using pre-revolutionary gold coins. The chervonets replaced some illegal parallel currency with a legal instrument.[26]

But, of course, the existence of a good substitute for the ruble was bound in time to assist in its already inevitable decline. After the fact Narkomfin experts liked to suggest that they had always known it was just a fling: the chervonets, they explained, had been merely a holding operation until the budget could be balanced. The record is, of course, more complex.

However, with the aid of chervontsy, foreign currency and indexation, the system managed to carry on and even to continue economic growth. Earlier stabilisation, in 1922, was considered either politically impossible or undesirable: the cost in unemployment and/or growth retardation of a balanced budget was judged too high. And in 1922 the inflation rate, from the government's point of view, was not too terrible. There is, in any 'inflation tax', an optimal level at which the forced 'revenue collection' is as high as possible, and this can be a very high rate indeed.

'Scissors' and money

Was anything much lost by delaying a reform from 1922 or 1923 to 1924? Much of the answer lies in the still murky connection of this hyperinflation with the 'scissors crisis' of 1923. That crisis was, as commentators have expressed in different ways, a 'seminal event',[27] a perceived turning point in the fate of NEP. This technical and still obscure debate over prices was nonetheless critical in many ways in the fate of the USSR and the twentieth century.[28]

[26]That is, it was legal to hold, though the category of 'legal tender' was reserved for the sovznak, to preserve some sort of role for it while the Treasury still felt it needed to pour them out. As Finance Minister Grigori Sokol'nikov was to note, the subsequent decision to accept taxes in chervontsy really 'signed the death warrant of the Sovznak'.

[27]Chris Ward, *Russia's Cotton Workers and the New Economic Policy* (Cambridge, 1990), p. 130.

[28]As Nikolai Simonov notes, 'It was the rare economist or political activist who managed to do without statistics on prices' as a result: 'V preddverii 'velikogo pereloma''', *Voprosy Istorii KPSS*, No. 3, 1990, p. 59.

The costs of economic reform:

The problem of the scissors, put at its very simplest, was that industrial prices were rising more rapidly than agricultural prices. To be more concrete, more poods of rye had to be exchanged for fewer arshins of cotton cloth. As a consequence there was worry in the spring and summer that peasants would not sell or were not selling their grain at these deteriorating 'terms of trade'. In the autumn there was an excess of industrial goods at the prices set by the trusts and syndicates.

In interpreting the 'scissors' there were at the time, and still are, two basic camps. The group which became the 1923 Opposition generally saw the cause of the relative height of industrial prices in the excessive weakness of the trusts, which made costs too high. The rest of the Party saw the cause in the excessive strength of the trusts, which could raise prices too high as a result of a monopoly market position.[29]

Members of the opposition argued that costs were high as a result of the lack of full recovery of the economy. Only a minority of capacity was being utilised, resulting in high per unit overhead costs. The only immediate fix was to concentrate industry further, even if this necessitated greater unemployment. In the autumn Trotsky was to accuse the rest of the leadership of failing to close factories because of political considerations.[30]

The opposition perceived deeper causes which lay in the underdevelopment of Soviet industry, compounded by the waste of bureaucratic mismanagement. For the latter they were to prescribe party democracy [inside the single party]. For the former only further industrial development offered a remedy. Prices were high in part because the entire country, and thus the infrastructure, was underdeveloped. This is strongly parallel to the argument for infant industry protection in less developed countries.

The other side argued that monopoly power led to arbitrarily high prices, and proposed therefore to set about controlling industrial prices. The opposition opposed 'commanding prices in the style of war communism'.

Individual economic writers and others then and later offered some alternative interpretation of the perceived economic problems which linked them to the monetary situation as well as to developments in industry and agriculture. But in the intervening years this has tended to fade from the picture.

Yurovskii made observations about peasant behaviour which explained

[29]See also M.M. Gorinov, 'NEP: Poiski putei razvitiya', Znaniye Series (Istoriya), No. 2, 1990, for a well-explained and documented account of the 1923 discussion. In 'Vserez i nadolgo, no ne navsegda: Trotskii o NEPe', in V. Lel'chuk (ed.), (Moscow, 1991), I offer a moderately full exposition of my view on the approach of the Opposition at this time.

[30]*Izvestiya TsK KPSS*, No. 5, 1990, reproduces Trotsky's letter to the Central Committee of 8 October 1923, previously known to us only from the retold version in *Sotsialisticheskii Vestnik*, 28 May 1924, which expresses this view. A reply from Stalin and other members of the Politburo, previously unpublished, is in *Izvestiya TsK KPSS*, No. 7, 1990, and a defence of political refusal to close factories is to be found on p. 178.

the fear that peasants had become reluctant to sell grain. He noted a reluctance which was not due to relative prices. Their reluctance was aimed at the rapidly depreciating sovznaki, which they did not want to take back to the countryside for a period. Thus, as Yurovskii explained, they were increasingly coming to town to sell only what they needed in order to finance their planned purchases. At the start of the day they would ascertain the price of their intended purchases, adding a bit for inflation in the course of the day. Having sold just enough to cover it, they would proceed home with their purchases, actually lugging their excess grain. It was a better store of value than money, and if need be it could be fed to the livestock as a more long-term method of storage.[31]

Monetary factors can also explain why the 'blades' of the scissors were wider the deeper into the backwoods one went. Tradesmen could not exchange their sovznaki for chervontsy in these areas, except with long delays. Thus they would demand a substantial premium on the price. This analysis was strongly supported by Mikoyan at the thirteenth Party Conference (January 1924), insisting that Soviet trade could not continue in the absence of a firm ruble.[32]

One damage done by hyperinflation is precisely socially the threatening distortion of relative prices. The particular form of the last year of the Soviet hyperinflation, the 'bipaper' standard – a seriously inflating chervonets but a hyper-inflating sovznak – certainly exaggerated this further.

The death agony of the Sovznak

As inflation became ever more rapid towards the end of 1923, the point was reached – and it was visible to the government – where further emission of ever more worthless sovznaki was self-defeating. Expectations about such emissions made the currency increasingly worthless. But no one thought the budget could yet be balanced.[33] All conventional wisdom suggested it was dangerous or impossible to try to stabilise the currency until that happened. *Chto delat'?*

It is here that the sophistication of the Soviet 'bankers' shows up astonishingly well. How have successful stabilisations ended hyperinflations elsewhere? In an exceptionally influential article, the American monetarist Thomas Sargent listed four characteristics of the 'Ends of Four Big Inflations' he made famous:[34]

---

[31]Yurovskii, *Na putyakh k denezhnoi reforme* (Moscow, 1924), p. 96.

[32]*Trinadtsataya Konferentsiya RKP(b)*, (Moscow, 1924), p. 77.

[33]Note that a balanced budget in Soviet terms has long meant only a budget in which printing money is not the means to plug the gap between expenditure and earnings. Loans, if they can be raised, can be used for 'balance'.

[34]Thomas Sargent, 'The Ends of Four Big Inflations', in R.E. Hall (ed.), *Inflation: Causes and Effects* (Chicago, 1982), pp. 41–96, and in his own *Rational Expectations and Inflation* (New York, 1986). The four are post-World War I Austria, Hungary, Germany and Poland.

The costs of economic reform:

1. Each country persistently ran an enormous budget deficit.
2. They took deliberate and drastic fiscal and monetary measures to end the hyperinflation.
3. This caused the price level and foreign exchanges suddenly to stabilise.
4. After the stabilisation the quantity of money increased rapidly, even though prices were stable.

To put it more simply, people were willing to hold onto the money now seen as having value. Velocity decreased, and more money was sitting in safes and pockets and under mattresses. There was more money about, but it was not having an inflationary impact. It was not chasing goods as fast.

All this seems to fit the NEP template well. Soviet advocates of a swift if risky monetary reform understood the last point well. Yurovskii, the head of the foreign currency section of Narkomfin, in a paper prepared at the request of a US Senate Committee gathering information on the situation in European currency and finance in 1925, explained that the monetary authorities came to recognise, especially in the light of the lessons of the just-prior German stabilisation, that the 'sudden transition from a rapidly depreciating currency to a stable currency' had 'opened the possibility of a "painless" issue of currency to an amount of ten, and possibly more, million chervontsy'[35]. In short they could continue to finance a budget deficit by printing money for just a bit longer, as long as people believed the monetary reform was indeed working. If they did so they would start wanting to hold on to more money, and this in itself would anchor the stabilisation.

Price controls, the 1924 Reform and the fate of NEP

The 1924 Reform did indeed end the great NEP hyperinflation. The old sovznak was removed from circulation, and a new treasury note with tighter rules about its emission replaced it in circulation. Steps were taken toward a balanced budget. It was promised to do this the following financial year. All this is called by economists 'a change in the monetary and fiscal regime'.

But did it all really go according to Sargent's orthodox formula? Yurovsky's testimony suggested more was going on. If it had been clear that things were not going to be tightened at once the whole manoeuvre could have foundered. In this price controls may have played a significant role in quickly establishing public confidence. They were instituted in December of 1923, and there were further campaigns in 1924. And it is from 1924 that the 'goods famine' first makes its appearance in the

[35]In J. P. Young (ed), *European Currency and Finance* (Washington D.C., 1925), Vol. I., p. 261.

USSR. This is the same pervasive shortage which stands as such an obstacle to reform today, by threatening galloping inflation even in the absence of a large store of unwanted savings (the ruble 'overhang'). As Novozhilov pointed out, insistently and to little avail, the goods famine and price controls are tightly tied together.

The 1924 Monetary Reform appears to have strong 'heterodox' elements in it. In the discussion of contemporary hyperinflations there is a relevant distinction between 'orthodox' and 'heterodox' ends to hyperinflation. In a 'heterodox' stabilisation use is made of wage and price controls to achieve the initial public sense that the measures are working, and often the exchange rate is pegged (fixed) against foreign currencies to increase confidence in the value of the money. If that works, then the budget need not be completely balanced, and money can still be printed to plug the gaps, only not as much as before. Theorists like Sargent tend to think that 'heterodox' endings are not very permanent or satisfactory. Others suggest that the distortions in the economy from the heterodox solution are worth it if there is a big risk that increasing unemployment is the alternative.[35]

The evidence that this 'heterodoxy' was policy are strong. Indeed, it seems unlikely that the other elements in the reform package could have produced success by themselves alone. The new treasury notes had no other effective backing to the population than that they could not exceed half the amount of the chervontsy in circulation. (The latter notes, in turn, were only partially backed by precious metals and foreign currency.) One critical account of price controls in the 1924 anti-inflationary process is to be found in Kuzovkov's 1925 critique of policy.[36] From Arnold's later vantage point in 1937 the reliance on price controls is clear, and perceptively put:[37]

> 'It was, then, the policy of price regulation rather than deflation that helped to produce a comparatively stable price level. Inflation under a regime of regulated prices apparently cannot be judged by the *height* of the index number of prices no matter how carefully computed. There enters a new factor – the extent of the unsatisfied consumers' demand.'

Thus a major consequence of stopping the hyperinflation, the suppressed or repressed inflation of 1925–29, seems to have been historically more costly and significant than the hyperinflation itself. A valid and important question remains as to whether there were serious real alternatives.

To most of the policy-makers price controls, even with the attendant goods famine, appeared the wisest choice. No doubt the acceptance of concentration of state industry in trusts as otherwise efficient seemed to reinforce the case for such control. Having taken this route some

[35]In J. P. Young (ed), *European Currency and Finance* (Washington D.C., 1925), Vol. I., p. 261.
[36]D. Kuzovkov, *Osnovnye momenty raspada i vosstanovleniya denezhnoi sistemy* (Moscow, 1925), especially p. 389.
[37]Arnold, *op. cit.*, p. 231.

bureaucrats no doubt quickly perceived the advantages of the power to dispose over things in short supply. Such a position might also be rather habit-forming.

In the end the full stabilisation resulting from the 1924 Monetary Reform lasted only two years. In the spring of 1926 the downward pressure on the exchange rate was too intense to sustain by continuing to prop it up through Soviet purchases of rubles with precious hard currency in the hands of the state. Narkomfin was opposed to devaluation, seeing the pegging of the ruble as an important measure of stability.[38] A critical decision was taken at this juncture to forbid Soviet citizens by law to trade in foreign currencies.

Socialist Unemployment

The 1924 currency stabilisation does not seem to have accelerated the already rising unemployment.[39] That is just as well, as unemployment was quite substantial. It is not much exaggeration to say that it came in with NEP and went out with NEP. To what extent was it the result of reform and the greater influence of the market?

There have always been some good alibis for this early attempt at market socialism. It has long been a commonplace that NEP unemployment, unlike 'traditional' unemployment, rose while employment rose. In fact such a pattern is also characteristic of less developed capitalist countries with abundant supplies of labour in the countryside. Another common assertion is that NEP was 'not at all industrial'. But that is disingenuous: neither was NEP Russia. But the proportion of the relatively small industrial labour force unemployed was substantial, especially in 1923–25.[40]

NEP unemployment appears to have been significantly higher than that prevailing in the pre-revolutionary boom period just before the war, 1909–13.[41] The reason why this was most likely to be so in the earlier period of NEP is completely clear: workers returned to the cities before workplaces fully recovered from the devastation and disorganisation. The

[38]See Manevich, *op. cit.*

[39]Unfortunately in July 1924, only a few months after the currency reform, the 'purge' of the labour exchanges rendered late 1924 unemployment figures valueless. This is the very worst gap in NEP unemployment data, which are generally passable. There are no published useful alternatives in this period. However, candid accounts to be found in the archives confirm the assessment that unemployment 'stablised' in reality in 1924. The then 'top secret' estimate made by Rabkrin estimates a sight real fall in the hish (1½ million) unemployment level from April 1924. (TsGAOR *fond* 374, opis' 8, *delo* 1828, page 66). Industrial unemployed numbers, in numbers and as a proportion of the unemployed, had been rising before the currency stabilisation. The purge denied registration to arriving peasants and displaced 'former' persons and the like.

[40]Note that tables omitted here can be obtained from the author.

[41]This comparison is the focus of my 'Unemployment', in R.W. Davies (ed.), *From Tsarism to NEP: Continuity and Change in the Economy of the USSR* (London, 1990).

economy did not return to its pre-war level until, at even the earliest estimate, 1926–27.[42]

In the later period another tendency elevating urban (and thus open) unemployment made itself felt, as the unemployed tended to remain in the towns upon losing work:

> 'In the past the workman, shut out from the factory, had a place of refuge in the village, where he was always a member of the village community and land stood at his disposal; now, however, the land is distributed, and, besides, the peasants . . . are anything but disposed to receive him.'[43]

These are problems of migration: at root, problems of modernisation and urbanisation. They belong much more to the Soviet past. But were there significant causes of unemployment apart from this in the NEP economy, more closely related to the general operation of market forces? In both the traditional Soviet account and in the new rose-coloured perestroika edition of NEP it has been common to deny this. To re-examine the character of NEP unemployment critically it is necessary first to introduce a temporal refinement.

In the first two years of NEP, from 1921 to mid-1923, the dominant group of the unemployed were the white-collar workers, often those who were dismissed from a state apparatus bloated from War Communism.[44] Women formed the majority of the unemployed in this period. They were crowded out of industry, first by demobilised Red Army men and then by former workers returning from the countryside to which they had fled.[45] The transfer to the conditions of the New Economic Policy was, then, a process of continuous increase in labour supply, coupled with a significant initial decline in labour demand from that of War Communism.[46]

The leading role in the second act of the drama fell to the 'real' unemployed (in Soviet eyes), the industrial proletariat.[47] The combination of industrial concentration and redundancies, and the increased flow of experienced workers back from the countryside, swelled industrial unemployment to its highest proportion. The summer of 1923 is a visible dividing line. The financial year 1923–24 was the darkest year in terms of the proportion of the urban labour force unemployed: both overall and industrial unemployed rates reached a peak of over 15 per cent. This

---

[42]For recent discussion see especially Paul Gregory, 'National Income'; R.W. Davies and P. Gattrell, 'Industry'; and the editor's Preface in Davies, 1990, *op. cit.*

[43]Anton Karlgren, *Bolshevist Russia* (New York, 1927), p. 202..

[44]L.E. Mints, 'Bezrabotitsa v Rossii', in A. Rashin (ed.), *Trud v SSSR: Statistiko-ekonomicheskii obzor*, October 1922–March 1924, (Moscow, 1924), p. 42. Mints, head of statistics in Narkomtrud's labour market section, was the most prolific analyst of NEP unemployment.

[45]Otdel TsK RKP po robote srede zhenshchin, *Voprosy bor'by s zhenskoi bezrabotitsei*, (Moscow, 1922), pp. 5–7. See also Mary Buckley in this volume.

[46]*Vestnik Truda*, No. 9, 1923, p. 39.

[47]For this sentiment, see, e.g., *Isvestiya TsIK SSSR*, 31 October 1925. However they remained a minority of the total unemployed.

predominantly industrial period for unemployment ended in mid-1925.

The third phase is the one most commonly visualised today: the unskilled worker rushed on to the stage in full force: often from the countryside, often young, quite often female, and very numerous. Although industrial unemployment did *not* decline either absolutely or as a proportion of the industrial labour force from 1925 to 1929,[48] it was overshadowed by this massive wave.

The denial of any industrial character to its unemployment does obscure important facets of NEP reality, especially in the mid-1920s,[49] but it must have been the enduring visual image left by the immense numbers who milled at the labour exchanges, filled up the night lodgings, poured into the towns from all corners.

The seemingly intractable problem of ending unemployment simply by the expansion of employment must have seemed very clear then.[50] Migration to new job opportunities overwhelmed the number of new places. Unemployment continued to climb right up until its final spectacular plummet in 1930.[51]

But if the last phase is the enduring image transmitted to us, what role did internal NEP factors play in the earlier years? There is evidence that a number of Soviet policy-makers quickly absorbed the full idea of the market and its advantages for efficiency, speaking in terms that seem very modern and even Thatcherite.

At certain points an attempt to enforce market discipline was important in increasing NEP unemployment. In 1923–24 in particular the deliberate concentration of industry, while handicapped by a certain 'softness' in budget constraints in favoured plants, definitely put industrial workers out of work. Rykov even indicated that this was intentional:

[48]Figures, calculated from *Kontrol'nye Tsifry Narodnogo Khozyaistvo SSSR na 1926–27*, pp. 254–55, 76–7, and the same *1929–30*, pp. 487–89, and *Planovoe Khozyaistvo*, October–November 1930, p. 343, and Soviet figures reported to *International Labour Review*. Statistics on Employment, November 1926–January 1930, are available from the author. There are a number of problems with the data. I restrain myself from dilating upon them here.

[49]Even later Mints, (*Voprosy Truda*, 1929, No. 6, 'Kon''yunkturnyi obzor za 1–e polugodie 1928–29g)' pointed out that intensive rationalisation had produced a rise in the industrial group of the unemployed in need of attention. Industrial unemployment was also increased by the 'revolving door' of immense amounts of temporary hiring. (See D. Filtzer, *Soviet Workers and Stalinist Industrialisation* (London, 1986), pp. 26–27; S. Kheinman, 'Trud v SSSR', *Ekonomicheskoe obozrenie*, No. 9, 1929, *Pravda*, 7 July 1927, for a typical press exposé of 'distortion of the regime of economy', hiring and firing workers each month to avoid issuing special clothing.

[50]See Hiroaki Kuromiya, *Stalin's Industrial Revolution* (Cambridge, 1988), Chapter 8, for an incisive treatment of the transformation of the labour market in this period.

[51]This occurred in the context of both previously unimaginable tempos of industrialisation, the development of managerial incentives to swallow as much labour as possible, and, especially, collectivisation. On the last, R.W. Davies, *The Soviet Collective Farm 1929–1930* (London, 1980, p. 166, presents a rather straightforward picture, in contrast to Nabuo Shiokawa's account in *Annals of the Institute of Social Science*, Tokyo, No. 24, 1982-83, which argues for a more complex pattern whose net effect is not so clear. This has also been a dispute in Soviet historiography.

'I'm afraid that we save too many and too often. When we introduced the New Economic Policy we introduced it on the reckoning that it would produce a selection of our best enterprises, and that it was inescapable some would go down the tubes. But many of our workers have a consciousness that it's obligatory that they be saved, that bankruptcy isn't permitted.'[52]

Unemployment came from the emphasis on cost cutting, on fiscal and monetary stringency. From the summer of 1923 the drive to eliminate subsidies clearly resulted in an increase in unemployment.[53]

A large number of people, even among the industrial work force, appear to have been willing to work at the going wage rate and unable to do so, one good definition of unemployment. (This does not contradict the conclusions of Chris Ward, based on his fine study of the NEP cotton industry, that much of the unemployment was of the type which economists call 'structural'. Unsatisfied demand for skilled workers confronted the unsatisfied supply of the unskilled.[54])

The combination of market forces and a wage policy which emphasised helping workers in work to recover their real incomes encouraged a higher rate of unemployment than before the war. In short, NEP policies represented a choice of a relatively smaller labour force with a higher wage over the possibility of a larger labour force with a lower wage and productivity. The trade unions also favoured this policy, as trade unions have often tended to do. Their employed members weighed on them more heavily than their rather alienated unemployed.[55]

The pattern of NEP unemployment has striking similarities to reform Yugoslavia, a point which bears exploration.[56] But if the *pattern* may owe much to 'market socialism', the *level* does not seem, however, to have been caused by the failure to carry the reforms through to capitalism. Many other nations suffered from elevated interwar unemployment. The crises particular to NEP, notably the scissors crisis, were less important in producing peaks of unemployment than the general secular trend.

NEP unemployment was the cause of a very real source of discontent with market forces. Some consider it played a pivotal role in the downfall of that system and the triumph of Stalinism.[57] Some of its causes are historically unique and unlikely to recur – but not all.

One of the most serious lessons from the 1920s is the fashion in which

[52]A. Rykov, VTsPS, Shestoi S'ezd Professional'nykh Soyuzov SSR (11–18 November, 1924), (Moscow, 1925), p. 287.
[53]*Khozraschet* did not forbid the payment of subsidies, but rather made them explicit.
[54]Ward, *op. cit*, especially p. 133.
[55]I have explored this in 'Unemployment and Politics in NEP Russia', SIPS Seminar Paper, CREES, University of Birmingham, 1988.
[56]For an insightful account of Yugoslav unemployment, see Susan Woodward, *Socialist Unemployment*, (forthcoming). Woodward argues persuasively that NEP was a conscious model for Yugoslavia.
[57]This unproven case is supported by scholars as diverse as E. H. Carr and Stephen Cohen.

unemployment reproduces itself. Only once it was clear that labour supplies were abundant did enterprises cease to hoard labour. Indeed they engaged in an unusually large use of temporary personnel, a 'revolving door' policy, as trade union activists complained.[58] In part this evaded the requirements that applied to permanent employees – notice before redundancy, safety equipment provision, benefits. Thus there were two very separate groups in a factory labour force.

A look back from today

Today there is a serious discussion on how many are openly unemployed in the USSR.[59] This chapter has focused so far on the geographic periphery, where unemployment is said to be substantial. It is, however, unclear whether this phenomenon is of very long standing. There is an even more earnest discussion on how many will be unemployed as a result of NEP-like measures, or even more determinedly capitalist measures. Goskomtrud's estimate of 35 million, which seems to be the number to be made redundant, has been accepted for no more particular reason than that nature abhors a vacuum. Even this gives very little basis for knowledge of how many of these will find jobs quickly.

Hyperinflation is another word that has entered the Soviet vocabulary of late. 1990 levels of budget deficit and monetary emission, unless controlled, threaten to make it a household word.

The historical record explored here can usefully be read as a thinly veiled parable. But what can we take that is concrete from this lesson? What is left after we abstract the colossal inflation and the widespread, high and ineradicable unemployment from that which is completely specific to that historic period?

[58]D. Filtzer, *op. cit.*, was the first to note the significance of this. I discuss it in some detail in my contribution in Davies, 1990, *op. cit.*

[59]D.J. Peterson, Radio Liberty, *Report on the USSR*. 'Unemployment in the USSR', August 25, 1989, pp. 5–10 and also January 5, 1990 contain useful surveys. See the thoughtful discussion on Central Asia in *Sotsiologicheskie Issledovaninya*, 6, 1990, and the conversation 'Bezrabotitsa', in *Molodoi Kommunist*, No. 1, 1990, with Alexei Lebedev for useful insights. Revived interest in NEP unemployment is also to be noted. See I. Zaslavskii, 'Zanyatost' i Rynok Truda pri NEPe', in *Sotsialisticheskii trud*, No. 10, 1989, pp. 87–92; and the more empirically grounded A.I. Chernykh, 'Rynok Truda v 20–e Gody', in *Sotsiologicheskie issledovaniya*, No. 4, 1989, pp. 118–26. These are the fullest examples; V.F. Bush's curious article in *EKO*, No. 10, 1989, passes over unemployment very swiftly (in one paragraph) in an article devoted to 'Rynok Truda 20–x Godov i Nashe Vremya'. Indicating that in the 1920s the 'labour market' was connected in the public mind with the existence of unemployment, he says a few words about how wonderful the labour exchanges were and moves on. All three of these journals carry material which attempt to estimate present and future unemployment. I think it should be noted that in the recent Soviet discussion there is an unfortunate tendency to ignore completely the careful and contentful, if mundane and politically dictated, work of Ludmilla Rogachevskaya *Likvidatsiya bezrabotitsi v SSSR 1917–1930*, (Moscow, 1973).

One major question demanding an answer is the extent to which the instabilities of NEP were a result of reform, and the extent to which they were the result of not enough reform.

An obvious deformation of NEP, seen from the capitalist West, is the conditional nature of the acceptance of private capital, and the increasing restrictions put on it. As long as state or social ownership is dominant, this pressure will arise whenever private capital is advancing economically. Though this essential hostility was a central part of the political process which decided the fate of NEP, it does not seem to have been particularly important in determining the costs of NEP in unemployment and inflation.

A more evidently relevant connection is to be found in the problem of monopolies, prices and price controls. At the time of NEP monopoly was accepted, and the economic organs sought instead to tame its side effects. But even when such old-fashioned socialist dreams of the immense economies of scale are finally abandoned, bureaucracies prefer monopolies.

They would, after all, prefer to have a relatively manageable number of entities to try to administer. In partially marketised conditions the tendency to 'streamline' can be even greater.

A consequence of the desire to continue with control while allowing a fair degree of nominal enterprise autonomy is also the desire to organise fewer units.[60] This tendency toward state organisation of monopolies was encouraged during NEP by that genuinely held, deep-seated old-fashioned socialist belief in the existence of large economies of scale. Moreover, the initial condition that not all fixed capital in the country could efficiently be put into action at once demanded concentration. To attempt to run it all would have meant continuing to run much of it well below capacity with concommitant heavy overheads.

The same ideological conditions are lacking today. Gigantism has lost its romantic charm. But the charm of 'regulation' is never gone. It provides the justification for bureaucracy: it is their work creation scheme. Thus one of the hardest nuts to crack is the question of monopoly, and one of the most important. Not only does monopoly stimulate the inflationary process. By that very act it justifies the continued need for price control, and thus bureaucratic intervention. The circle is complete.

But demonopolisation of Soviet industry is far harder than the break up of 'trusts'. The distortion of the Soviet economy is at a far more basic level, in the actual concentration of production in plants. (In the present hypershortage conditions it plays a particularly pernicious role. The entire supply of detergents can be upset by events in Sumgait, to take an example.) 'Anti-trust' cannot be accomplished principally by the legislative process. When we urge the Soviets to break up the monopolies as

[60]This is dealt with in an intriguing way by Wim Swaan, in *Comparative Economic Studies*, Winter, 1989, 'Price Regulation in Hungary'. Indirect but Comprehensive Bureaucratic Control.

part of the reform sequence, we should pause a moment to contemplate the sheer magnitude of the task.

Yet without this there will either be inflation or price control with suppressed inflation. If there is a major lesson from NEP inflation, it may well be that the suppressed inflation of 1925–29 was far more damaging than the hyperinflation of 1921–24:

> 'The shortages of industrial goods were a major factor in the reluctance of the peasantry to supply grain in the required quantities from 1927 onwards. The goods famine acted as a deterrent to increased production by the industrial workers. It created conditions for speculation on the free market and a drift of capital into the hands of private traders. It ultimately forced the government to adopt a complicated rationing system.'[61]

We have, in sum, a Gordian knot: a system of irrational prices is administered by bureaucrats who derive much of their power and privilege from their role in supervising this network of shortages. But they oversee immense monopolies which cannot be divided at a stroke. Prying loose the central administrative grip in these conditions is likely to achieve massive inflation but little of the benefit deriving from competition. But there is one way to cut this knot, or at least to loosen it. Genuinely open foreign trade and international economic relations with a freely convertible currency can immediately reduce the monoploy power of the behemoths by providing new competition, apart from the other more intuitively obvious benefits of reducing isolation. Yet even in the few brief years when NEP achieved a freely convertible currency the decisive foreign and domestic economic policy makers seemed almost as if to conspire to seal off the Soviet state. There seems increasingly less basis for the hope that here again history will not repeat itself.

The 'Soft Budget' constraint

Even in NEP conditions, closure of factories was sometimes eschewed on political grounds. ('Budget constraints' can, after all, be soft even under capitalism when bankruptcy is politically threatening.) NEP, however, had a Narkomfin which seems very different from today's Ministry of Finance. There does not, as yet, seem to be anybody in the Soviet Union trying to take the 'treasury view'. In the presence of new pluralistic pressures for expenditure, and old bureaucratic ones, this would at least offer a degree of balance.

The very first step toward monetary rectification would be the publication of some believable figures, though it is not even clear the authorities have any means to make a reliable estimate. The cumulative – quite

---

[61]Davies, 1958, *op. cit.*, pp. 89–90. Davies goes on to argue that inflation did not carry with it some of the consequences which flow from it in under-developed economies with a smaller degree of state control than in the USSR.

possibly explosive – character of the Soviet emission of money and the creation of non-cash money for enterprises by bank credit threatens to take a sudden turn towards open hyperinflation if public expectations alone alter.

In the contradictory interim, the transition to the transition, the resemblance has been more to the last period of War Communism than to NEP, a system 'where all the wires had been cut'. The slide towards virtual barter is all the more absurd and potentially dangerous for being acted in modern dress. In such depressing circumstances it may be at least lukewarm comfort to reflect on the fact that the Soviet economy did begin to recover in early NEP in the midst of conditions of threatened and then actual hyperinflation.

NEP offers fewer lessons on how to overcome unemployment. Despite a certain recent Soviet tendency to romanticise NEP labour exchanges more can be learnt from elsewhere. An active labour market policy seems to entail a professional and generous boost to 'investment in human capital' and a generous hand in assisting workers in geographic mobility. The NEP labour exchanges were simply too overwhelmed with numbers and under-resourced to do this seriously.

Without additional incentives employers will not normally finance most industrial training in anything resembling normal labour market conditions. That is, they will suffer shortages of skilled workers for some time without undertaking to retrain the unemployed. This is a fairly definite proposition derivable from neo-classical economic propositions, not prejudice.

Without an active labour market policy frictional unemployment will turn into structural unemployment. Unemployment will become chronic, and the 'natural rate' of unemployment will rise. But such a policy may be more expensive initially than unemployment compensation. It requires a commitment to work for full employment to choose this path. A commitment simply to alleviate individual hardship will encourage quite different choices.

In place of a conclusion

Georgy Arbatov recently addressed the West in a stern voice on just the subject of this chapter:[62]

> 'I cannot understand those economists at home and abroad who intimidate people by the prospect of the great suffering which the market will supposedly cause them. I can see why our economic functionaries are doing it. . . But why should others swallow the bait?'

Arbatov reasonably pointed to anticipated objections:

> 'Some readers may wonder whether I think the transition to a market

[62]*Financial Times*, 2 May, 1990.

economy will be painless, and whether society will have to pay a price for it. But does Soviet society not pay daily a very high price for the absence of a market? . . . . My own view is that the second price is much higher than the first.'

On this last point it is difficult to disagree with Arbatov. But why not, then, concur with him that it is dangerous or silly to present the market as 'a cloud of danger promising all kinds of trouble for the man in the street, rather than prosperity, consumer goods, and opportunities to earn good incomes and live well?'

An over-arching fear of the consequences can, of course, be paralysing to any economic reform. But there is good reason for even the most ardent pro-market economist to command a certain concentration on the problems of the market. The NEP experience demonstrates that the results of dealing with hyperinflation and mass unemployment can be as consequential as the original difficulties. It is also important that, in contrast with the present Soviet context, protest and discontent were muted by the increasingly repressive political system. A wider historical perspective provides a salutary warning.

If people are drunk on the heady wine of Arbatov's tempting vision, what sort of a hangover will they have when they wake up to reality? The likely result is some sort of turn to a populist vision, whether Soviet Peronism or neo-Stalinism, to protect them from the chill winds Arbatov does not want to forecast. This is one of the most important reasons for a close examination of the dark lining in the silver cloud of NEP.

IV Ideology and Culture

10
Construction . . . reconstruction . . . deconstruction

Julian Cooper

Since 1985 the edifice of Soviet socialism has been undergoing reconstruction. The very term perestroika signals that Gorbachev and his supporters conceive the process in terms of the same ideological discourse that has held sway in Soviet politics at the level of political leadership since the October Revolution. At the core of Bolshevik–Marxist–Leninist ideology has been the conviction that socialism must be *constructed* by conscious human action according to a preconceived plan. Not only was socialism conceived as a task of social engineering on a grand scale, but this very mode of development was understood to express the superiority of the new social formation over all antecedents.

'But what distinguishes the worst architect from the best of bees is this, that the architect raises his structure in imagination before he erects it in reality' (Marx). Here we have one of the original sources of the constructivist discourse. For the Bolshevik tradition the undisputed achievements of pre-socialist humankind, of civilisation, were regarded as little more than the achievements of the best of bees. But even the worst of the Bolsheviks understood themselves to be the conscious builders of a new, superior form of society. No ordinary architects were the Bolsheviks and their later adherents. The structures to be erected were not simply the fruits of prior imagination; they were the scientifically substantiated products of the law-governed processes of history. It was from this core ideological conviction that the Russian Marxists derived their extraordinary confidence and *élan*, not to say arrogance, in the face of overwhelmingly unpropitious circumstances.

Taking their lead from Plekhanov, over a century ago, what attracted Russian socialists to Marxism was above all its self-proclaimed scientific status. This was scientific socialism, a socialism, it was believed, that had rendered redundant all utopian projections. As Lenin was to acknowledge, one could still dream, but now policy was to be determined on a strictly rational, scientific basis. For many Russian and Soviet revolutionaries the socialist movement was the true inheritor of the project of Enlightenment. It was perhaps Bukharin who expressed this view with the strongest conviction.[1]

[1]Most strikingly in his collection of essays, *Etyudy* (1932; reissued in 1988).

Under way in the USSR now is the deconstruction of the ruling ideological discourse of Soviet Marxism–Leninism. It is perhaps not surprising that to the forefront for reconsideration have come precisely the long-transcended first terms of the ideology's antinomies: utopia/science, spontaneous social process/conscious social construction, reform/revolution, and now, increasingly, private/social and capitalism/socialism. What is being challenged is the ideology's extraordinary one-sidedness, its absence of genuine dialectical tension. In my view it is precisely this one-sidedness that constitutes one of the most significant, core, distinguishing features of Soviet Marxism–Leninism. But it is also the methods and modes of though characteristic of the discourse that are also being reconsidered, permitting the addition of dialogue/struggle. Soviet Marxism–Leninism has always been combative and partisan. From the very beginning the realm of ideas has been viewed in terms of a medieval battleground. Beyond the boundaries of the discourse have been alien ideas to be demolished in struggle; within its walls, suspected heresies to be hunted down and slain like dragons.

A constantly recurring theme is that of utopia. Many argue that Soviet socialist ideology was essentially utopian, bearing little relation to the reality of the society in which socialism was being built. This gap between the idea and reality, it is argued, was bridged by two basic means: firstly, under the banner of the construction of socialism, reality was forcibly accommodated to the requirements of ideology; secondly, the backward and refractory reality was mythologised, 'utopianised' in such a way as to present it as the true realisation of the socialist idea. To a surprising degree, partial success was achieved on both fronts and, indeed, this helps to explain the longevity of the Administrative System and the current difficulties of reform. Perhaps here also lie the roots of the dualities that have characterised Soviet development: above all, coercion and heroism, tragedy and triumph. It could also be argued that the urge to universalise the ideology, to extend it into every sphere of life of the society (another of its fundamental distinguishing features) stems to a large degree from the need, understood consciously or not, to have the mythologised representation accepted as widely as possible as the true reality. On this interpretation, the extraordinary, unrelenting drive for the universalisation of the ideology, and perhaps also the intolerance of the ideology itself, registers no more than the profound insecurity of a ruling éite committed to a utopian project, but experiencing at every step the gulf between desire and attainment.

Utopia is now being reassessed. Reflections on Stalinism and history in general are promoting a new interest in a long-neglected topic. As the critique extends back to Marx there is interest in exploring the 'pre-scientific' 'utopians'. Shakhnazarov now admits that from his youth he found it strange that Fourier and Owen were called utopians.[2] Aleksandr

---

[2]*Kommunist*, No. 4, 1990, p. 56. In the same issue (p. 11) Aleksandr Yakovlev makes a passing reference to Fourier and Saint-Simon.

Tsipko, perhaps the most resolute of all the deconstructors, has also praised Fourier. Implicit is a questioning of the claims of *scientific* socialism, the growing acceptance of the legitimacy of a plurality of possible socialisms. This is novel because until recently Soviet Marxists (and, to be fair, most Marxists in the West), following Engels and Lenin, have taken for granted the claim that Marx converted socialism from a utopia into a science. In my view a case can be argued that Marx's celebrated break with utopianism in the *Communist Manifesto* was achieved by a method of direct relevance to our theme. The 'utopians' were charged with an inability to fill the gap between their socialist visions and the real circumstances of the present. In contrast, Marx claimed that his socialist vision (many of the programmatic elements of which were directly borrowed from Fourier, Owen and Saint-Simon) was firmly grounded in the real trends of social development. But to a large extent Marx achieved this by resort to a systematic overstatement of the maturity of the actually prevailing economic and social conditions of the day: early capitalism was 'utopianised' in order to transcend utopianism. At its very birth Marxism took over and reworked the utopian impulse, transposed it from the future vision to the lived reality; at the birth of 'real' socialism the same transposition recurred.

From the very beginning a core, fateful element of Soviet Marxism–Leninism has been its extraordinary belief in the malleability of both social institutions and the human personality. Here the ideology's characteristic one-sidedness has blended with a dubious legacy of the Enlightenment. Marx's dialectic of social development in terms of material content and social form has been interpreted in such a way as to privilege the latter, amounting to a denial of the continuities of history and civilisation. Social relations, usually interpreted in narrow, oversimplified class terms, have been viewed as all determining, shaping material content at will. This theoretical position has underpinned the utopian endeavour. Some Soviet writers now acknowledge that this approach amounts to vulgar sociologism, or social/class reductionism. Worst of all, understanding of the nature of the human personality has been dominated by a one-sided interpretation of Marx's sixth thesis on Feuerbach (the essence of man . . . is the ensemble of social relations), effectively denying the existence of an intrinsic, universal human nature as the relatively unchanging, if not unchangeable, material content of human beings.[3] In addition, as Tsipko and other Soviet writers have observed, Soviet thinking has been influenced by an Enlightenment belief in the essential goodness and perfectability of man: Rousseau has been as influential as Marx. Confident belief that a new socialist man could be formed through the conscious adoption of appropriate social measures remained a constant theme from the earliest times (in the writings, for example, of Bogdanov, Lunacharskii and Trotsky) to

---

[3]Soviet Marxists could read with profit the splendid little book by Norman Geras, *Marx and Human Nature: Refutation of a Legend* (Verso, 1983).

the present (as shown by the curious nature/nurture debate of the 1970s and early 1980s: those stressing biological determination were attempting to undermine one-sided orthodoxy). Only now is that belief being subject to serious challenge.

In the ruling ideology the intoxicating brew of utopianism, the perfectability thesis, and vulgar sociologism undoubtedly contributed to an instrumentalist approach to the individual. It is as if the enlightened aristocracy of 'architects' viewed the mass of citizens as toilers, 'bees' in the cellular, collectivist 'hive' of Soviet society. But that image is too organic, not reflecting the modernism of the project. We should not be surprised that the chief site engineer viewed the population as little screws in the machine-like structure of the new society. An interesting question is the extent to which the ground for such pervasive instrumentalism was prepared by the early Proletkultist and productivist cultural movements. With perestroika there has been acknowledgement of the 'human factor', but this concept remains embedded within a profoundly productivist discourse. In this connection it is worth noting that in some respects even the 'utopian' Fourier had a more modern understanding of the individual than that frequently met in Soviet ideology, or for that matter, in the writings of Marx. Fourier had a keen awareness of the reality and complexity of human desires; not for him humans reduced to bearers of labour power.

It has been argued by Tsipko and others that Marx was responsible for the 'original sin' which fatally deformed Soviet socialism. Lenin and the Bolsheviks followed Marx in their belief that commodity production was alien to socialism, and this non-market conception became a core element of Soviet ideology notwithstanding gestural acknowledgement at various times of a transitional role for market or quasi-market forces. I believe that this charge is essentially correct, but the question remains: why did this understanding of socialism come to predominate as it did? Firstly, no doubt, because the market was considered to be the ultimate expression of spontaneous forces not subject to conscious human control. To have economic life shaped by forces as blind as those of nature was considered incompatible with humankind's attainment of the true realm of freedom. Just as nature had to be conquered, so had natural forces at work in society.

Also relevant here is another important dimension: the understanding of scarcity. Marx's vision of the future amounted to a transcendence of scarcity: instead of generalised want there would be abundance, and abundance was conceived as the essential condition for the full realisation of human capabilities. But with abundance there would be no need for a special mechanism of distribution, such a mechanism was only required on a temporary basis until the unleashed productive forces achieved the rapid elimination of want. Russian and Soviet Marxists took over this understanding: why adopt the market if tomorrow, or the day after, the need for it will disappear? But today we have generalised want. As Xenos observes in his pioneering study, the short-term Soviet solution owed more to Rousseau than Marx: a policy which 'sought to suppress desire in order to hasten the arrival of communist abundance . . . a twentieth-century version of a Rousseau-like revolution from above against scarcity'.[4] From this perspective Soviet ideology, as 'civil religion', had a vital repressive function: it became an instrument for the repression of desires in the interests of the communist future. Given this general ideological cast of mind, is it conceivable that the market could really have displaced the central plan?

Almost to the present Soviet Marxism–Leninism has retained an extraordinary innocence. Cut off for more than sixty years from the mainstream of world intellectual life, even from non-Soviet Marxism, it has clung to positions long discarded or modified elsewhere. Only now are some leading party intellectuals beginning to recognise the enormous price paid for this self-imposed isolation. Entire intellectual traditions have been ignored, neglected, or crudely anathematised, including those of Weber, Freud, Wittgenstein, the Frankfurt School and the Austrian school of economics. To a remarkable degree Soviet Marxism has maintained its allegiance to intellectual traditions of an earlier age, notably those of the Enlightenment and nineteenth century evolutionism and progressivism. At a time when, for good or ill, discourses of post-modernity dominate Western thought, Soviet Marxism remains committed to the project of modernity, to a large extent innocent of its critique – not only of the 'dialectic of Enlightenment', but even of the earlier spectre of the Weberian 'iron cage' as the outcome of social rationalisation. As the walls come down Soviet intellectuals find themselves theoretically ill-equipped to comprehend the increasingly de-utopianised reality they inhabit, and it is perhaps not surprising that many turn to earlier, non-Marxist Russian thinkers, notably Berdyaev, Vernadskii, Dostoevskii, and the authors of 'Vekhi', taking up intellectual traditions cut short by the Revolution or Stalinism.[5] It is their concern with moral issues that makes these thinkers so attractive to Soviet intellectuals at the present time, but there remains a deep gulf between the traditions of Russian philosophy and the ideas now influential in the Western world.

Soviet Marxist–Leninist ideology is itself a construct, an assembly of

---

[4]N. Xenos, *Scarcity and Modernity* (1989), p. 54: Xenos's summary of Rousseau's solution for a transcendence of scarcity is worth quoting in full: '. . . the society would be subjected to a kind of political education from birth, with institutions molded toward the purpose of minimizing the effects of emulative competition. Such a society, though not rich, would be one that did not experience scarcity. . . . But to effect this solution in reality rather than a utopian way – to solve the problem for a fully grown modern society rather than one being born – would require authoritarian means, as recourse to a legislator would suggest. It would require the repression of desires already stimulated and the transfiguration of a socially mobile order into one with strict limitations on wealth and its acquisition. It would entail, too, the maintenance by the state of a rigid moral code, a civil religion, with the aim of fostering a regard for the collective over the self. In Rousseau's infamous phrase, such a society would be "forced to be free".'

[5]Tsypko is now championing the latter: 'Perhaps, a return to our "Landmarks" will reveal the true, and so far hidden sense of our perestroika?' (*Moscow News*, 1990, No. 26, p. 3).

elements exhibiting striking structural coherence. Its core dogmas have remained essentially unchanged for decades, reflecting the stability of the principal features of the Administrative System. Since 1985, at an accelerating pace, the basic supports have been withdrawn or modified. Very soon the entire structure must surely collapse – indeed, concealed by the fog of the general ferment of ideas, it may have done so already. As the constructivist project of Soviet communism comes to a close, so also will perestroika as its final stage. The USSR, or Russia and the other republics, will become 'normal' societies in the sense that they will no longer be subject to political leadership exercised in the name of a single, universalised, utopian ideology. The end of Ideology; but not the end of ideologies.

Soviet ideology has always had difficulties with the concept of civilisation. One-sided emphasis on social forms, vulgar sociologism, has made it difficult to acknowledge the reality of a core of human achievement of universal significance not directly reducible to specific social formations or classes. This unease was registered in the late Brezhnev period when there was an effort, unsuccessful, to gain acceptance for a new concept, 'socialist civilisation', in all respects superior to 'capitalist civilisation'. In effect this represented a modernised version of the discarded 'two camps' thesis. It is a sign of the breakdown of traditional Soviet ideology that civilisation is emerging as a key concept, now invoked frequently by many writers. It is indicative that Gorbachev himself now appeals for support for a market economy on the grounds that the market is an achievement of human civilisation. Some have gone further, suggesting that the entire Soviet experience has been a diversion from the mainstream of civilisation. This is now Butenko's position: he argues that the Soviet Union has turned off the main track of human development into a cul-de-sac. Now the task is to return the country to the 'natural-historical path' of progress, to go back to restore its 'general-civilisational principles'.[6] In this new discourse, civilisation is synonymous with 'normal'. From this standpoint the Soviet experience explicitly, or implicitly, is being presented as a pathological condition: what is required is not a restructuring but a cure.

These observations are founded on a belief that ideology has been of profound significance as a determinant of the course of Soviet development from 1917 to the present day. Throughout this period the Soviet Union has had a political regime of an essentially theocratic nature, the policies and actions of its leadership being shaped and bounded by a relatively stable body of ideas consistently presented as the highest achievement of human science. Taking perestroika in historical perspective, what is striking about the ruling ideology is its long-term coherence and stability. The continuities from the Revolution (or at least, War Communism,

---

[6]A. Butenko, 'Krizis ili tupik?', *Moskovskaya Pravda*, 15 May, 1990. Butenko argues that perestroika cannot succeed so long as it is maintained that the country is simply in a crisis and not a 'social–economic cul-de-sac'.

the experience of which has cast a shadow over all subsequent decades) to the present are more in evidence than discontinuities. This immobile ideology played a major role in 'freezing' the basic structures of society. But what of other ideologies that have, often with great difficulty, coexisted with the discourse in dominance? Have the continuities been equally as strong? This is a topic for another paper, but it could be of decisive importance for the future of the post-communist USSR.

11
Literature under Gorbachev – A second Thaw?

Julie Curtis

We are now witnessing the death throes of 'Soviet literature', a strange creature which was born in 1917, reached the age of consent in its teens in 1934 at the first Congress of Soviet Writers, and which is currently breathing its last, both as a literary genre and critical mode (Socialist Realism), and as a State institution (the Union of Writers). Its prime passed with the death of Stalin in 1953; the 'Thaw' of the late 1950s and early 1960s dealt a first blow to its vigour and stimulated the onset of a long-drawn out decline. This 'era of stagnation' (*zastoi*) was the equivalent of a comatose state in which a number of life-support systems maintained some sort of functions alive, while very little that could be described as worthwhile living was being achieved. From the mid-1960s to about 1987, the only vigorous part of literature written in Russian by individuals born as Soviet citizens was to be found outside 'Soviet literature', either in desk-drawers, in *samizdat*, in *tamizdat* or else in emigration. Just as vivid scenes from childhood and later are said to flash through a person's mind on his or her deathbed, so the 'return' of a great many texts of poetry, prose and drama to the Soviet reader under glasnost' has provided a final, uncharacteristic blaze of variety, beauty and profundity to mark the end of 'Soviet literature' as we have known it. This crabbed individual has lived out his allotted span of threescore years and ten, and we must now look forward to a new literary culture which, however it turns out, will not resemble the old. Perhaps it is time to proclaim that 'Soviet literature' is dead, long live Soviet literature!?

The purpose of this chapter is to offer some reflections on the decline of the Soviet literary system during its death throes under Gorbachev. The onset of glasnost' in the second half of the 1980s may initially have seemed to represent a second 'Thaw', but it has now become clear that the process initiated by Gorbachev has led to far more destructive consequences than those that were achieved under Khrushchev. I shall hope to show that any comparison between the phenomenon of the 'Thaw' and glasnost' is a comparison between a relative change and something which, however unintentionally, has become absolute and irreversible.

The achievements of the 'Thaw' period, which took its name from the title of Il'ya Erenburg's 1954 novel, must be viewed above all in contrast to the period of blight that had preceded it under Stalin. The term may in fact be misleading rather than helpful, since it seems to suggest a process, whereas in fact what is most typical about the Thaw is its erratic nature. Did it last three, or six, or eight years, or were there three separate thaws? Or does the term cover the whole period of Khrushchev's rule from 1953 to 1964, defining its identity, in other words, by contrast also with the grey Brezhnev years which succeeded it? The nature and the fate of three works, Erenburg's *The Thaw* (published 1954), Pasternak's *Doctor Zhivago* (completed 1955) and Solzhenitsyn's *One Day in the Life of Ivan Denisovich* (published 1962), reflect this contradictory picture. Erenburg's work, which is undoubtedly a slight piece, was courageous enough to allude to the fact that a great gulf between official art and true genius had developed in the Stalin period; it unmasks the self-interested hypocrisy of the Soviet bureaucrat; and it is above all concerned to bring the four couples in the novel to recognise the legitimacy of their emotions, and therefore culminates in an ending where the private is accorded primacy over the public. In crude terms, *Doctor Zhivago* shares similar preoccupations, although it is rooted in a Christian faith and represents a much greater artistic achievement; nevertheless, it seems perverse that it was denied publication in the USSR in 1956, just two years after the publication of *The Thaw*.

The scandal around the figure of Pasternak when the novel was published in Italy in 1957 and he was awarded the Nobel Prize might have seemed to augur the end of the Thaw period, although in fact its peak had not yet been reached; this was to be the publication of *One Day in the Life of Ivan Denisovich* in 1962. This novel represented a much bolder step in questioning the role of the State; picking up the themes of Khrushchev's 'secret speech', it confronted the truth about the Stalin period and the existence of the prison camps in a way that was never to be repeated in an official Soviet publication until recently. For the generation that initiated the policy of glasnost', a generation now mostly in its fifties, the publication of *Ivan Denisovich* remained a symbol of freedom and publishing integrity to which they have aspired to return ever since. It seems very appropriate that it should be the full publication of Solzhenitsyn in the 1990s which marks the fulfilment at last of those aspirations; Solzhenitsyn's works, in other words, have now become emblematic of glasnost' in the same way that they were emblematic of the 'Thaw' thirty years ago.

The 'Thaw', however, differed from glasnost' in a number of important respects. Khrushchev's goals, both political and cultural, were surely far more limited than Gorbachev's, and carried out far less systematically and determinedly; his goal was to correct, not to transform. It is perhaps characteristic that the style of Khrushchev's 'secret speech' in 1956 at the twentieth Party Congress is far more naturally vivid and outspoken than any of Gorbachev's published speeches, especially when Khrushchev is painting his portraits of Stalin and Beria as monstrous tyrants. But when it came to justifying the Leninist tradition and the Communist Party's hold on power, Khrushchev in his 1956 speech was as mealy-mouthed as any Brezhnevite hack.[1] In a speech of 1957 he did not hesitate to heap reproaches on Soviet writers and artists:

'. . . one feels bitterness and regret at how rarely writers and painters succeed in depicting our people adequately in works of literature or of art, or in showing that these are new people, born and brought up in the epoch of socialism . . . . The Communist Party considers those who are active in literature and the arts as its loyal friends, assistants and reliable support in the ideological struggle . . . . Our people need works of literature, painting and music which reflect enthusiasm for labour and which the people can understand. The method of social-ist realism provides unlimited opportunities for the creation of such works.'[2]

Khrushchev's handling of cultural affairs was in reality largely a matter of the exercise of power, as his coarse hectoring and bullying of art-ists and writers in 1962 and 1963 was to demonstrate. But the legacy of Khrushchev's 'Thaw' was vital to the process that is going on today.

There has been some disagreement about whether the 'Thaw' was ini-tiated from above or from below,[3] but obviously once a signal had been received from above, those below seized the initiative and kept pushing to see how far they could go. During the Brezhnev period, as many commentators have noted, things were not always entirely bleak – as G. Hosking points out:

'Khrushchev's 'thaw' of the late 1950s and early 1960s was a prelimi-nary outburst of . . . plain-speaking,and even after it ceased, a degree of *frondisme* never quite disappeared from at least the literary journals . . . discreet establishment non-conformity was a regular feature of the literary scene in the 1970s and early 1980s.'[4]

The cinema remained often independent and innovative, while in the theatre directors such as Lyubimov, Efros, Efremov and Tovstonogov were producing some brilliant work.[5] Perhaps it is not surprising that the new Minister of Culture appointed on 22 November 1989, Nikolay Gubenko, emerged from the senior staff of Lyubimov's Taganka Theatre; and he is rapidly transforming the Ministry into something more closely

---

[1]For a Soviet publication of Khrushchev's speech, 'O kul'te lichnosti i ego posledstviyakh', see *Svet i teni 'velikogo desyatiletiya' – N.S. Khrushchev i ego vremya*, Leningrad, 1989, pp. 46–106.
[2]*Ibid.*, 'Iz vystupleniy N.S. Khrushcheva na soveshchanii pisateley v TsK KPSS 13 maya 1957g.', pp. 125, 129.
[3]See, for example, the discrepancy between *émigré* views that it came from below, reported by J. Graffy during his talk on '*Glasnost'*' given at Cambridge University on 10 March 1989, and the opinions of N. Eydel'man, reported in *Ogonyok* 44, 1988.
[4]G. Hosking, 'Introduction' to *Culture and the Media in the USSR Today* (hereafter *Culture and the Media*), J. Graffy and G. Hosking (eds.), (London: Macmillan/SSEES, 1989), p. 3.
[5]See Ian Christie, 'The Cinema', in *Culture and the Media*, p. 64; and A. Smeliansky, 'An Act of Freedom', *The Guardian*, 16 September [?] 1989.

resembling the Arts Council. But the literary scene under Brezhnev, by contrast, was particularly badly damaged, and many of its leading figures were dispersed into dissidence, *samizdat*, imprisonment or emigration.

Gorbachev's approach to the cultural intelligentsia has been more sophisticated than Khrushchev's; instead of treating them like recalcitrant children, he has been prepared to allow them to make their own decisions about what should be viewed and read; at the same time he appears to hope that, having gained their trust, it will be possible, nevertheless, to persuade the cultural intelligentsia by comradely exhortation to create works which would further the cause of perestroika. The fact that glasnost' is seen by Gorbachev as part of a much larger policy may be one of the important distinctions one can make between it and the 'Thaw'; after all, one could ask whether the 'Thaw' was a policy as such at all?

My observations of glasnost', perhaps inevitably, have had to be based on journalistic materials, and on discussions with friends and colleagues during a number of visits to the USSR I have made since 1985.[6] For one thing, few extensive studies have yet been made of the literature of glasnost'.[7] Like our Soviet colleagues, Western literary scholars have found themselves reading texts and analytical studies alike in journals and newspapers rather than in books during the last five years, and as publications have proliferated, so the impossibility of covering the full range of materials has become increasingly apparent. One of the main sources I have used has been *Literaturnaya Gazeta*, the official organ of the Union of Writers, not because it has been the most radical and adventurous of the glasnost' press (this accolade must be reserved for *Ogonek, Moskovskiye Novosti* and *Argumenty i Fakty*), but because the demise of Soviet literature, precisely as a branch of ideology, can be traced most directly from its pages. For a Westerner in particular, magazines and newspapers have been far more interesting in recent years than book publications of texts, many of which have long been familiar and available over here.

In literary terms glasnost' has meant above all the retrieval of a great many texts from the oblivion to which they had been consigned by State censorship, and the filling in of the 'blank spaces' of literary history. This process of restoring texts to the public was one which had been embarked upon but not completed during the 'Thaw', when some works by Bulgakov, Platonov, Babel', Akhmatova and others were re-issued or published for the first time. Since 1985 many other such texts have been published in the Soviet Union for the first time, even though they had

[6] I would like to record my gratitude to the British Academy, the British Council, and Robinson and Trinity Colleges, Cambridge, for their support in enabling me to visit the USSR for research purposes at least once every year since 1985.
[7] A distinguished exception is Julian Graffy's article, 'The Literary Press', in *Culture and the Media*, pp. 107–57. This provides an extraordinarily comprehensive account of the major trends of glasnost' and of most of the significant publications in books and journals.

long been known in the West. Little acknowledgement was made during the earlier years of glasnost' of the fact that Western publications and critical studies of a given work had existed, in some cases for several decades; this situation changed perceptibly early in 1988, when official attitudes to Western culture were dramatically revised, and it became possible to acknowledge Western achievements in all fields, including literary studies, rather than automatically decrying or ignoring work by Western scholars. A different category of 'new' publications by living authors was also slow to gather momentum; this was the publication of *émigré* writers, hitherto unmentionable or labelled as enemies. But the publication of works by *émigrés* alive and dead has now extended all the way from Nabokov via Voynovich to Solzhenitsyn. In May 1990 the sight of a Soviet edition of *The Gulag Archipelago* in book form in Leningrad (in a Beriozka shop, of course) was still enough to make one blink at the transformations wrought in five years of glasnost', and clearly 1990 is to be the *annus mirabilis* of Solzhenitsyn publications. A third category of 'new' publications in the Soviet Union comprises works by authors such as Rybakov or Shatrov, who had remained more or less within the Soviet establishment, but who had kept hidden away in their desk drawers works, often from the 1960s and the frustrating late 'Thaw' period, which they had not been able to publish before and are now presenting for public scrutiny for the first time. Other authors had remained inside the Soviet Union but further outside the establishment, such as Yerofeyev or Yevgeny Popov. And a final category of 'new' literature with which the Soviet reader has been bombarded in recent years is of course that of 'world literature', works by innumerable authors hitherto considered undesirable, and ranging from George Orwell to Umberto Eco.

This process of 'returning' literary works appears, however, to be drawing to a close. And one might be forgiven now for asking what there is left to publish? After Solzhenitsyn there are virtually no skeletons left in the cupboard, and the next few years are clearly going to see the mopping up of publication of the last remaining formerly 'banned' texts of any substance by any author. Many have commented, indeed, that this sudden surfeit of riches has been so overwhelming that readers have been put off; not only do the exigencies of normal life render it quite impossible to find time to read all these items, but there is also a sense in which people's appetite for these works has been blunted by their ready availability. A certain edge has been lost now that they are no longer forbidden fruit. This has had an unusual impact on the repertoires of theatres, which have very frequently responded by dramatising hitherto unavailable novels and attracting audiences to watch rather than read these works.[8] In terms of literary history too, we are now faced with an

---

[8]In April 1990, for example, Moscow theatres were performing, amongst others, stage versions of Erofeyev's *Moscow–Petushki*, Ginzburg's *Into the Whirlwind*, Nabokov's *Lolita*, Pasternak's *Doctor Zhivago*, Bulgakov's *Heart of a Dog* and *Theatrical Novel* and Solzhenitsyn's *Gulag Archipelago*.

unparalleled phenomenon; how, for example, is it going to be possible to 'date' a work in the long run as a component of Russian literature in the Soviet Union? Does Akhmatova's cycle of poems *Requiem* date from its time of composition (1935–40), its time of publication in the West (1963), or its time of publication in the USSR (1987)? And since some copies of it circulated covertly within Russia or were smuggled in from abroad throughout this period, should we date its literary impact from the time when it was only patchily and relatively narrowly known, or from the time when it first became officially and publicly available? This might appear a somewhat abstract problem of literary scholarship, but it is in fact one crucial factor which explains why literary activity has in some respects ground to a halt at the moment: a very necessary process of digestion and assimilation of texts is taking place for new writers and established writers alike, and it would not be surprising if little work of substantial interest were to emerge now before at least the mid-1990s. There is virtually no glasnost' literature, in the sense of important new works written between 1985 and 1990, of any great significance; nor indeed, has much literature emerged that deals with the recent past, with the 1970s and early 1980s, let alone with the period of glasnost' itself. Prose fiction in particular has reacted slowly to the new circumstances, while poetry and drama have responded more quickly. In due course it is probable that the main focus for 'new' prose publications will be largely documentary: the 1990s will undoubtedly see an enormous upsurge in the publication in Russian of memoirs, autobiographies and biographies, diaries and travel journals alike, some new, but many extracted from the archives, both private and state-run, which have belatedly begun to release their treasures.

But in this matter of how literature 'reacts' to new circumstances, it is not sufficient to assume that, once the yoke of censorship and administrative control of literature has been lifted, what will emerge will be a literary scene which is much the same as that which obtains in most Western countries. Since the beginning of the nineteenth century literature in Russia has been considered a vehicle for political, moral and social debates, and this attitude has shaped the literature of the Soviet period, even including Socialist Realism. There is no guarantee that the lifting of State restrictions on Soviet literature will bring about a transformation in society's expectations that literature should remain a morally responsible medium. A number of factors contribute to this situation, but a consideration of what has happened to the Writers' Union and to other unions of cultural workers will be helpful in illustrating it.

The opportunities which seemed to be opening up with Gorbachev's advent to power were fairly rapidly seized upon and exploited by members of most of the State organisations that controlled culture; 1986 saw the miniature coup in May which produced the election to power of the film-maker Elem Klimov to run the Union of Cinematographers; this would soon lead to a policy of dusting down films which had long been languishing under a censor's ban and reconsidering their plight; many films in this way were taken 'off the shelf' and released, and this encouraged a boldness in cinema programming which led in due course to the highly influential screenings of *Repentance* (completed in 1984 and released in 1986), *Is it Easy to be Young?* (1987) and *Little Vera* (1988), amongst others. In December 1986 the All-Russian Theatre Union underwent a similar transformation when it redefined itself as a new organisation, the Union of Theatrical Workers, under the leadership of the actor Mikhail Ulyanov. 1986 also saw at least the election of a former inmate of the Gulag, Vladimir Karpov, to lead the Writers' Union, although that organisation remained more intractably conservative than the cinema and theatre unions when it came to radical reforms. Most conservative of all, however, has been the Union of Composers, which after its Congress in April 1986 retained the 73 year-old Tikhon Khrennikov as First Secretary, as he has been, astonishingly, since 1948.[9]

In the world of literature, as I have suggested, the moves towards change have been slow. The role of the censors has been diminished, with responsibility being transferred more and more to the editors of journals and the editorial boards of publishing houses. This has meant a slow but steady widening of the limits within which publications have been operating, leading to a situation where now virtually anything goes. It is salutary to recall, however, the degree of pressure exerted, apparently by Gorbachev himself or by people in circles very close to him, even as recently as the end of 1988, when the proposed publication of Solzhenitsyn was forbidden.[10] The process of democratising the Writers' Union itself has also been inordinately slow. For this reason a number of influential and pro-Gorbachev writers got together in April of 1989 to form a new group, *Aprel'* (consciously adopting an image reminiscent of the 'Thaw'?), to press for change in the Union of Writers. This group, which includes figures such as Bitov, Tolstaya, Okudzhava, Yevtushenko, Shatrov, Voznesensky, Iskander and others, moved fairly cautiously at first, but has become increasingly outspoken as its members discover the depth of resistance to their reformist proposals. Things intensified after 18 January 1990, when there was a widely publicised attack by a group of anti-Semitic thugs on a meeting of the *Aprel'* group in the Writers' Union Club (Tsentral'ny Dom Literatorov), an attack that involved physical violence and that appears to have been carried out with the connivance at the very least of the officials responsible for order and security in the Club.

In advance of their founding congress, scheduled for April 1990, the group issued a press release in the name of the organising committee of the *Aprel'* association, which claims the subtitle 'Writers in support of perestroika'.[11] This document, effectively a manifesto, is couched in perhaps surprisingly 'conventional' terms for a supposedly radical group. It states its support for political pluralism as well as artistic pluralism;

[9]Christopher Rice, 'Soviet Music in the Era of *Perestroika*', *Culture and the Media*, p. 92.
[10]J. Graffy, 'The Literary Press, *Culture and the Media*', p. 137.
[11]*Aprel'-Inform – Press-biulleten' orgkomiteta uchreditel'nogo s"ezda vsesoyuznoy assotsiatsii 'Aprel''* (*Pisateli v podderzhku perestroyki*), Nos. 1–2, March 1990.

demands freedom of speech; condemns the Union of Writers of the RSFSR for spreading dissension between the nationalities, an obvious reference to the apparent support for anti-Semitism and its most vocal proponent, the *Pamyat'* organisation, within the Russian branch of the Writers' Union; and it also demands an end to the pyramidal, hierarchical structure of the Writers' Union, seeking instead a federative structure with democratic elections to self-governing organs of management. Two things are striking here: firstly, that *Aprel'* appears determined for the moment to seek for reform of the Writers' Union from within, rather than aiming to abolish the organisation altogether; and secondly, the extent to which the *Aprel'* group's struggles and aspirations for the Writers' Union appear as a microcosm of those of the centrist–radical groups in the political world, and seem analogous in particular to the Democratic Platform's fragile – and now waning – hopes for a reformed Communist Party in relation to a new, federative Soviet Union. The *Aprel'* group talks of fostering co-operative publishing, trying to satisfy what has become known as the 'book-hunger', a problem now largely determined by acute problems in the supply of paper; and they ask that the role of the 'Litfond', the body that determines many of the practical and financial aspects of the professional life of a Soviet writer, should be reviewed. They call on other writers to join them so that the *Aprel'* organisation should come to embrace the whole nation, and declare that:

> 'The purpose of the existence of the Union should become the pro-
> tection of the civic and professional standing of the writer and of his
> right to create freely in any field, without any ideological, linguistic,
> thematic, genre, stylistic or other restrictions; and the protection of the
> social, economic, legal and other rights of its members, as well as the
> protection and support of young writers.'[12]

To many foreign observers it might seem strange, however, that Soviet writers should feel any need henceforth to function through a powerful Union organisation; do not writers in other countries operate more or less successfully without one? Furthermore, the setting-up during the spring of 1990 of branches of the International PEN-Club in the USSR under the presidency of Anatoly Rybakov would seem to afford the *Aprel'* writers, many of whom also belong to the PEN-Club, an attractive alter-native organisation to the Writers' Union, which would work towards the very goals they seek. As in other branches of perestroika, the 'new thinking' is still very much shaped by the old, and consists in dramatically enlarging the limits of action rather than throwing caution to the winds and abolishing those limits altogether. All writers have remained depend-ent on the Writers' Union until very recently for access to everything from paper to publishing houses and pensions; and, of course, for a great many privileges in the way of access to good housing and pleasant holiday schemes and travel abroad. Just as one might speculate as to how long the Democratic wing of the Communist Party will retain any significance if

[12]*Ibid.*

the Party's monopoly of power is removed, so the *Aprel'* group is liable to lose its *raison d'être* if the Writers' Union is swept away altogether by market forces.

What the *Aprel'* platform does make clear, largely by omitting any discussion of it as presumably being completely irrelevant to the present-day literary process, is that the concept of Socialist Realism is defunct. Senior officials of the Writers' Union fought a rearguard action from 1987 onwards to defend the concept in discussions on the pages of *Literaturnaya gazeta*.[13] During the Brezhnev period it had still been proclaimed the official method of all Soviet art, but once the strictly imposed certainties of the Stalin period had been questioned under Khrushchev, it was actually very difficult for both writers and critics under Brezhnev to discover what the Socialist Realism of the 1970s was supposed to achieve. There has been a marked lack of conviction, or rather a yawning vacuum, both in the pronouncements of writers on the subject and in the analyses of literature provided by critics and academics during the last 30 years. Attempts to defend it now as a central concept defining the unique contribution of socialist literature to world culture are largely greeted with derision, and it seems clear that in the new constitution for the Writers' Union which is due to be debated in the autumn of 1991 at its ninth Congress, the concept will be abandoned.

However, a different way of looking at the concept of Socialist Realism, which has certainly proved somewhat elusive since its promulgation as the official method of Soviet literature and criticism at the Writers' Congress in 1934, is to regard it, as Katerina Clark has put it, as 'the official repository of State myths' in the Soviet Union.[14] Texts should not be measured, in other words, against a putative model of a literary genre, but instead analysed as official inspirational propaganda tailored to the needs of the moment. In the early years of glasnost' Socialist Realism continued to be very important in this sense of State pressure seeking to shape the behaviour of the Soviet population. If we in the West are to view 'Socialist Realism' as a convenient tag to describe the prevailing cultural myths of Soviet society, then we can note the way in which officially inspired literary debates have taken their cue from the political debates which appeared to be most significant in the early Gorbachev years: namely the nationalities issue, and the ongoing crisis over ecological issues. This latter was particularly exacerbated by the Chernobyl' crisis, which is sometimes held to have been the stimulus for the introduction of the policy of glasnost', but which is increasingly coming to appear as glasnost''s greatest failure of 'openness of information' in communications with the public. Be that as it may, the officially defined tasks of literature in the 1990s have looked since about 1988 as though they were going to be to reflect and shape national debate

[13]See, for example, *Literaturnaya Gazeta* on 1 April, 22 July and 29 July, 1987, and 9 March, 13 April, 18 May, 25 May, 20 July and 24 August, 1988.
[14]K. Clark, *The Soviet Novel – History as Ritual* (Chicago and London, 2nd ed., 1985), p. xii.

about the need for national unity and for environmental protection in the Soviet Union. We may observe, for example, the enormous influence of Valentin Rasputin, a doughty campaigner on behalf of the increasingly polluted Lake Baykal, and of Chingiz Aytmatov, the Kirghiz writer whose novel, *The Executioner's Block* (1986), first raised the delicate issue of a Soviet narcotics problem, and whose own commitment to national unity as a non-Russian Soviet citizen may well have been instrumental in his appointment, alongside Rasputin, as one of the only two writers to hold seats in Gorbachev's new Presidential cabinet, created in March 1990.

Gorbachev himself still clearly thinks of literature in largely utilitarian, conventionally Soviet terms. In June 1986, for example, when he held a meeting with 19 authors who were also members of the Supreme Soviet, he spoke of the 'need for works of art which would inspire confidence in victory for the ideas and plans of the twenty-seventh Party Congress'.[15] When it suited Gorbachev in 1987 to re-open the debate on Bukharin and Trotsky, possibly in order to reassure the West that the Soviet Union did not subscribe to the latter's ambitions for world revolution, Mikhail Shatrov's 1962 play about these men, *The Peace of Brest-Litovsk*, was allowed at last to be published and staged at the Vakhtangov Theatre in Moscow:

> 'Shatrov's special position as the leader of glasnost' in the theatre was dramatically stressed on the play's opening night when none other than Gorbachev came to the theatre to honour Ulyanov, the actor playing Lenin, and to embrace Shatrov.'[16]

In January 1988, addressing a group of journalists, Gorbachev was still defining glasnost' in terms highly reminiscent of Socialist Realism:

> 'We are for glasnost' without reservation or limitations, but for glasnost' in the interests of socialism. To the question of whether glasnost', criticism and democracy have limits we answer firmly: if glasnost', criticism and democracy are in the interests of socialism and the interests of the people they have no limits! This is our criterion.'[17]

Two years later, as the twenty-seventh Party Congress opened, Gorbachev had ceased to appeal to writers for their support in such naïve terms, evidently realising that he could no longer hope to treat them as servants of the State.

This shift, especially since about 1988, away from orthodox views of 'Soviet literature' has been cautiously reflected in the pages of the principal newspaper of the Writers' Union, *Literaturnaya Gazeta*. This worthy publication provides information, if often belatedly, about events organised by the Writers' Union, and occasionally publishes interesting

[15]Quoted by M. Walker, *The Guardian*, 25 June 1986.
[16]M. Glenny, 'The Thaw Turns into a Flood', *Sunday Times Magazine*, 3 July 1988, p. 54.
[17]Quoted by M. Dejevsky from a speech to journalists from *Pravda* on 13 January 1988 in '*Glasnost*' and the Soviet Press', *Culture and the Media*, p. 39.

polemical articles or new works of note; however, all this used to be set in a dull lay-out which has improved only slightly as the period of glasnost' proceeded. Nevertheless, the circulation of *Literaturnaya Gazeta*, like that of many of the other journals, soared in the first few years of glasnost', although like the others it has also slipped from its peak of nearly 6.5 million at the beginning of 1989 back down again, to about five million: evidently economic constraints have begun to bite and the public's appetite for sensational new publications has become sated. In recent months there has been an attempt to revamp *Literaturnaya Gazeta*, especially since the appointment of the political commentator Fyodor Burlatsky, a fluent spokesman for Gorbachev's ideas, as the paper's new editor on 15 March 1990. On 2 May 1990 the newspaper began to appear in a redesigned format which is more attractive to read and which has experimented with some use of colour photographs; it no longer claims to be an organ of the board of management of the Writers' Union, but speaks now just for 'the Writers' Union'. The holy Soviet portrait of Gor'ky has been summarily jettisoned from the masthead, leaving Pushkin in sole occupation, and the paper now proclaims its Tsarist credentials as having been founded in 1830 before it was relaunched in 1929. These are more than cosmetic changes, for they are clearly meant to inspire readers to rethink the relationships between Russian and Soviet literature, and between writers and their Union.

Hitherto, certainly, *Literaturnaya Gazeta* had reflected the slow pace of change in the official thinking of the Writers' Union. Some indication of the way in which the Union had fossilised was provided by Natal'ya Il'yina, who in a remarkable profile of the Union's membership published early in 1988 in *Ogonek* reported that the average age of its 10,000 members was 60.[18] In December 1987 *Literaturnaya Gazeta* published discussions of a new constitution for the Union. By December 1988 the newspaper had got as far as sending out a questionnaire to members of the Writers' Union asking for views about the reform of the Union and of its constitution; and in March 1989, some fifteen months after the first discussions, the newspaper carried a new draft of the constitution. However, it was scarcely a model of glasnost' thinking. This astonishingly reactionary document proclaimed a commitment to *partiynost'* and *narodnost'*, the traditional twin pillars of Socialist Realism even though the latter was not actually named as such; a loyalty to Lenin and to something called 'revolutionary perestroika'; and a promise of freedom of aesthetic innovation in creative work, although it also offered its support to works which would be 'realistic in method and socialist in ideal', a garbled rephrasing of the 1934 definition of Socialist Realism ('a truthful, historically concrete depiction of reality in its revolutionary development'). It is scarcely surprising that the *Aprel'* group felt impelled to seek a new form of organisation after this blinkered refusal on the part of the old guard to contemplate change. Discussions have continued to rage

[18]Referred to in *Literaturnaya Gazeta*, 20 January, 1988.

since then, with the establishment displaying remarkable tenacity, but it is difficult not to believe that the 9th Congress of the Writers' Union in 1991 may well be its last in its present guise.

As with the concept of Communism, so the attempt to repackage the ideological concept of Socialist Realism has spun out of control. While members of the Communist Party and of the Writers' Union agonise over the precise nature of their future ideologies, the rest of the country is getting on with the task of innovation and experimentation regardless of these redundant debates. In literature we have seen a mushrooming of independent and informal groups, whether it is the student group at Moscow State University with its scurrilously impertinent remake of Lenin's newspaper *Iskra*, the nearest thing to *Private Eye* to emerge so far; or the dozens of attempts at co-operative publishing which have now finally begun to get off the ground after many obstacles had been placed in their path.[19] The market has begun to reach publishing, with the result that consumer demand is now capable of being satisfied, even if prices for the new publications are relatively very high. Hundreds of theatre studios have sprung up – Smeliansky estimates there to be 300–500 new ones, while Michael Glenny notes that the number of official theatres in Moscow increased from 30 to 45 between 1986 and 1988; even if few of them survive, there is no doubt that they have already changed the whole framework of theatrical culture entirely.[20] In June 1990 Elem Klimov decided to retire from the Union of Cinematographers to get on with his creative work, presumably feeling that the task of campaigning to achieve creative freedom has been successfully accomplished.[21] On 12 June 1990 the Soviet Parliament passed an unprecedented bill guaranteeing press freedom and eliminating censorship of the mass media, permitting any organisation or individual over the age of 18 to launch a publication, and providing for officials to face criminal charges for hampering journalists or refusing them information.[22] This all bodes well for creative freedom in every branch of the arts.

The 5 years from 1985 to 1990 are beginning to appear more and more as a transitional phase. After it will come something completely different, for the evolutionary process so deftly controlled by Gorbachev and his men between 1985 and 1988 has now surged forward out of their hands. In the past, literature has served as many things; it was a substitute for journalism and social sciences even in the nineteenth century, functioning as a forum for the raising, often in disguised form, of political and social issues which could not be discussed overtly in the press or in academic studies. After the 1917 Revolution, literature was permitted to become a

---

[19]For an account of these difficulties, see the journal *Glasnost'* for June 1987, reprinted in Radio Free Europe/Radio Liberty's *Materialy Samizdata* 24/87.
[20]A. Smeliansky, 'An Act of Freedom', *The Guardian*, 16 September, 1989; and M. Glenny, 'Soviet Theatre: *Glasnost'* in Action – with Difficulty', *Culture and the Media*, p. 80.
[21]*Literaturnaya Gazeta*, 13 June, 1990.
[22]Jonathan Steele and John Rettie, *The Guardian*, 13 June, 1990.

kind of substitute for religion, a new opiate for the masses. Grafted on to the Russians' genuine love of literary works, and of poetry in particular, was a somewhat mindless cult of the writer as a saint, which turned their homes into shrines, their lives into bowdlerised hagiographies, their works into crudely distorted political sermons, and their archives into sepulchres. Literature is now freeing itself from all of these responsibilities, with the result that it finds itself in a state of considerable uncertainty about its future role and identity. A great many Russians still think it should serve the interests of the State, and many think it should fulfil a didactic function, telling young people how to behave and discouraging the peoples of the Soviet Union from slaughtering one another; others are content for literature to throw some sort of truthful light on historical events, which is why one of the most characteristic texts of this glasnost' period has been Rybakov's *Children of the Arbat*. This novel of the 1960s was published to great acclaim in 1987, for it offered a portrait of Stalin which accused him of direct involvement in the 1934 murder of Kirov. It is, however, a very poorly written work which, although utterly sincere, tacks its courageous political message on to a Socialist Realist construct. But this phase, where poorly written works are tolerated for their political integrity, will surely pass; Marietta Chudakova has already noted the beginning of a decline in the production of this sort of semi-publicistic fiction.[23]

More skilful work is currently being produced by a number of writers such as Tolstaya and Petrushevskaya, whose great achievement, typical of that of much feminist writing and particularly potent in the Soviet context, is to write what one might call a 'real realism', honest accounts of real life which are not burdened by excessive political, philosophical or moral purposes and certainly disregard the Socialist Realist tradition. Instead they pursue an art which exists for its own sake – something Russian literature has seen little of since the Silver Age at the beginning of this century. Maybe Russian literature in the Soviet Union is coming at last to cease to feel the need for a function? It is doubtful whether the reputations even of Tolstaya and Petrushevskaya will survive to rank them among the greatest writers of the century, but their achievements suggest that new shoots will be coming through. It is the generation which enjoyed the 'Thaw' which is the generation which has created glasnost', a generation skilled in the art of negotiating compromise; the young are more impatient, and see no need for further caution. At present the picture is not so much of a second 'Thaw' as of a deep winter, with few visible signs of new growth; but undoubtedly there are some writers around who have been keeping temporarily silent over the last few years, as well as other new ones we know nothing of who are beginning to stir. It is they who, after glasnost', will start to create a new Russian literature for the twenty-first century.

[23]M. Chudakova, interviewed in *Literaturnoye Obozreniye* 1, 1990.

V The Republics

The Republic

12
Obstacles to reform:
The Siberian dimesion

Caroline Humphrey

The policy of 'de-nationalisation' (*razogosudarstvleniye*) envisages transferring ownership of at least some of the basic resources of the Soviet
Union, 90 percent of which is now state property, to workers, co-
operatives, and other small groups of citizens. One might well ask
what difference this transfer of property rights would make. In order
even to begin to approach this question it is necessary to have some
understanding of the actual situation, economic and legal, political and
social, in which Soviet enterprises find themselves. This chapter focuses
on the situation in the provinces of the RSFSR, especially the vast region
of eastern Siberia, which differs significantly from either the metropolitan
cities or the National Republics. Much of the region is comprised of
Autonomous SSRs and Autonomous Oblasts in which ethnic minorities
have formal authority, but exist in an uneasy relationship with a vast
Russian majority. This means, nevertheless, that local élites have their
own, varied, cultural-political bases, which have developed historically
from pre-revolutionary times. These structures were strengthened, if
anything, by Soviet local institutionalisation, and have now come into
the open with the reduction of repressive centralised authority. It will be
suggested here:

1. That local state-owned enterprises and organisations already have
   considerable, and growing, autonomy, which is linked to the local
   nomenklatura and socially constituted in quite specific ways.
2. That these already place considerable obstacles in the way of economic and democratic reforms.
3. That conflicts between those inside these organisations and the
   underprivileged and 'disenfranchised', who are outside them, often
   takes an ethnic form.
4. That an alteration of legal titles may not affect much in the way of
   change for some time.

We need, first of all, to discuss general economic conditions shared by
the whole provincial population. In many Siberian towns the hardiest and
most determined queues are not for basic foodstuffs but to buy gold. In
the autumn of 1990 the author spent several weeks in Ulan-Ude, capital
of the Buryat ASSR. One night, as we saw a crowd huddled against the

wall of a building in the dark, a Buryat friend told me, 'They stand there all night, and in the morning many more people come. Even though gold has become so expensive in the last 2 years everyone is trying to get hold of it. They even buy and sell places in the queue'.

A move to gold indicates a lack of trust in the value of the ruble. In Russia today this is combined, as everyone knows, with excess money savings, severe shortages of goods in the shops, general inflation and impossibly high prices in markets, supply and production blockages in farms and factories, a chaotic legal situation, and the introduction of 'rationing'. But the social implications of the situation are less well known and understood. One might imagine a parallel with the time after the Second World War, when many of these economic features were present. However, for reasons explained below, the present situation should be seen as different even from that of Russia in the 1940s. Internal historical analogies can be drawn for some aspects of what is happening today, but they also are to be found further afield, and anthropology may be useful to elucidate them.

Here is a very brief outline of the situation in provincial Russia. The declaration of 'sovereignty' and other forms of autonomy vis-a-vis the USSR, not just by the RSFSR but by regions within it, such as the Buryat ASSR, and counties within regions, such as the Aga Autonomous Okrug,[1] means that there is widespread uncertainty about government and law at 'higher' levels of the body politic. Consequently, organisations and enterprises in the localities, run in a personal way almost as 'suzerainties' by local bosses, have strengthened themselves and increased their social functions in order to protect their members. What are the relations between these organisations? It is not possible to rely on the law, or even know what it is these days, and at the same time government, which used to regulate flows of goods and allocation of labour – including decrees by Soviets and plan-orders by Ministries – has ceased to be universally or even generally obeyed. One could see this situation as the beginning of the reforms, the loosening of centralised authority and the devolution of power. But the social structures that are now toughening themselves are in contradiction with the goal of a free market, even with that of a regulated but all-USSR market. Symptoms of this are that economic relations

---

[1]Within the USSR, the Russian Federated Soviet Socialist Republic is the largest of the National Republics. It is divided into large regions, which are called Oblasts in areas populated by Russians and Autonomous Soviet Social Republics in areas where there are significant ethnic minorities. Oblasts and ASSRs have approximately the same formal powers. At the next level down the hierarchy, inside the Oblasts and ASSRs, there are smaller administrative 'counties', called National Okrugs, for lesser ethnic groups. These, and the Oblasts/ASSRs are then divided into local districts (called Raion). Virtually all ethnic groups, such as the Buryats, live not only in their own Buryat ASSR but also in National Okrugs within Russian-dominated Oblasts, and elsewhere, i.e. simply as citizens in other Oblasts and Raions.

between local 'suzerainties' are increasingly conducted by distinctive methods (of which the general public in the west has little knowledge): by coupons and 'orders', by means of direct barter, or via what is widely known as 'the Mafia' – a heterogeneous collection of racketeer associations whose common feature is that they contain their own 'protection'.

Sometimes Russians use a metaphor to describe the local corporations which I have called suzerainties. They are 'icebergs': of different sizes, perhaps melting a little at top and bottom, or maybe growing imperceptibly, floating and jostling one another in an unfriendly sea.

Western newspapers often inform their readers that the USSR has introduced rationing to cope with the situation. This may give the wrong impression. There is a distinction in principle between generalised rationing and limited 'coupons'. What actually is being used is the latter, a multifarious collection of food-cards (*kartochka*), coupons (*talon* and *kupon*), orders (*zakaz*) and coupon-orders. This is an important factor which differentiates the current situation from that at the end of the Second World War. Then, the centralised government was able to make an assessment of stocks and production-flows in the country and assign goods to cities and regions by a single system of rationing. The system differentiated between social categories (soldiers, mothers, pensioners, etc.) but in principle it was universal for the whole country and population. Today, no one knows what goods there are, and even if general rationing is introduced it will be impossible to establish universal norms. Entitlements to purchase are limited by a host of local factors. The coupons and orders enabling people to buy things are issued not centrally but by all sorts of regional organisations and at different administrative levels. Even local Soviets seem to have side-stepped responsibility for the regulation of allocations as a whole.[2] Crucially, the coupons and orders can be issued by the places where people work (the 'suzerainties' or 'icebergs').

Long ago the anthropologist Mary Douglas (1967) explained the socio-political consequences of the use of coupons in her analysis of certain tribal economies in New Guinea. She contrasted three types of primitive economy, controlled, freely competitive, and mixed, and argued that the 'currencies' found in the more controlled economies were more like coupons than money. 'I would expect primitive coupon systems to emerge where there is some danger that the effective demand for scarce resources may so disturb the pattern of distribution as to threaten a given social order'.[3] Both rationing and coupons (or licensing) are instruments of social policy, but whereas rationing is *egalitarian* in intent, coupons are not. The object of coupons or licensing is *protective*: to limit access to particular goods to certain groups of

[2]*Dialog*, 1990, 2, p. 58.
[3]Mary Douglas, 'Primitive Rationing', in R. Firth (ed.), *Themes in Economic Anthropology* (London, 1967), p. 127.

people. An important side effect of coupons is to create advantages, even sometimes monopolies, for those who issue them and those who receive them. 'Both parties become bound in a patron–client relation sustained by the strong interests of each in the continuance of the system'[4].

In Russia today coupons thus have social implications both within and between 'suzerainties'. How does this work? Let us take the food-card (*kartochka*),[5] which is the most prevalent form in the provinces. Such cards are for specific products sold in state shops which are scarce in a given town or region and they are issued only to people who have a residence permit (popularly known as *vizitka*). Important for the argument of this chapter is the fact that not just residence permits but food-cards too are personalised: they include the person's name and address, and must be stamped by an authority from his or her place of work. The products people are entitled to buy with them have changed many times during the past few years, and since 1 December 1990 have extended to virtually all products in many places. This means that outsiders cannot buy such products at all. If a villager goes on a visit to Ulan-Ude for a month he or she will have a hungry time of it without friends to feed him. As for those out of work, as people say, '*Kto ne rabotayet ne yest . . .*' (He who doesn't work doesn't eat). Even for respectable citizens there is often no alternative to buying a forged *vizitka* on the black market.[6]

Coupons (*talon*) are similar to food-cards, but even more limited in the social groups able to use them. They enable certain categories of people (workers at a factory, members of a collective-farm, war-veterans of a town, mothers of many children, etc.) to buy specific products. They are extremely heterogeneous. Sometimes coupons are limited to a specific shop, sometimes not. Sometimes they are allocated per head in a family, sometimes by the number of adult workers. They may be distributed randomly (drawn out of an urn) or they may be allocated to people who have worked especially well. Coupons may be given out by various organisations, from local Soviets to work-places. They are far more common in the provinces than in Moscow,[7] because, according to Soviet popular opinion, the metropolitan authorities are afraid of widespread rioting by the great numbers of the 'disenfranchised' who would not be eligible for them in the city.

In the Ukraine a curious variant, called the *kupon*, was introduced from 1 November 1990. This is a card, personalised like the *kartochka*, to which is attached a number of stamped squares (one ruble, two rubles,

---

[4]*ibid.*, p. 131.

[5]The reader should not be confused by this term. At present it has the character of a local coupon as described, but the expression *kartochnaya systema* is used for the general rationing brought in during World War II and which some economists advocate introducing for the USSR as a whole in the future.

[6]In autumn 1990 these were being sold for 30–50 rubles in the Ryzhskii market in Moscow.

[7]At the end of 1990 sugar was the only common item in Moscow for which *talony* were issued.

five rubles, etc.) up to a given sum. Food products can only be bought by means of the *kupon:* each time something is bought a square is cut off (but change, apparently, is never given!). These coupons are officially available only to people in work, being paid as a proportion of wages, and to registered pensioners and invalids, taking the place of most of the pension. This system is widely seen as the beginning of a move to a separate Ukrainian currency. As one Soviet economist has put it, discussing the various coupon systems in general, 'The cards only divide the market into 'apanage princedoms' and protect resources that have been 'beaten out' from "aliens"'.[8]

'Orders' (*zakaz*), which exist in several guises, are also common. A large factory, for example, may have its own grocery shop. In Moscow local government insists that such shops be open to the general public at least one day a week, and perhaps to pensioners another day a week. The other five days are reserved for the factory. All shopping at the store is done 'by order', i.e. purchase of a limited bundle of products (the 'order', e.g. 300 grams of cheese, 1/2 kilo of sausages, three tins of fish, etc.) which the shop changes from time to time according to its supplies. Another prevalent form is for shops selling scarce goods, such as shoes and boots, to take a consignment directly 'by order' to an office or factory where they are sold to employees by coupons which have been distributed beforehand. Just as common is a system whereby departments of an organisation such as an Institute of the Academy of Sciences fetch in their own orders and distribute them at the work-place. In this case, at set times the contents of the 'order' are advertised and people queue to put their names on the list. When the set time is up the department sends people down to the shop to collect the goods, they are brought back to the Institute, and distributed. These orders are more or less 'powerful' depending on the social weight of the organisation concerned (academics, it goes without saying, rank rather low). The shops may give better or worse quality goods, or fulfil only 100 out of 300 orders on the list, for example. However, many whole families live entirely on the regular 'order' of one of their members, perhaps a Party stalwart or a veteran of World War Two.

The situation is clearly unfair. Meat, for example, may be available by two different systems in neighbouring towns, in one by coupons and in other only by orders made at the work-place. In the 'deep countryside' (*glubinka*, which may in fact be found not so very far from Moscow[9]), people often have access to none of these systems and therefore have to provide their own basic subsistence. A woman working as a secretary in a state farm, for example, has an exhausting day as she rushes to com-

[8]*Dialog* 1990, 2: 57.
[9]Conditions in these areas, depopulated because of their proximity to large cities, are often far worse than in central Siberia. Farms produce little and therefore can provide very little for their members. Even essential infrastructural services, such as roads, electricity and telephones, have disappeared from many areas.

bine her job with milking her cattle, tending her pigs, and so forth. To give an example: in 1988 in Kalmykia 4214 tons of meat were distributed through state outlets only by coupons and orders. Of this 70 per cent was sold in the capital city of Elista, but Elista does not contain anything like 70 per cent of the population. A meat coupon in the capital therefore 'weighed' considerably more than in the country towns, and farmers were not given coupons at all.[10] But despite their unfairness these systems are widely popular as most people think they have something to gain from them.

Inside the organisation there are many possibilities for deploying patronage and they extend to hangers-on. In Kalmykia orders for meat were also made by work-places. The construction group Kalmykstroi, for example, sent their order to the butcher shop only for it to be discovered more or less by chance that the director of the group had personally added 110 names to the list. Since many people may get left off these lists for one reason or another (e.g. their official residence is in another town, they do not work, or have part-time or unofficial employment) one could interpret the director's action as charitable, but it is also clear that the boss (*khozyain*, 'owner', 'master') only stood to gain himself by his increased patronage.

The coupon systems naturally have social effects at the receiving end too. An example is the allocation of vodka coupons in regions such as Tuva which are still subject to the 'dry law' against alcoholism. Here coupons are allocated by committees within work-places and I was assured in 1989 that they take it upon themselves to judge whether someone is 'suitable' to receive a monthly coupon. Drunkards and 'unsuitable' people are refused, and must prove themselves before their work-mates in order to get back on the list.

The coupon system itself, however, is beyond the law. You can be prosecuted in some regions for illegal distilling, but not for issuing coupons. In Yakutia recently a large cartel printed thousands of counterfeit vodka coupons. When this was discovered several hundred people were arrested. But they were released because no law could be found under which to prosecute them. They had not sold the coupons and benefited financially, all they had done was to issue their own licence to get drunk (depriving other people of vodka). Counterfeiting is not difficult because coupons are printed on ordinary paper. At the end of October 1990, two days before the official introduction of the Ukrainian coupons, they were being sold openly at the main city market of Odessa. It was unclear whether these were counterfeits or genuine coupons that had escaped through the back door, since the authorities had just announced a decision to print an extra million. As an observer commented, 'In the present system the consumer is protected by precisely nothing'.[11]

[10]*Dialog* 1990, 2, p. 58.
[11]*loc. cit.*

The result is that people are increasingly dependent on the services provided by their work-places, especially in the countryside, where illicit help is more hard to come by. It is not always realised in the West quite how all-embracing these may be. Again the situation is utterly heterogeneous. No matter if the old Victory Collective Farm has renamed itself the Victory Agrarian–Industrial Firm, one must look closely at the individual farm to see what the reality is. In September 1990 I returned to the Karl Marx Collective Farm in Barguzin, Buryat ASSR, where I had first done fieldwork in the 1960s.[12] I found that it was now rather successful, having undergone a period in the doldrums in the 1970s. But the striking fact was that it was organisationally almost entirely unchanged. Even the Chairman was the same man as in 1967, and the other officials had merely shifted round among the top jobs. As in the old days, what I called the 'manipulable resources' (the surplus product over the amount supplied to the state under the plan-order) were used to provide services for the members as the Chairman saw fit. In this case he had decided on cultural investment: a magnificent club had been provided, an ethnographic museum built, an integrated Buryat educational programme was under way in the schools, and a sports stadium was under construction. But Gorbachev's agricultural reforms were here resolutely refused. Although one or two young men had managed to winkle out lease-hold fields, they were of such low quality as to discourage all but the most determined, and the Chairman was adamant that classic collectivised farming was the only realistic possibility in Siberian conditions.[13] Indeed, he, like most farm chairmen I met, saw individual farming as a threat: it would claim his best workers, who would put their energies into their own profits rather than those of the collective farm. Such bosses will certainly oppose any new law on individual land-ownership.

On the other hand, in the relatively untypical Bodongut State Farm, also in Buryatia, the Chairman had gone over to the lease-hold system entirely, even before it became government policy. The farm was divided into 22 lease-hold brigades. Darmayev's calf-raising brigade, for example, last year sold produce worth 90,300 rubles to the state via the farm. During the year the four families in the brigade lived on an advance worth 15 per cent of their estimated income. Payment for any farm machinery used, for fodder, and for amortisation, housing and repairs was deducted from the 90,300 rubles at the end of the year. The rest of the income belonged to the families, to dispose as they wished. For this system to be profitable to the farm, the accounting office had laboriously to work

---

[12]See Caroline Humphrey, *Karl Marx Collective: Economy, Society and Religion in a Siberian Collective-farm* (Cambridge, 1983).
[13]His arguments, which were echoed by several other farm Chairmen I met, have a good deal of force. They were that local infrastructure (roads, housing, electricity) were all centralised, that technology (tractors, milking machines, etc.) was not available in the numbers or types required for small-holdings, and that the workers had become specialised in their abilities and were no longer capable of mixed, independent farming.

out two new internal sets of prices. Taking into account the prices paid to
the farm by the state for deliveries of the plan-order, the farm had to set,
for each item, its own prices paid to the lease-holders for their products
and the set of prices at which the workers acquired machinery, fodder,
etc. from the farm. The result in this case was a brilliant success.[14] The
farm made such a profit that it was able to provide thousands of rubles to
its workers for loans to build houses and acquire private livestock, to pay
each year 300 rubles to mother-heroines, 200 rubles to families with many
children, 130 to war invalids, 100 to veterans, to provide paid maternity
leave for three years for each child, to hire a farm postman, club worker
and kindergarten staff, to build a medical centre, a general store, and an
abattoir and meat-packing shop.

What these two otherwise different farms had in common is the decisive power of the Chairman. This has undoubtedly grown recently with
a relative weakening in the authority of the Communist Party – not that
there are any other political parties in much of provincial Russia as yet.
Both men had translated their economic authority sideways into politics:
the Chairman of the Karl Marx Collective was also executive head of the
local Soviet and the Chairman of Bodongut was an elected deputy to the
Soviet of the Buryat ASSR. The relationship between political power and
the heads of local enterprises and organisations in the provinces deserves
some further discussion.

A recent article in *Argumenty i Fakty* (no. 37, 1990, p. 4) shows that
huge areas of Siberia[15] have what the journal calls a negative democratic
coefficient, meaning that their deputies to the First Congress of People
Deputies of the RSFSR voted more with the 'Kommunisty Rossii' bloc
than with the 'Demokraticheskaya Rossiya' bloc. According to this calculation,[16] while the average for the whole RSFSR was +7, and Moscow had +29, the central Siberian regions ranged between −10 in Irkutsk
Oblast to deep 'lows' in the two Buryat National Okrugs (−72 and −100
respectively). Too much should not be made of this. Nevertheless, the
authors of the article, A. Sobryanin and D. Yur'yev, make the point that
the election laws have made close tie-ups between the local *nomenklatura*
and the deputies extremely likely, since candidates were proposed and
supported within local enterprises and institutions to begin with. Many
intellectuals I met, both Buryats and Russians, were disappointed with
the quality of their deputies, whom they saw as 'toadies' of an archetypal

[14]Some farms, and brigades within them, have failed to make ends meet with the lease system, resulting in 'on paper' bankruptcies. At present these, and the 'family contracts' are
still covered by loans from the state (see C. Humphrey 'Perestroika and the pastoralists',
Anthropology Today, June 1989). Observing these failures, the vast majority of farms
have stayed firmly with the old collective system.

[15]Namely, Tuva ASSR, Irkutsk Oblast, Evenk National Okrug, Yakut ASSR, Buryat
ASSR, Chita Oblast, Aga Buryat National Okrug, Ust-Ordynsk Buryat National Okrug,
Amur Oblast, Khabarovsk Krai, and the Jewish Autonomous Oblast.

[16]Reckoned as follows: if a delegation contained 20 members and voted on 10 issues, 130
votes for the democratic position and 70 votes for the communist one (i.e. 65 per cent
and 35 per cent), then the coefficient of the region would be (+ 65) + (− 35) = + 30.

Soviet kind, minor officials, factory-workers or shepherds supported by a deluded electorate, mainly on the basis of their class or ethnic background. The point is that by this same token, which makes such deputies people of 'our' sort and hence kindly viewed by the working-class electorate, they are also subject to the very practical and definite powers of the local bosses. In some cases, of course, deputies are not just the subordinates of the regional *nomenklatura* but are these masters themselves. Thus, for example, by far the most important man in the Aga Buryat National Okrug is Ts. N. Nimbuyev, who is both a member of the Presidium of the Supreme Soviet of the USSR and the Chairman of the group of Agro-Industrial Firms (collective farms of old) of Mogoitui district, the richest area of Aga. As his biography shows,[17] his political career has been stormy and his inclinations are by no means conservative – and this is why the 'democratic coefficients' mentioned above may be misleading – but what is clear is that he emerged through the traditional institutions and he has a rock-solid local power base.

The rapid personnel changes of Moscow and Leningrad in recent years have not been copied everywhere in the provinces. It is difficult to generalise about this, because clearly regions differ markedly from one another. But it is possible to see that in eastern Siberia, at any rate, the stability of cadres at district (raion) and even regional (oblast, ASSR) levels has several institutional supports. One important factor is the ability of the Communist Party to marginalise new independent and democratic movements. Although the Party has lost both legitimacy and members recently, it still provides the training (perhaps 'inculcation of a political culture' would be a better expression) considered necessary in the provinces for someone to be considered by local masters as 'one of us' – or to challenge them on their own terms. A period as a Party instructor is a regular part of most higher careers, whether the person then goes back to work in an productive enterprise or on to a political post. Party officials within local institutions are not much more than keepers-of-order for the director or chairman, but

---

[17]Nimbuyev, a Buryat, started life as a shepherd and then a construction worker in a kolkhoz in Aga. He had no father at home and left school early to support his brothers and sisters. He joined the Komsomol, went to a technical school for evening classes and returned to the farm to work as a Brigadier. He entered the Party and soon was made Party Secretary of the farm. Then, after as spell as an instructor at the Raikom Party headquarters he was nominated Chairman of Red October collective farm. This farm was apparently tottering on the edge of total collapse and had had forty Chairmen in forty years, but Nimbuyev started up a leasing system (five years before perestroika) and got good results. He built houses and clubs for his workers. He also instituted democratic reforms, elections for key farm posts. Soon all this aroused the ire of the Chita Obkom Party, but Nimbuyev went to Moscow and personally argued his case there. In the recent Soviet elections he was opposed by the chairman of the Obispolkom, but because of his good relations with the workers was able to organise a successful campaign. Recently he was able to arrange a 40 million ruble grant for Aga from the central government, arguing that this was in fact only repayment of a debt to Aga, which for decades had been supplying meat to the state at low prices and getting nothing in return.

at higher levels the jowly Brezhnev look-alikes of the Party are still the people who can get things done. This is partly because they have funds, buildings, cars, manned and working telephones and traditional authority at their disposal, and partly, perhaps, because the new deputies are unsure as yet of their rights (and so, therefore, is everyone else). Furthermore, it is not always realised by those whose main knowledge of Soviet society comes from the major cities, to what extent the various local authorities are practically intertwined with one another. They are often, perhaps usually, housed in the same or adjacent buildings and use the same facilities. For example, in the Aga Buryat National Okrug, all of the important institutions of Mogoitui district, the Party Raikom, the Rai-Soviet, the trade unions head, the education authority, the Agro-Industrial Union, the procurator, the Red Cross, the bureau of statistics, and so forth, have their home in various offices within one strange red fort-like building of modernistic design. It is outside town and can be reached only by car (or a long trudge on foot, a sure sign that a person is not 'one of us'). These people are in touch with their colleagues in the countryside, whom they telephone with advance warning of visits by officials, or summon to frequent meetings.

This situation is compounded by national political traditions. In the Tuva ASSR, for example, clan loyalties are still strong, and everyone knows that clan A controls this district, clan B that district, that clan C dominates in cultural institutions in the city, and that clan D has provided the ASSR leadership for generations. In Buryatia, clan loyalties have little political significance, but here traditional domination by a geographical group, the 'Western Buryats', who had earlier and closer contacts with the Russians during the Tsarist period, still obtains. Although the 'Western Buryats' come from Irkutsk Oblast, outside the Buryat ASSR, they entirely dominate political life in the ASSR. The resentment aroused by this situation among the local 'Eastern Buryats', who are Buddhists rather than Christians converted by Tsarist missionaries, is now coming into the open, and it is they (who maintain supremacy in the Aga Okrug) who are now exploiting their 'eastern' cultural links by making business deals with Mongolia and China (see below). Perhaps we could conclude that it is because of the strength of traditional national élites in areas such as Buryatia and Tuva, for generations adapted to working within the single Communist Party system, that new parties have so far failed gain power (in Buryatia they had yet to emerge at all by autumn 1990).

Such a local nexus of bureaucrats and managers is not necessarily 'conservative' in the sense of wishing to return to a centralised economy. Some Buryats, including the officials of Aga, are eagerly seeking new international economic links and have set in train their own business deals with Mongolia and China. These innovative ventures include the introduction of Chinese contract labour not only to produce vegetables for local consumption, but also to make furniture which can be sold or exchanged elsewhere in the Soviet Union.[18] But local élites are self-protective and determined to hold on to their power, and this means not only that they oppose new 'free' organisations and upstart deputies (who might switch new opportunities to themselves), but also that they tend to be disciplinarian with regard to their own 'subject' work-forces. In this they have a great deal of leeway.

It may be surprising to some readers that so little has changed in this respect since the 'period of stagnation'. As in the 1960s and 1970s[19] patronage is still distributed through spreading networks of kin. Furthermore, a factory director or farm chairman can still get rid of workers, or alternatively effectively prevent them from leaving, even though this is against the labour laws. In the former case he can make life impossible by withholding essential benefits (e.g. coupons, housing, or, in the case of farms, the *uchastok*, the vegetable plot). In the latter case, if he wants to keep a worker he can simply refuse to sign the *prikaz ob uvolneniya* (discharge decree) without which it is very difficult for the worker to find a new respectable job.[20] Many people are kept inside the 'suzerainty' primarily by housing problems. Even Siberian cities require residence-permits and all have immense waiting-lists for accommodation. Farms and factories, on the other hand, provide housing for their workers. The kind of people tied in this way are families with children, and the sort of people who can, and do, leave are young men and women who are prepared to travel, squat in friends' apartments, and take risks. Let me give an example of a person tied against her will, the source being an editor from a readers' letters department of a local newspaper. The woman in question had four children, no husband, and lived on a collective farm. She had had no work provided by the farm for three years and the reason for this was simply that she had quarrelled with the chairman. She lived on the 35 rubles pension of a mother with young children and the produce from her vegetable plot, a miserable existence. But she could not move, though the farm was willing to let her go, because her house was there. She complained of her lot to the newspaper, but her letter was not published, because, as the editor said, 'We have far too many of such terrible stories'. Dictatorial actions by chairmen

[18]I met a delegation of Chinese officials being entertained lavishly by managers in Aga and also several workers, most of whom knew not a word of Russian. Although the Chinese workers live insulated lives in their own barrack-type accommodation there has reportedly been some hostility towards them from local people and some of the contracts have been discontinued for this reason. However, the search for advantageous international deals continues to be very active. A group of Buryats, including delegates from the Ust'-Ordynsk and Aga National Okrugs as well as the Buryat ASSR, are planning a visit to Australia to make contact with Buryat emigres there. This was aimed not just at reviving links with compatriots but at some kind of hard-currency financial help.

[19]Humphrey, *op. cit.*, pp. 333–52.

[20]The work-place is allowed to retain 'essential labour' for two months according to law, but in many cases this can in fact be dragged on for an indefinite period.

within their own domains are frequently given protection by other local authorities.[21]

Although there is nothing new about this particular situation, farms and other enterprises have now become economic sub-systems with noticeably greater autonomy than previously. They can make their own peculiar internal arrangements. For example, I went into one farm general store and saw, prominently displayed against a rack of ordinary coats, a few glossy furs and shiny Japanese anoraks. They had notices pinned to them: they were only for sale to people who had sold 300 kilos of potatoes or 70 kilos of meat to the farm. But the Bodongut state farm went much further. It *printed its own money*. All internal transactions in the farm were paid in this money, which was only converted into rubles at the end of the year when the farm itself was paid by the state. The initial reason for this internal money was that no-one would give the farm a loan to pay its first year advances to the lessee brigades, but it continued to be used because, as the Chairman said, it prevented people and rubles seeping out of the farm during the working year.

A Soviet legal specialist has summed up the situation:

'Empty shop counters, as history tells us, are the initial syndrome of social discontent. Towns, oblasts, republics are fencing themselves off with palisades of rationing in defence against 'migratory demand', they are bringing in nothing more or less than 'buying tickets'. The scale and consequences of this mutual alienation are unpredictable. A large number of people support such methods, and mass consciousness brands those who penetrate into 'foreign' enclaves of the rationed market through a prism of confrontational mythology as *pokupanty* [a pun, combining the idea of those who buy up too much, *pokupat'*, with occupying forces, *okkupanty*, C.H.] or *plyushevyi desant* (plush landing-forces) .... In almost every region such epithets are widespread. The market is divided-up, and aggressive particularism is growing'.[22]

What are the relations between these defensive 'suzerainties'? It should be noted:

1. That their 'manipulable resources' are frequently goods and labour rather than money.
2. That the law gives little protection to informal contracts.

[21]For example, a farm chairman in provincial Russian driving through his lands found one of his cowherds sleeping under a tree, completely drunk. The cows had wandered off and trampled a field of buckwheat. Infuriated, the chairman strung up the cowherd in the tree by his jacket and drove off. On his way back, he found the cowherd blue in the face and on the point of death. The cowherd subsequently complained to the Party secretary of the local town. The official listened to his story and said, 'Come back in two days'. He then rang the farm chairman and agreed to fix the matter. When the aggrieved cowherd reappeared, he said, 'We'll support your complaint if you still wish to make it, but if you do there will be a fine of X rubles for the ruined buckwheat'.

[22]A. B. Vengerov, writing in *Dialog*, 1990, 2, p. 58.

3. The virtual absence of commercial banks in the provinces.
4. The controls still exercised over farm markets.
5. The inequalities in access to scarce resources between regions.

It is these conditions that give rise to barter and the operations of the 'Mafia'. As governmental decrees become less effective[23] the sheer number of informal contracts has risen, and it is these in particular that are neither serviced by banks nor protected by the law.

Factories and farms have always, if they are at all successful, ended the year with some manipulable resources in products. In the past the state plan-order was supposed to mop up all such assets, but now that enterprises are all officially based on self-accounting it is official policy to allow them to dispose of their surplus as they see fit. In theory this could be done through the medium of money. Similarly, individual citizens with disposable assets (potatoes they have harvested, a dacha they wish to change, etc.) could use money. But in practice they frequently do not, and one reason is the absence of both commercial banks and personal bank accounts.

In the USSR today there are only a handful of banks *offering services* to individuals or institutions, and none in places like Buryatia, as far as I know. Sberbank SSR, Promstroibank SSR, Agroprombank SSR and the other state banks still play a traditional role. This means that they do not trust customers who might wish to bank with them, indeed they restrict access by placing fearsome militiamen at their doors to examine identity documents. In effect they still operate virtually entirely on instructions from above. They are ordered to finance X or Y project, and they do so, without regard for its further viability (this is one reason why so many construction projects lie unfinished in the Soviet Union). State banks even liquidate the assets of enterprises, or move funds between the accounts of various customers with impunity. Not surprisingly there is a widespread desire to keep out of their grasp. Individuals can place their money in a savings bank, but this is not a bank account as we know it. There are no cheque books and the idea of making loans available to people who ask for them on their own initiative is a novelty. Rather than see their money eaten away by inflation people are increasingly turning to saving in commodities (for example, gold).

The result is that both enterprises and individuals turn to barter. This

---

[23]The desperate attempts of the old system of decrees to maintain control is illustrated in relation to the 1990 potato harvest in Buryatia. Heavy rains during the late summer made the fields water-logged and delayed the harvest. As usual in such situations the ASSR government declared a situation of emergency and ordered all institutions such as schools and institutes to send labour to the fields. What was unusual this year is that the government increased the rates of pay, lowered the work-norms, and ordered farms to pay the helpers on time (!). But this was not sufficient to make enough people come out. Meanwhile city-dwellers needed potatoes. The result was that many people made their own arrangements with the farms, harvesting in return for a direct payment in potatoes. Many farms were in such disarray that they turned a blind eye to people simply helping themselves in the fields.

is not a new phenomenon, but it is growing.[24] In farms and factories barter has always been essential to maintain production, not just to dispose of surpluses. Simultaneous barter is the kind of contract which can best dispense with trust. It has no need for the generalised trust epitomised by confidence in the value of a national currency. The transactors see what is on offer, come to an agreement, swap their products, and can then walk away from the deal never to meet again. However, such direct barter is extremely rare, especially in agricultural economies. This is because the various products are available at different times of year, and because, since agriculture is cyclical and needs for supplies recur, it makes sense to repeat exchanges with the same partners rather than seek new ones each year. Unlike simultaneous barter, delayed barter or repeated barter requires a high degree of trust and fair-dealing. Only this can ensure that a return is made later for an item given today, or that both sides will wish to repeat the transaction in the next cycle. As a result transactors tend to establish exchange networks with 'known people'. But these can never provide the fluid, all-pervasive links of a monetary system, since they are limited by these very personalised relations, by the lack of generalised trust and information. Barter, therefore, is not only a symptom of a disintegrated economy but also perpetuates it.[25]

All barter, whether immediate or delayed, requires information as to what is available where, when, and at what rates. In the Soviet Union this is provided not by central exchanges but by special individuals or departments within each enterprise. These 'supply departments' as they are known are staffed by highly-valued people, *snabzhentsy* (suppliers) or *tolkachi* (pushers). Their task is to travel round the country getting information and making deals. Although the products transacted may be valued in rubles no money changes hands. Let us take an example. In the Aga Buryat Autonomous Okrug the eastern region is treeless steppe-land where sheep-farms produce wool and meat, the western part is heavily wooded. Farms of the two regions have set up their own regular exchange relations whereby meat and wool are exchanged for timber and fodder. Barter can be combined with the system of 'orders' and this may result in further trading. It can also be used to pay for services as well as goods. Such arrangements have their own vocabulary. *Barternaya sdelka* (barter exchange) is a respectable term for an open arrangement, often made 'with a (written) agreement' (*s dogovorom*). But a simple *sdelka* is perhaps more shady, and *sgonoshit'sya* is to come to some definitely private agreement.

The barter contracts are unregulated by the state and exchange ratios vary from year to year. As one farm director from Aga told me smugly, his single state farm producing meat was now worth more than all of the seven timber and fodder producing farms put together. Thus although

[24]Soviet friends told me that around 60 per cent of the Soviet economy is conducted by barter. This seems an exaggeration, but it shows how the phenomenon is perceived today whatever its actual dimensions.

[25]C. Humphrey, 'Barter and economic disintegration, *Man*, March 1985.

barter establishes little pools of trust and mutual help, it does not necessarily save a transactor from relative decline engendered by the wider external economic situation. The whole system is carried out in circumstances of doubt about its legality and merges with a new generalised sense of uncertainty.

As a lawyer from Buryatia has recently written:

'Why has it happened that we are building the law-governed state (*pravovoye gosudarstvo*) with the help of . . . ever spreading legal nihilism, and they even try to persuade us that this is a natural process? In countries with a developed parliamentary tradition corrections to the Constitution take years to work out, but we are prepared to take them up almost by ear. The next step is quite logical – generally to ignore the law in favour of some 'higher goal'. Republics and regions of the country are establishing their own acts in contradiction to the Constitution. And not just regions! Districts, even village Soviets give out declarations of their sovereignty, with the obligatory paragraph: the laws of all higher organs of power will be effective in their territory only after local ratification. This means chaos. . . . Rolan Bykov recently said to Gorbachev that one presidential decree is lacking, a decree which could provide the fundament of unity for all republics - on the sovereignty of the individual.

. . . But would such a decree help when our people do not even understand that chaos does not lead to freedom but to dictatorship, that a man cannot count himself free unless he knows that his house is protected from a disaster, that he cannot be driven from his work because of what he looks like, that his right to elect and be elected is secure? We need a state which can guarantee these elementary human rights. A state is powerful when its subjects can not only insult it but can also observe its laws, and, if they are imperfect can change them only by parliamentary means, being guided by that wise principle which preserves stability, "The law may be bad, but it is the law" '.[26]

Concern with freedom/sovereignty at the level of government has resulted in a situation which effectively 'legalises' (or makes unprosecutable) hitherto criminal activities. Let us take 'speculation', for example. Speculation involves buying something in one place, taking it to where there is greater demand, and selling it at a higher price. It has always been illegal (because no good productive labour adds value in the process) and today in theory still is so. But what about barter, which could be seen as speculation doubled, and carried out by officials at that?

Most people have no objection to barter, but they do feel very strongly about the new co-operatives (small private firms) which are only a step away. Co-operatives, to look at things from the outside, could be a

---

[26]A. Subbotin, writing in *Pravda Buryatii*, 7 October 1990, p. 2.

solution to many of the problems of Soviet distribution. But in provincial Russia, as elsewhere, they are widely disliked, mistrusted, and even feared. Partly this is because of their great financial gains: according to a recent estimate the state paid five milliard rubles to farms for food grains last year but the co-operative sector had an income of 40 milliard.[27] The author's cry, 'Yet we all eat bread!' explains a great deal. No one in the west expects bread producers to be very rich, even at subsidised state prices, yet in Russia different, age-old values prevail. Many co-operatives are involved simply in moving scarce products around the country, in pure 'speculation' in Soviet terms, or in the production of low-quality, yet glamorous, goods which are then sold expensively. When this is done by an officially-registered co-operative it is not illegal, but legitimate business. No wonder ordinary people are dismayed. From this it is another short step to 'Mafia-type' operations. These have homed-in even more specifically to areas of extreme demand and vulnerability, but the point is that these foci for threatening activity are multiplying with increased scarcity. So it is not just the expected areas of drugs and prostitution which see such operations, but also meat sales in town markets, black-market alcohol, Western-fashion clothing, taxi-networks (particularly in cities where there are foreigners with dollars, or where there is petrol scarcity), video-parlours, and home and vehicle repairs.[28] There is even a specialist area of 'queue-management', which consists of taking money from people who do not have time to stand for days or weeks themselves.

In everything that has been said it is apparent that belonging to a 'suzerainty' is almost a necessity, even if it results in dependency, even if some people can perceive the general social alienation involved. How else to get 'orders' or 'coupons', let alone somewhere to live? In effect, this means having a steady job, and preferably an established position under a powerful and successful boss. But many people do not have such jobs. Pensioners, the disabled, school-leavers without training or diplomas, demobbed soldiers and refugees from areas of civil unrest may find themselves out in the cold. Ex-prisoners find it almost impossible to get good jobs. In many areas of the RSFSR this problem of dislocation has become aligned not just with social class, or the penumbra of great cities, but specifically with ethnic boundaries.

This is not invariably the case. Some non-Russian cultures encourage their own forms of integration. The Buryats and Yakuts have both strong ties to the land, hence relatively stable and loyal populations in collective farms, and also have a tradition of literacy and thus include a large administrative/intellectual class well integrated into regional institutions. This has a historical dimension in that the Tsarist government gave land

[27] *Dialog*, 1990, 2, p. 73.
[28] It is difficult to tell to what degree ordinary people's fears about these operations are justified. However, I certainly met several householders whose flats were in disrepair, who were unable to arrange for official repairs, and yet were afraid to ask for help from a cooperative because they thought their homes might be ransacked.

rights to these nationalities on a 'clan' basis[29] and encouraged ties with the state in other ways.[30] The Koreans, to take another example, have maintained their tradition of intensive vegetable cultivation, for which they were originally encouraged to come to Siberia in the nineteenth century, and now they successfully engage themselves as temporary summer brigades all over the RSFSR, returning home during the winter to live on the proceeds.

But we find the reverse case in Tuva.[31] Here there is a particularly entrenched political élite, much separated from ordinary people. Young Tuvinians do not want to work on the farms and yet many of them have not adapted to the urban work-ethic either. Rootless gangs of young men, with no jobs or only temporary employment, roam the towns, living any way they can. These days people do not dare wear valuable fur hats in Tuva for fear they be snatched from their heads; muggings, knifings, and attacks on buses and cars are common. It is this anomie which lies at the base of the Tuvinian 'nationalist' riots, which have caused hundreds of Russians to flee the province. In fact, there is no real Tuvinian nationalist party or political agenda, though one may develop.[32] The situation is that many young Tuvinians simply resent the Russians: it is Russians, who are better trained and more culturally attuned to industrial work who dominate in the 'suzerainties' and who have access to better facilities, especially accommodation, and it is mainly Tuvinians who find themselves left outside.

Furthermore, Tuvinians, amongst whom worship of sacred mountains, rivers, trees and springs is virtually universal, hate the Russians for their careless attitude to the environment. The dislike extends to Russified Tuvinians. For example, gangs frequently stop someone in the street with a simple question; unless the answer is given in fluent Tuvinian, the person may be knifed or even shot. In provincial Russia hunting guns are to be found everywhere, and these days they are frequently stolen and taken to the cities. The stated reason for concerted attacks is often economic, especially the smuggling in of vodka, and there have been serious economic results.

As already noted, Tuva is subject to the 'dry law' while neighbouring regions are not. Until recently construction projects, entirely staffed by well-paid Russians, have provided a cover for the smuggling in of vodka

[29]By 1917 these 'clans' were to some extent a legal fiction, since the mid-19th century allocation ceased to correspond to actual population distribution, but nevertheless the system gave all Buryats a sense of having a home territory even if they did not live in it.

[30]This was done through Orthodox missionising, education, and the awarding of titles, etc. to native rulers.

[31]Tuva, then known as Tannu-Tuva or Uryanghai, was part of the Manchu Empire until 1911 and only formally joined the Soviet Union in 1944. Its peoples have consequently been subject to Soviet norms for a shorter time than elsewhere is Siberia.

[32]There is a rather disorganised movement called the Democratic International Movement of Tuva, headed by Dr. Kaadyr-Ool Alekseyevich Bicheldey, an historian, but it is not this which lies behind the attacks on Russians; what he wants is just to revive the culture of the Tuvinians.

together with building supplies. So violent have been the attacks on the workers and lorry-drivers by resentful Tuvinians that many Russians have lost their lives. Factories and mines staffed by Russians have had to close as the workers have fled in panic. In reprisal the neighbouring, and much richer, Russian regions have halted all capital investment in Tuva. Poor Tuva has hardly any paved roads, few bridges, and much of the rural population lives in felt yurts.

Russians also attack native peoples for directly economic motives. All over the forested regions of Siberia there are logging enterprises (*lespromkhoz*). They are entirely Russian staffed and have begun to be much resented by native peoples as the swathes of desolation become more and more apparent. The Udegei are hunters living in the Amur River region and for them destruction of the forest is the destruction of their subsistence and way of life. With the new political conditions their protests apparently met with some positive response from the local authorities. The reaction of the Russians in the logging village to this threat that their enterprise might have to close was to cut off the supply of electricity to the Udegei village.[33] Such disputes are everywhere and are bound to increase, since there is as yet no effective law in the RSFSR to establish rights to land for any group apart from the state.

One result of all this 'aggressive particularism' is that 'protection' of various kinds is emerging all through society. This is not the night-watchmen of old, but new organisations and rackets, staffed it seems often by the very dislocated people who have lost their footholds in the 'suzerainties'. The old underworld is prominent, but so are former soldiers and even ex-members of the KGB. Local bosses may be important employers of the more legitimate forms of protection. The chairman of another Buryat collective farm where I did fieldwork in 1967 had fairly recently been shot by angry workers. The precise reasons are not known, but it is easy to see that the immense power of such bosses over ordinary lives might give rise to occasional, or even not so occasional, acts of violence, especially when there is the hazy and exciting idea of 'democracy' around.

We are witnessing the falling apart of civil society in Russia. Local defensiveness in economic, social and political spheres in the result. Many of the ethnic movements of small minorities in Russia are primarily defensive in character. Their aim is to preserve or resurrect different cultures, not to impose on the Russians. But every barrier which is raised (or to put this in the language used in Russia itself, these 'pallisades' surrounding 'icebergs' or 'apange princedoms', this view of outsiders as locust-like 'occupying forces' buying-up everything in sight), is also a barrier against the ultimate goal of the economic reforms, at least as envisioned by metropolitan liberals. It is difficult to see how a free market, even a relatively free market, can be attained through

[33]Valery Sharov, Far Eastern correspondent of *Literaturnaya Gazeta*, personal communication.

the hedges of coupons, orders, and local barter systems which are now beginning to form a veritable maze. It is also difficult to see how genuine democracy can flourish when all except the bravest spirits among local deputies must take account, for themselves and their families, of the practical power of the masters of local domains. In the current state of combined ignorance, disregard, and mistrust of the law, no new merely legal edicts are likely to have much force for some time. The numbers of the economically 'disenfranchised' are growing, and they may become an increasing destabilising force. Perestroika has revealed historically entrenched political cultures and local 'suzerainties' forged in the Soviet period. Unless it succeeds in loosening and democratising them, rather than allowing them to align with ethnic divisions, as in Tuva, it is bound to fail in its aims.[34]

[34]An earlier version of this article appeared in 'Icebergs', barter, and the mafia in provincial Russia'. *Anthropology Today*, vol 7 no. 2, April 1991, pp. 8–13.

13
The state, nationalism and the nationalities question in the Soviet republics

Graham Smith

A turning point occurred on the 66th anniversary of the Soviet federation which threatens its undoing. Following the Gorbachev administration's decision to open up the previously closed society, ostensibly to facilitate 'reform from above', autonomous ethnoregional movements began to take shape throughout 1988, whose intentions quickly became the achievement of national self-determination for their communities, if not outright independent statehood. Such aims, accompanied by an escalation in ethnic demonstrations, violence and inter-ethnic conflict, have questioned the ability of the centre to retake control of the so-called nationalities question. As Gurr reminds us, 'rebellion from below' is not simply based on expectations greatly outstripping the capacity for attaining them, conditions already present and increasingly evident throughout the union republics. Rather, an organisation is also required with mass mobilisation potential capable and willing to challenge successfully the state's very legitimacy, a prerequisite already in place for the first time in the federation's history in the Baltic republics, Georgia, Armenia and Moldavia.[1]

Yet the polity bequeathed to the Gorbachev administration in 1985 was politically stable. This chapter begins by exploring the nature of this ethnoregional stability in the two decades preceding Gorbachev's succession, and then examines why the nationalities question can now be legitimately considered as representing probably the greatest crisis to befall the Soviet state in modern times.

Developed socialism and centre–periphery relations

During the Brezhnev-designated era of 'developed socialism', there was little evidence to suggest that nationalism posed a threat to the Soviet state. Confined mainly to dissident politics in the Ukraine and Baltic Republics, it was relatively easily contained by a state willing and able when necessary to use coercion. There were, however, other reasons why nationalism remained on the fringes of political life. Underlying this was the regime's preference for preserving the status quo over engaging in social and economic reform. Reflecting this conservatism of Brezhnev's rule and its ability to ensure social stability was the detectable emergence

[1]T. Gurr, *Why Men Rebel* (Princeton, 1970), p. 2.

of a new set of centrally-managed practices, which displayed some of the features of corporatist politics. As Bunce argues, developed socialism represented 'a corporate vision of a consensual society, in which conflict could be managed by deals struck between the state and functionally-based interests'.[2] Under state corporatism, the state imposes, rather than voluntarily enters into, relations with functional interest groups in order to pursue the aims and purposes of securing the conditions for economic growth, social stability and national cohesion. Such Soviet corporatist practices also reflected an important but neglected territorial dimension, in which a political compromise existed not only between the centre and the non-Russian union republic leadership but extended to union republic society through centrally declared social commitments. Three such components of centre-periphery corporatism are worthy of consideration: the relationship between the centre and the union republic leadership, regional policy and social welfare, and the function that the federal structure played in the social reproduction of native cultures and identities. Yet, as I will want to go on to argue the discordances challenging this centrally determined compromise were already evident before the election of the Gorbachev leadership.

A detectable change occurred in the character of centre-union republic leadership relations with the end of the Khrushchev administration. Under Khrushchev, relations were volatile and uncertain for both Moscow and the non-Russian republics in which it was not always clear to the republics' political leaders of the purpose behind Moscow's policies. A degree of regional economic autonomy had been granted, only to be taken away after the centre had lost control over the regions, while claims that nationality-based union boundaries 'were losing their former significance'[3] were interpreted by some as an attack on national statehood. Thus, in contrast to Khrushchev, who succeeded in complicating centre-periphery relations and in alienating local political leaders, Brezhnev engaged in extensive fence mending. There was, in effect, a willingness on behalf of the centre and republic leaders to administer their particular territorial and political spheres of influence. Republic *apparatchiki* wanted security of status and autonomy, while from the regions Moscow required political stability and commitment to moderate and more realistic republic economic growth. As part of its 'trust in cadres policy', Moscow was also prepared to allow greater flexibility in native appointments, a policy that facilitated the growth of patron–client networks within the arena of republic and local politics.[4]

[2]V. Bunce, 'The Political Economy of the Brezhnev Era', *British Journal of Political Science*, vol. 13 (1983), p. 134.
[3]*XXII S''ezd Kommisticheskoi Partii Sovetskogo Soyuza. Stenograficheskii otchet* (Moscow, 1961).
[4]See, for example, J. Moses, 'Regionalism in Soviet Politics: Continuity as a Source of Change 1953–83', *Soviet Studies*, Vol. 37 (1985), pp. 184–211; and M. Urban and R. Reed, 'Regionalism in a Systems Perspective: Explaining Elite Circulation in a Soviet Republic', *Slavic Review*, 43 (3) (1989), pp. 413–31.

This was also complemented by the less evident frequency of 'outsider' appointments to key republic posts. The type of Russian officials appointed also changed. In many cases they were either descendants of Russian settlers or had climbed to the top of the republican bureaucracy after serving time at its lower levels. Key posts in republic party and state organisations displayed far lower rates of personnel turnover, particularly among natives. In short, the centre's greater trust in native and local cadres made party and state life in the republics less uncertain and more comfortable. In return, the native political leadership could be relied upon to ensure regional stability.

Although the republic leadership closely identified with the centre's conservatism, they also were able to exercise influence. Lobbying for central allocations became an acceptable, indeed routinised, part of life.[5] Moscow was also prepared to examine initiatives and proposals from the regions, but issues which arose either from the centre or the periphery were to do with tinkering with current policies rather than with pushing for systemic changes. In all, the native political leadership were prepared to engage in politicising republic needs but only in so far as they did not undermine the Brezhnevite compromise. Moscow's policy of 'trust in cadres', combined with its increasing benign neglect of republic political and administrative life, had also furnished native leaders with a degree of power and patronage probably far greater than at any time in Soviet history. Local empire building, nepotism and widespread corruption became characteristic features of political and social life in many of the republics, particularly in Central Asia.

Corporatist features of centre–periphery relations were not just confined to the political apparatus. A number of centrally declared commitments within the general material and cultural sphere of social life also existed. This invariably represented a continuity from the previous regime, in which populist policies enabled social citizenship to remain important to regional stability. Full employment continued to be created for natives within their own republics, even where an over-abundance and over-concentration of particular skills existed. A regional policy, based on taking into account state commitment to fostering inter-regional equity in resource and investment allocations, also provided an important social weapon. During the 1970s, the non-Russian union republics were able to retain a higher proportion of their annual turnover tax than previously; in Central Asia's case, this meant retaining the full amount.[6] Yet, particularly from the late 1970s onwards, there were evident signs that Moscow was less prepared and able (in the absence of economic reform) to meet the growing social expectations, particularly of the demographically fast growing and least developed southern republics.

[5]D. Bahry, *Outside Moscow. Power, Politics and Budgetary Policy in the Soviet Republics* (New York, 1987).
[6]V. Koroteeva, L. Perepelkin and O. Shkaratin, 'Ot biurokraticheskogo tsentralizma k ekonomicheskoi integratsii suverennykh respublik', *Kommunist* 15 (1988), pp. 22–33.

In terms of relative levels of *per capita* consumption, in contrast to 1960 when the coefficient of variation between the republics stood at 0.10, by 1985 it had risen to 0.14, with the Russian and Baltic republics surging further ahead. This inability to realise through a purposeful regional policy fulfilment of the growing material expectations of Muslim Central Asia, was of increasing concern to many in both Moscow and the region. A decline in relative levels of growth in *per capita* consumption by the early 1980s compared with the 1970s, however, was affecting all republics, and in three republics (Lithuania, Turkmenistan and Uzbekistan) real *per capita* consumption actually fell.[7] There were, therefore, clear signs that the unprecedently high living standards reached throughout the republics could no longer be assured.

Preservation of those union republic institutional supports that facilitated the social reproduction of native cultures and the upward mobility of nationalities within their administrative homelands also constituted an important part of the social compromise.[8] In particular, reaffirmation of the federal structure by the Brezhnev regime following heated debates leading up to the formulation of the 1977 constitution as to whether nationality boundaries should continue to form a basis of social and economic life under developed socialism, meant that membership of the eponymous nationality-republic continued to provide territorial privileges for natives in further education, status employment and party membership. Such institutional supports were particularly vital given the growing social location of the titular nationalities throughout the Brezhnev years within the increasingly multi-ethnic and competitive environment of their native cities, precisely because assimilation into the dominant (Russian) culture was not a precondition of gaining position and status within their urbanised societies. Federalism also continued to ensure demand for a large native intelligentsia able to read and speak the native tongue. This community of native speakers continued to grow throughout this period and showed no signs of foregoing their native tongue for Russian in spite of the social pressures to communicate in the lingua franca of the state.[9] The continuation, then, of native-based republic institutions preserved niches for incumbents adhering to the native culture. This enabled ethnic divisions to remain an integral part and reference point of native public life and an organisational basis for reinforcing ethnoregional identities.

[7]G. Schroeder, 'Nationalities and the Soviet Economy', in *The Nationalities Factor in Soviet Politics and Society*, L. Hajda and M. Beissinger (eds.) (Boulder, 1990), pp. 43–71.
[8]V. Zaslavsky, 'Ethnic Group Divided: Social Stratification and Nationality Policy in the Soviet Union', in *The Soviet Union, Party and Society*, P. Potichnyi (ed.) (Cambridge, 1988), pp. 218–28.
[9]In the 1959–79 inter-censal period, the proportion of each union republic nationality declaring their namesake nationality language as their native tongue remained relatively static at over 98 per cent; only the two Slavic nationalities, the Ukrainians and Belorussians, recorded a lower proportion of native speakers, at 89.1 per cent and 83.5 per cent respectively. *Naselenie SSSR. Po Dannym Vsesoyuznoi Perepisi Naseleniya 1979 goda* (Moscow, 1980).

During the Brezhnev years, then, a native intelligentsia was able to flourish. Indeed, during this period it constituted the fastest growing social group within the union republics. Such representation was particularly notable in the culturally related professions like teaching and the arts,[10] which reflected employment opportunities available as a result of union republic status and of the monopoly that the native intelligentsia enjoyed over access to the language and culture of their indigenous communities (Russian migrants are notorious for their unwillingness to learn the eponymous language). The increasing nativisation of the upper echelons of republic life was not just restricted to the cultural professions; natives had also come to play a far more prominent role within the local economic, political and administrative machine. Moreover, this native social stratum contrasted with previous generations who had gained position more by their political credentials than by educational qualifications. Such changes reflected what Lewin has more generally referred to as Soviet society's urban revolution of the Brezhnev years, a process characterised by the growing strength in all spheres of public life of a new urban intelligentsia of diploma-holders who increasingly came to displace and challenge the hegemony of the previous social formation.[11]

Although the growth and interests of this ascendant stratum cannot be analytically divorced from the privileges which accrued from federation, neither centralism nor the erosion of cultural freedoms were likely to endear the humanistic intelligentsia to a social compromise which undermined professionalism or inhibited both their symbolic and material interests in the creation of a more culturally pluralistic and decentralised society. It is a stratum conscious of and frustrated by the tensions of the Brezhnev years: by a system which largely confines native mobility opportunities to the namesake nationality-republic; of an overly centralised production system stifling local professional initiative; of a migration policy which increasingly brought Russians into competition with natives for urban jobs, based on Moscow's lack of understanding of local labour markets and insensitivity towards the poor state of urban service provision and housing needs; of a culturally standardising centre (increasingly by the late 1970s) insisting on fluency in Russian as a necessary condition for professional employment and to expanding opportunities for the teaching of Russian in republic schools and universities; and of centrally managed and sectorally organised industrial ministries running roughshod over the local environment. It was this new social stratum (which, at least initially, identified with the Gorbachev revolution) that came to form Gorbachev's natural constituency of support. But it was also this stratum, particularly within the culturally related professions, which was to take advantage of the unfolding liberalising climate, and was to prove pivotal in demanding more than perestroika was prepared to deliver.

---

[10]Yu V. Arutunyan *et al.*, *Sotsial'no-kul'turnyi oblik Sovetskii Natsii (Po Materialam Etnosotsiologicheskogo Issledovaniya)* (Moscow, 1986), p. 66.

[11]M. Lewin, *The Gorbachev Phenomenon. A Historical Interpretation* (Berkeley, 1988).

Nationalism, in short, enabled this section of society to articulate the injustice of their arbitrary exclusion, and to forward a comprehensive ideology of appeal on behalf of their underprivileged co-nationals by appealing to the collective sense of nation-ness.

Perestroika and ethnoregional movements

Despite far-reaching proposals for economic modernisation, and later for social democratisation, the Gorbachev leadership continued to treat the nationalities question as of incidental concern. It was only when the reform programme triggered off growing ethnic discontent that Moscow was prepared to include the nationalities question in its political agenda. Thus, in his honeymoon first year as General Secretary, Gorbachev preferred to reiterate Brezhnev's faith in the deeply felt sense of belonging to 'a single family' (*Sovetskii narod*), and of the continuing flourishing and rapproachement of inter-ethnic relations.[12] At the 1986 twenty-seventh Party Congress he did go so far as to concede that success with the socio-economic convergence of the nationalities was not in itself sufficient to erase nationality-based identities, but this did not mark any departure from the viewpoints of either Brezhnev or Andropov.[13] In his programme for economic modernisation, which was extended at the Congress to include proposals for devolving economic powers to the larger nationality republics, no attempt was made to link such policy shifts to the nationalities question. In playing down the more balanced development of the regions, as part of his drive towards securing economic modernisation, Gorbachev chose to emphasise the continuing contribution of all republics to the development of an integrated Soviet economy which 'should match their developed economic and spiritual potential'.[14] Large-scale capital intensive projects, particularly important to the future of the less developed republics and regions, were either to be abandoned or given lower priority.[15]

Gorbachev's failure to give adequate weight to the possible problematic consequences of restructuring a multi-ethnic based society cannot simply be put down to the fact that he had no experience with the national question.[16] Although the first Soviet leader since Lenin without a career background in a non-Russian union republic, he was probably not totally inexperienced in handling ethnic issues. His duties as First Secretary of Stavropol town Komsomol, and as a member of the district

---

[12]M. Gorbachev, *Ibrannye rechi i Stat'i* (Moscow, 1985), p. 52.
[13]M. Gorbachev, *Politicheskii doklad tsentral' nogo komiteta KPSS XXVII S''ezdu Kommunisticheskoi Partii Sovetskogo Soyuza* (Moscow, 1986), p. 101.
[14]*Ibid.*
[15]See, for example, A. Bond, 'Spatial Dimensions of Gorbachev's Economic Strategy', *Soviet Geography* (1987), pp. 490–523.
[16]Z. Gitelman, 'The Nationalities', in S. White *et al.* (eds.), *Developments in Soviet Politics* (London, 1990), pp. 137–59.

Komsomol bureau, must have carried some responsibilities for overseeing the late 1950s resettlement of the Karachi and Cherkess peoples.[17] Whatever influence this might have had it did not detract from a naïve optimism characteristic of the occasional pronouncements which he made throughout the 1960s and 1970s on the nationalities question.[18]

For the new administration, reform was not simply to do with revitalising the Soviet economy in order to improve living standards. It was also to do with social justice.[19] Both were linked to ensuring social stability which also demanded reasserting central control over the republics and regions which had been weakened during the later Brezhnev years. In short, Moscow required a reform-minded and loyal party machine free from what was unacceptable local nepotism, corruption and empire-building. 'At some stage', Gorbachev noted at the 27th Party Congress, 'some republics, territories, regions and cities were placed outside the bounds of criticism . . . In the Party there neither are nor should be organisations outside the pale of control and closed to criticism, there neither are nor should be leaders fenced off from party responsibility.'[20] In stepping up Andropov's campaign to wipe out *razlozhenie* (abuse of power), a purge of largely Brezhnev era appointees, focusing on Central Asia and Kazakhstan, began on a scale not seen since Stalin's time.

Such reaffirmation of central control also illustrated the insensitivity of the Gorbachev leadership to nationality sensibilities. This was notably evident in Kazakhstan, where Russians outnumbered Kazakhs by 41 to 36 per cent. Following a series of criticisms from Moscow throughout the latter half of 1986, directed against the Republic Party and leading personnel concerning economic mismanagement, corruption and 'report padding',[21] the native First Party Secretary was replaced by a Russian from outside Kazakhstan, which broke with the hitherto All-Union convention of appointing a native to such a post. It also triggered off the December 1986 riots in Alma Ata, the first major blow from the ethnic periphery to the reform programme. From Moscow's point of view, bringing in an outsider in order to reassert control over a republic crippled by élite mismanagement and corruption may have made rational sense, but for many Kazakh, numerically outnumbered and limited in the social and economic opportunities open to them within their own homeland, it showed the new regime as insensitive to their particular needs.

From that point onwards, and as incidences of ethnic unrest unfolded across the country, the illusion of a multi-ethnic society living in cultural harmony was shattered. Throughout 1987, ethnic demonstrations

---

[17]Z. Medvedev, *Gorbachev* (Oxford, 1988), pp, 31–32.

[18]A. Motyl, 'The Sobering of Gorbachev: Nationality, Restructuring and the West', in S. Bialer (ed.), *Inside Gorbachev's Russia* (New York, 1989), pp. 149–73.

[19]V. Shlapentoch, 'The XXVIIth Congress – A Case Study of the Shaping of a New Party Ideology', *Soviet Studies,* vol. XL, No. 1 (1988), pp. 1–20.

[20]Gorbachev, *op. cit.* (1986), p. 157.

[21]*Pravda*, 7 July 1986, and 9 December 1986.

followed throughout the cities of the Russian and Baltic republics and in the Ukraine. It was not, however, until the Nagorno-Karabakh Soviet unexpectedly called for their region's transfer to neighbouring Armenia in February 1988 that Gorbachev was goaded into declaring that the national question was now a vital issue on the Kremlin's agenda.[22] Rather than incorporating the nationalities question into the reformist programme, Moscow simply dealt with each crisis as it arose on a case by case basis in an attempt to contain events in the regions. For the Kazakhs, this meant promises of better educational facilities for native language teaching and additional economic resources for the republic. At the same time, in response to Crimean Tatar demands to re-establish their homeland, a hurriedly constituted State Commission was set up which, although accepting the right of Crimean Tatars to resettle in the Crimea, rejected demands for the reinstatement of an administrative homeland.[23] As for the Armenian irredenta of Nagorno-Karabakh, recognition of the negative geopolitical spillover of meeting such demands resulted in a policy of muddling through, first by offering a regional development package, then, as the Armenian-Azeri conflict escalated and martial law proved ineffective, by transferring the enclave to direct control from Moscow in January 1989, only to cede control back to Azerbaidzhan ten months later, further fueling conflict over the disputed territory.

What was crucial to the emergence of nationalism as an organised political force, however, was the centre's acknowledgement that socio-economic reform could not be effectively implemented without civil society's participation as catalyst in facilitating 'reform from above'. Having disabled the state-censored society through the twin policies of glasnost' and democratisation, the centre in effect purposely invited a multi-ethnic society to engage in the making of perestroika, without having considered the likely repercussions of its actions. Thus the most remarkable feature of the new Soviet politics was the speed by which ethnoregional movements emerged to become a central focus of union republic political life.

To varying degrees, ethnoregionalism followed a three-stage pattern. Firstly, with the advent of glasnost', a national consciousness was reawakened. It enabled the nationalities to rediscover their history, to bring openly into sharp relief the long-held national beliefs and prejudices rooted in the collective imagination, and publicly to re-examine the reality of past and current ethnic inequities. The national, territorially organised media in particular played an important role at this stage, providing a distinctively republic-based focus on events and issues which did much to facilitate discussion within 'a national context' and to raise the consciousness of peoples around national concerns. Glasnost' also enabled a constellation of locally-based and issue-orientated informal

[22]*Pravda*, 18 February 1988.
[23]*Pravda*, 9 June 1988.

groups to emerge, espousing a variety of cultural, linguistic, environmental and other concerns, but whose rudimentary organisational scope and geographical appeal was confined to the parameters of the nationality-republic. At this stage, environmental groups, in particular, enjoyed a high profile. That they should have done so was not simply due to their organisational capabilities or to the political saliency of centrally-imposed environmental degradation, but also to the fact that at this early stage the environment was allowed on to the local public agenda because it was judged not to pose a direct challenge to regime legitimacy. Nor was environmental lobbying motivated solely by environmental concerns. For example, opposition to plans to construct a nuclear power plant in Western Latvia was also bound up with widespread concern in the republic that the project would bring in an estimated 40,000 labourers from other republics, thus reflecting the politicisation of more 'national concerns'.[24]

Stage two, beginning in the Baltic republics in mid-1988 but quickly spreading to Transcaucasia and Moldavia, and eventually to other republics, saw the mobilisation of issue orientated groups behind the republic-based Popular Fronts. Integral to their formation was the role of the cultural intelligentsia, with members of the Republic Union of Writers and Journalists invariably playing an initiating role. Although set up as movements in support of perestroika, to which Moscow gave its blessing, they quickly (although not exclusively) emerged to become movements championing ethnoregional interests and national autonomy. Increasingly, however, the Popular Fronts faced the dilemma of whether to prioritise the civic interests of those living and working within the republic or to orientate and secure support around the interests and demands of the titular nationality. This has necessarily meant that within the localities, for both the titular and minority nationalities, citizenship and the meaning and scale of national self-determination have emerged to become explosive issues.

The establishment of ethnoregionalism as a co-ordinated and organised political movement was followed in some republics by a third stage in which the 1989 and 1990 elections played a crucial part. This involved the increasing weakening and marginalisation of the local Communist Party and the emergence of the Popular Fronts as the focus of political power. In some republics, this entailed the fragmentation of the Communist Party, with its more radical wing throwing in support with the Popular Fronts, but even where the Communist Party still held on to power, Popular Fronts have been able to exert considerable pressure upon conservative political leaders who recognised that in order to exercise effective rule they would have to go along with at least some national aspirations. Setting the pace have been the Baltic republics, with Lithuania becoming the first nationalist elected government to declare its republic's political independence from Moscow. By the end of 1990, all

---

[24]*Padomju Jaunatne*, 3 June 1988.

fifteen union republics had declared their right to some form of political sovereignty (Table 13.1).

Table 13.1: **Sovereignty Declarations and Ethnoregional Linkages in the Union Republics**

Union Republic	Sovereignty declaration	Ethnoregional Linkage (Date of movement's foundation)
Russia (RSFSR)	June 1990	No single over-arching Russian nationalist movement, although the Russian Popular Front (founded December 1988) began as playing this role.
Estonia	March 1990	Estonian Popular Front (April 1988).
Latvia	May 1990	Latvian Popular Front (July 1988).
Lithuania	March 1990	*Sajudis* (June 1988).
Ukraine	July 1990	Popular Front of the Ukraine for Perestroika *(Rukh)* (November 1988).
Belorussia	June 1990	*Adradzhen'ne* (Renewal) (June 1989).
Moldavia	June 1990	Moldavian Popular Front (*Al Moldovei*) (January 1989).
Armenia	August 1990	Karabakh Committee (February 1988) superseded by the Armenian National Movement (Spring 1990)
Azerbaidzhan	September 1989	Azeri Popular Front (July 1988).
Georgia	November 1990	Committee for National Salvation (October 1989), but in May 1990 split into two organisations, 'The Round Table' and 'The Co-ordinate Committee'.
Kazakhstan	October 1990	Coalition of groups, the most prominent of which is the Nevada-Semipalatinsk Movement (February 1989).
Uzbekistan	June 1990	*Birlik* (Unity) (November 1988) but fell apart by May 1989.
Turkmenistan	Autumn 1990	*Agzybirlik* (Unity) (January 1990).
Kirgizia	Autumn 1990	*Ashar* (Openness) (July 1989)
Tadzhikistan	July 1990	*Ashkara* (Openness) (June 1989)

The conditions in which the Popular Fronts have been able and willing to mobilise support for national separatism does, however, vary from region to region. There is the extent to which the social bearers of nationalism – the cultural intelligentsia – can draw upon a sense of national community, based on a territorial relationship which subsumes other crosscutting cleavages (e.g. language, possibly religion, class/occupation, party/non-party membership, urban/rural divisions) in order that the communal sense of nation-ness can become politicised and mobilised behind the nationalist cause. Contained within the image of the nation must be the ideal of being sovereign, and economic viability is important. In this regard, notable differences exist between the Baltic and Central Asian republics.

In many respects it is not surprising that Gorbachev should first give his blessing to the setting up of popular movements in the Baltic in order to ensure the success of reform from above. Convincing the population of the necessity of perestroika and of the type of reforms which were identified as integral to its success was not difficult. The enterprise culture was no stranger to the Balts. Both private enterprise and the co-operative idea had formed an integral part of their national economies during the inter-war years of independent statehood, and under successive post-Stalin regimes, the Baltic republics had proven to be a receptive laboratory for market-orientated experimentation. The idea of opening up Soviet trade through joint ventures with foreign companies was also attractive to a region with a long history of western trade which could foresee the material benefits likely to accrue from such a reorientation. Moreover, in contrast to Russia proper and to many other regions, there already existed a pre-Soviet civic culture of democracy, embedded in the years of independent statehood, and one which is more conducive than in most other republics to facilitating political participation and pluralism. Gorbachev's five day 'meet the people' visit to Estonia and Latvia in February 1987, which included visits to factories and farms where co-operatives, private enterprises and more effective work practices were already in place, must have underlined for the General Secretary the potential receptiveness of the region to economic restructuring.[25]

The Popular Fronts that emerged in the Baltic republics, first in Estonia in April 1988 and then in Latvia and Lithuania in that summer, quickly became mass-based political movements moving from their initial position of vaguely talking about political and economic sovereignty to demanding independent statehood. That support for full national separatism should have so quickly emerged as commanding such mass political support had not only to do with the possession of a cultural intelligentsia willing to champion such a goal, but it was also able to draw upon a sense of nation-ness, embedded in national cultures which Soviet modernity had been unable totally to transpose, and national symbols of recent independent statehood. This provided nationalists with a yardstick with which to highlight contemporary social and economic inequities and a basis upon which to reconstruct society by appealing to a continuity with history. Moreover, the willingness of a native local Party leadership to open up Baltic society and to empathise with economic and political independence was also pivotal in putting national self-determination on to the agenda of federal politics; a process due largely to ethnodemographics, which proceeded more smoothly in Lithuania and Estonia than in Latvia. In many respects, for the Balts, achieving national separatism is similar

[25]See, for example, G. Smith, 'The Latvians', in G. Smith (ed.), *The Nationalities Question in the Soviet Union* (London, 1990), pp. 62–68.

to what Habermas has referred to as Eastern Europe's 'rectifying revolutions' of 1989, because it offers to fulfil the popular desires of connecting up with the inheritance of constitutional democracy and with the styles of commerce and life associated with late capitalism.[26]

In Central Asia the Popular Fronts have been far slower to develop and did not emerge as an important political force until 1989. Their duration has also been limited and they have tended to remain more fragmented, localised and issue-orientated, with environmental issues dominating much of the oppositional agenda. Consequently, their impact on republic politics has been more limited and the ability to influence the direction of their republics and that of the centre confined to more acceptable cultural, environmental and economic matters. Although gradually moving towards embracing greater economic and political sovereignty, the appeal of national separatism is limited.

The conservatism of the local party leadership has played its part in imposing limits on the effectiveness of grass roots organised opposition in Central Asia. Despite the high turnover in personnel following Gorbachev's anti-corruption policy, Moscow has been unable to retake control of the region or to rely on its political leaders to implement glasnost' and perestroika. This widespread reluctance amongst both society and political élites has much to do with a weak political culture of activism and tolerance of plurality, and of a native society deferential to authority. Besides actively discouraging the formation and development of Popular Movements, political élites have remained critical of the more radical stance taken by their Baltic counterparts, labelling developments there as unacceptable 'rally-type democracy', and raising the question as to whether Moscow 'made mistakes in our choice of the teachers of perestroika'.[27]

The belated and more volatile history of the region's Popular Fronts is also a product of more complex, cross-cutting and overlapping identities which weaken the potential for mobility behind peculiarly 'national interests'. One of the most pervasive in this regard concerns the relationship between an urban secular faith like nationalism and religion. For the small urban national intelligentsia, it has been a difficult task to reconcile politically these two dominant but inseparable orientations which pervade the consciousness of Central Asians. The mobilising potential and effectiveness of the region's largest Popular Front, the Uzbekistan-based *Birlik* (Unity) organisation, has been undermined by factionalism between its Islamic-orientated wing (whose frame of reference and appeal is trans-national and whose social base is more firmly rooted in the countryside) and by a national-orientated wing whose social location is more urban-based and which aims to promote the also often conflicting national and republic interests of Uzbekistan. In contrast

---

[26]J. Habermas, 'What Does Socialism Mean Today? The Rectifying Revolution and the Need for New Thinking on the Left', in *New Left Review*, No. 183 (1990), pp. 3–22.
[27]*Izvestiya*, 30 November 1988.

to the Baltic then, such cross-cutting social divisions inhibit mobilisation behind the cause of home rule in a region where national conscious-ness has had no prior relationship with national self-rule, and indeed, where, before the formation of Soviet-created administrative homelands, national identities were weakly developed. Finally, the autonomist appeal is circumvented by economic realism. In contrast to the Balts, who have long since viewed their relative overdevelopment as self-generated and their economic assistance to more backward regions as inhibiting the more balanced development of their economies, Central Asians treat economic self-reliance with caution. So although demands for greater economic self-management and distributive justice are openly couched in a language of Moscow-imposed internal colonialism, it is also recognised that without the material benefits of membership of the Soviet federation there would be little prospect of overcoming the increasing economic and social problems that the region now faces. It is therefore not surprising that since the notion of republic *khozraschet* ('self-accounting') was mooted at the June 1988 All-Party Conference, these aid-receiving repub-lics have been far from enthusiastic about restructuring their economies on a more regionally self-accountable basis.[28]

Federation as stratagem

Moscow's belated attempt to seize the initiative from the localities and incorporate the national question into the reformist agenda is a recog-nition that the ability to restore central initiative is inextricably bound up with perestroika's success. As Gorbachev noted in a 1989 summer address to the country, 'interethnic conflict threatens to determine, not only the fate of perestroika, but also the integrity of the Soviet state'.[29] Gorbachev's attempts to manage the national question should therefore be understood within the context of this inseparable linkage between saving 'the revolution from above' and preserving the Soviet Union's territorial integrity.

Rethinking the national question followed a similar logic to many other aspects of economic and political reform in which the 'command admin-istrative system' provided the framework for critique of past failings, and the return to Leninist principles as the basis for preserving the unity of a multi-ethnic polity and legitimising 70 years of Soviet socialism in the regions. It was not the original conception of Leninist federation which was deemed faulty, but rather 'the command administrative sys-tem' that followed it. As a leading 1989 article in *Kommunist* put it, Lenin's notion of national self-determination and social justice for the nationalities had never been effectively implemented, for it was the command-administrative system which was responsible for deviating from

[28]Koroteeva, *et al.* (1988), *op. cit.*
[29]Gorbachev's television speech, the text of which is reproduced in *Soviet News*, 5 July 1989, p. 218.

the path of preserving the right of nations to self-determination, and which caused the current nationality unrest.[30] As Gorbachev noted, the sources underlying present day ethnic tensions emanate from a variety of distortions and past acts of lawlessness, the result of which was a nationalities policy that displayed 'indifference towards ethnic interests, the failure to resolve many of the socio-economic problems of the republics and autonomous territories, deformations in the development of the languages and cultures of the country's people, the deterioration in the demographic situation, and many other negative consequences'.[31] Social scientists were also singled out for presenting an overly optimistic and misleading view of ethnic relations. As Bagramov, a nationalities expert now acknowledges, 'in practice, the sphere of national relations had been treated as if everything was harmonious and that which did not fit into this harmony was simply dismissed and stigmatised as a manifestation of bourgeois nationalism'.[32]

The Leninist ideal of federation, as eventually endorsed by the specially convened September 1989 plenum on the Nationalities, and as reflected in the more recently proposed New Union Treaty, forms the basis for Moscow's stratagem for managing the nationalities question. Fashioned in dialectical terms, it envisages a nationalities policy that simultaneously recognises the rights of nations to independence (*samostoyatel'nost'*) and the need to further the unity of Soviet society as a multi-ethnic socialist state.[33] Under a New Union Treaty, the republics would be able to choose voluntarily what powers to delegate to the centre and decide what republic laws have priority over All-Union laws, and vice versa. But this notion of renegotiating centre-union republic relations does not imply dismantling the present territorial arrangement followed by the establishment of a genuine confederation. To do so would in effect mean the *voluntary union* of the sovereign republics,[34] a strategy that would most certainly result in the end of the Soviet Union in its present geopolitical form. Moreover, although Gorbachev's federal stratagem includes the right of nations to secede from the Soviet Union, exercise of such a right would occur over a period of five years and would be subject to referenda in the national republics. It is thus a political strategy aimed at preventing secession, and one which Moscow is likely to pursue at all costs. Thus, consistent with Leninist thinking, the CPSU Central Committee Platform reaffirms the Party's commitment to Lenin's principle of the right of nations to national self-determination, including succession, and supports the adoption of a law on a mechanism for the exercise of this right (as passed by the Supreme Soviet in April 1990), but continues:

[30] *Kommunist*, No. 9 (1989).
[31] *Soviet News*, 5 July 1989, p. 218.
[32] *Pravda*, 14 August 1987.
[33] *Pravda*, 17 August 1989.
[34] For a fuller discussion, see S. Kux, 'Soviet Federalism', *Problems of Communism*, March/April 1990, pp. 1–20,

> 'We are convinced that the weakening and disruption of reciprocally diverse and inter-related ties could lead to negative consequences for all peoples, to say nothing about individual destinies – consequences that are very difficult to foresee. That is why we resolutely oppose separatist slogans and movements that could lead to the destruction of the great multi-ethnic democratic state.'[35]

Unless it preserves some of the mechanisms which ensured the preservation of empire, federalism is unlikely to contain the nationalities question and to alter the separatist goal of creating new nation-statelets in the Baltic and in Transcaucasia. Federalism requires agreement on shared sets of interests. Mutual economic advantage is certainly one that would accrue from an appropriately constructed looser economic federation, in which the Russian Republic would remain pivotal. But the idea, as proposed by the Russian parliament, of a voluntary reconstituted federation of states centred on Russia, the Ukraine, Belorussia and Kazakhstan, in which other republics could join if they wish, has no appeal to the Baltic republics, Moldavia and Georgia. They do, however, recognise that establishing sound economic relations with Russia and other like-minded republics is crucial to their future national economic well-being and have already gone some way to securing such a future by bypassing Moscow and signing economic treaties of co-operation.[36]

An impasse has therefore been reached between Moscow and the union republics in which a reconstituted federation whose architects seem incapable of freeing themselves from the psychological and political thinking of Leninism is unlikely to provide a means of reconciling the demands of particularistic nationalisms. Having given authority through economic sovereignty to the regions and permitted through glasnost' national rights and entitlements to be placed at the centre of the local agenda, Moscow is, in effect, trying to reclaim a federal initiative which for the more nationalistically-minded republics has little, if any, appeal. If this does not work, testing Gorbachev's resolve to preserve the Union at all costs[37] may mean sacrificing democratisation. The stratagem of imposing direct rule over problematic regions, which has already been employed in Nagorno-Karabakh, and one which was threatened in January 1991 to resolve the 'war of laws' between Moscow and the popularly elected national governments of the Baltic republics, would do little more than speed up the Soviet Union's disintegration. Whatever future shape Soviet federalisation takes, it is unlikely to be achieved in an orderly and controlled fashion.

---

[35]*Pravda*, 13 February 1990.
[36]*The Economist*, 1 February 1991; G. Smith 'The Soviet Union: a confederal treaty?', *Oxford Analytica*, March 1991, pp. 8–9.
[37]*Pravda*, 7 February 1991.

VI Foreign Policy

14

The Soviet Union as a revolutionary power[1]

Alexander Dallin

I

If we wish to explore whether the Soviet Union has been a revolutionary power in the international system – and if so, when and how – we first need to establish what we mean by revolutionary power. Several possible definitions come to mind.[2]

We may view as a revolutionary power in the international system a state that seeks to upset the status quo, presumably in favor of itself and of its (real or potential) allies. Such a definition would require us to include not only Hitler's Germany in the 1930s but also France in the days of Bismarck, after 1871. In these terms Russia would have to be adjudged to have been a revolutionary power after the Crimean War, and so would Japan prior to 1941. It is debatable whether the term 'revolutionary' should be applied to this category of states, but I will try to test its applicability to the Soviet period.

A second approach would limit the reference to states whose leaders were or are committed to remaking the world, or a significant part of it, in their own image. By extension, this would include appeals to class war, civil war, and/or revolution within other states. Such a definition would certainly include the Soviet regime in its early days, though for how long and at what price are questions that remain to be addressed.

It might well be argued that such a messianic definition would include other systems as well – at certain times even the United States in its commitment to the ostensible promotion of political democracy and human

[1]This draft was prepared during a residency at the Rockefeller Foundation's Study and Conference Center at Bellagio, Italy. It is based on research undertaken with the help of a grant from the Carnegie Corporation of New York. The author is profoundly grateful for both.
[2]I have not found a definition of a revolutionary power in any of the standard texts or encyclopedias. However, K.J. Holsti in his discussion of national role conceptions (based on the content analysis of policy-makers' speeches) includes states that might describe themselves as 'bastions of revolution', whose roles might include (a) 'liberating' others, (b) providing physical and moral support to foreign revolutionaries, and/or (c) offering ideological inspiration. See K.J. Holsti, *International Politics* (Englewood Cliffs, 1983), pp. 116–17. Public statements need not be true indicators of intentions, but this role conception comes close to the second approach proposed below.

rights abroad.[3] The questions this is bound to raise again are: how serious and lasting a commitment, and at what price?

Or finally, do we mean 'revolutionary' not so much in regard to goals as with respect to methods? The use of secret services, agents and 'terrorists' scarcely qualifies a regime as 'revolutionary': the company of users would be numerous and varied. I would maintain that the existence of a Moscow-centred network of communist parties does not in itself constitute *prima facie* evidence sufficient to classify the Soviet Union as a revolutionary state.

The preceding is not intended as an effort at hair-splitting but rather to suggest that the very definition of the problem is not without its difficulties – a point to bear in mind as we survey the Soviet record.

II

There can be little doubt about the mindset, and the rhetoric it gave rise to, with which Lenin and his comrades came to power. For years, the slogan of transforming international–imperialist-war into just–civil-war had been reiterated by the Bolsheviks; belief in the inevitable world revolution was axiomatic; the Russian revolution had only momentarily managed to succeed ahead of its analogues abroad, and in fact the German revolution in particular was eagerly awaited as essential to bailing out the embattled Bolshevik regime.

But with characteristic dexterity the Leninists embarked on shaping their relations with the outside world in rather pragmatic terms. Over the protests of the purists in their own midst, they signed at Brest-Litovsk – an early instance of realism, regardless of ideology, and also of placing the Soviet state ahead of revolution abroad – a pattern that was to be repeated time and again in later years.

It would be wrong to say that the ideological constructs of Leninism were ignored by the makers of Soviet foreign policy: willy nilly, they saw the world in categories of class conflict, exploitation, either/or, and revolution. To this extent ideology no doubt shaped their perception and contributed, then and later, to a number of serious errors of judgement. It also gave rise to the Communist International and its various satellites and acolytes. Instead of waiting for foreign revolutions to save the Soviet regime, now Russia became the sponsor of efforts to promote revolutionary, 'proletarian' movements abroad. In retrospect, it is striking how obedient were most of the comrades abroad; but also how amateurish, incompetent, doctrinaire, gossipy, and quixotic the whole Comintern apparatus turned out to be. While it became the scarecrow

---

[3]A recent Soviet paper suggests an interesting criterion by proposing that the end of the Cold War came at the moment when each of the two superpowers stopped seeking to transform the other.

of the Western world, and while it was indeed in some respects a unique international network, on balance it was a remarkable failure. Only its blindest partisans and its most extreme enemies denied it.

Soviet diplomacy by contrast could be pursued with relatively few doctrinal constraints and inhibitions. Over time, the foreign ministry emerged unmistakably as the lead horse, and the Comintern syndrome began to shrink to the status of a subordinate and none too promising instrument of Soviet foreign policy.

Initially, in the 1920s, the revolutionary jargon was kept alive. But soon world revolution – having been Russified and Bolshevized – was also Stalinised.[4] Internationalism was equated with the interests of the Soviet state; and if authentic revolution – from above or below – had proved a failure the world over, its surrogate would be carried abroad on the bayonets and guns of the Red Army. Revolution was nationalised – in both senses of the word: it was taken over by the Soviet state, and it now served as an instrument of Russian policy. It would take an act of faith, clever ideological juggling, or a far-fetched analogy to the Napoleonic wars to argue that (unless we see all challenges to the status quo as revolutionary) Stalinist expansion – from Bessarabia to Xinjiang, or a few years later, from Valona to the Kurile Islands – was indeed the product of a truly 'revolutionary power'.

III

The Soviet record surely validates the first definition cited above. Throughout virtually its entire history from the October Revolution until the accession of Mikhail Gorbachev in 1985, the Soviet state has driven to alter the international status quo in its favour. Starting from an (accurate) perception of its own weakness, isolation, and inexperience in 1918–20, the Kremlin's perspective – rooted in the notion of an inevitable struggle between 'us' and 'them' – reduced the international contest to a zero-sum game whose score was measured by the 'correlation of forces' between the two incompatible world systems: an outlook that made Moscow strive uphill, to catch up with and ultimately – it was understood – to overtake the adversary camp. (Never mind that the correlation of forces was more of a rhetorical device than a measuring rod, or that Soviet propagandists could at all times adduce evidence which ostensibly demonstrated that the correlation was shifting in 'socialism's' favour.)

This uphill drive required a great variety of means – among other things, trading space for time (Brest-Litovsk); building a formidable armed force and a military–industrial complex (both before and after World War II); launching a massive 'peace' campaign (in the final

[4]This triad is suggested, among others, by Franz Borkenau in his *World Communism* (Ann Arbor, 1962).

Stalin years); seeking to acquire a variety of territory, from East Prussia to the Sea of Japan; controlling the East European 'bloc'; venturing (unsuccessfully) into Northern Iran and Afghanistan; stealing atomic secrets abroad; and sponsoring the Warsaw Treaty Organization, the Council for Mutual Economic Assistance, as well as other institutional ties among its client states in Eastern Europe, East Asia, and beyond.

This effort to enhance Soviet power and influence also witnessed numerous miscalculations and misperceptions, either out of ignorance or because of ideological blinders – from a misreading of the nature of fascism (in the early 1930s) to a miscalculation of Soviet prospects in the Third World (in the 1960s), from a misunderstanding of American attitudes in the 1970s to a misjudgement of armed forces and attitudes in Afghanistan (in the 1980s). What remained constant throughout this entire period (with very few exceptions, such as the defence against attack from abroad, be it in 1920 or in 1941 – and even there Moscow typically sought to grasp victory from the jaws of defeat) was the commitment to 'catch up and overtake', both in economic development and in military capabilities. In the end, it never even came close to closing the gap in economy and technology, but it did attain, *grosso modo*, strategic parity with the 'other' superpower in the 1970s and 1980s.

The remarkable transformation of the infant Soviet republic into the superpower of recent vintage was indeed the product of a prodigious effort, and in retrospect its high costs – including the distortion of economic development, the over-centralization of resource allocation and the setting of targets, and the sacrifice of other goals, such as boosting the availability of goods and services – were among the causes of the crisis that Mikhail Gorbachev faced when he came to power.

IV

Within this general continuity, we find significant markers indicating a gradual shift toward the acceptance of, and adherence to, the international political system. One such instance came in December 1933 – January 1934 when the Soviet Union (or rather, some of its key leaders) stopped identifying with the victims and 'revisionists' of Versailles (i.e. above all Nazi Germany) in opposing their erstwhile enemies number one and two – Britain and France. Before long Stalin and the Comintern were persuaded to abandon the 'ultra-leftist' argument of the Depression years that there was nothing to choose between 'bourgeois' democracy and fascism insofar as both were variant expressions of virulent capitalism, 'not antipodes but twins'.

What was important here, within the problematics of our topic, was the unprecedented Soviet shift to the defence of the international status quo, which was now perceived as preferable both to war and to the Nazis. While coexistence in general had a habit-forming quality, and while the change in Soviet and Comintern strategy in 1934–35 was characteristic of the periodical left/right shifts in their policies, this one went significantly further in opening the door to alliances with Western democracies (notably, France and Czechoslovakia), adherence to the much maligned League of Nations, and (after the Comintern's Seventh World Congress in 1935), as part of the new 'popular front' strategy, support, rather than sabotage, of the defence build-up and military preparedness of 'capitalist' countries. Psychologically it generated the sense in official Soviet quarters that, under certain conditions, the status quo was preferable to change. This was the starting point of an evolution that would land Soviet diplomacy in August 1990 alongside the Western powers in opposition to Iraq's seizure of Kuwait.

V

The shift just described, carried out over the opposition of dogmatic adherents of a particular 'class analysis', was only one in a chain of events in what has amounted to a gradual and almost continuous evolution down to the 1980s, in which:

1. The Soviet Union got stronger, or was so perceived.
2. Soviet attempts to stimulate and/or support revolutionary attempts and movements abroad proved remarkably and uniformly unsuccessful.
3. The Soviet Union, through a sequence of experiences, came to identify increasingly with at least some aspects of the existing international order.

The increase in economic power was widely heralded by Soviet media, and while the data were often selective and falsified, no doubt such a growth did in fact take place, as did the 'advances' in the spread of literacy, educational attainments, and urbanization. The corresponding growth in military power was even more impressive.

True, some observers discounted Soviet capabilities – because of the purges in the officers' corps or on the strength of performance in the Winter War against Finland (1939–40) and the initial response to the German attack (1941), or later as characteristic of Nikita Khrushchev's bluffing (1957–58). Others questioned perceived Soviet legitimacy at home, as well as popular morale and dedication. But in the end, the performance of the Red Army in World War II and, after Stalin, the modernisation of the Soviet armed forces, with ICBMs and nuclear weaponry, were bound to contribute to a sense that the Soviet Union could effectively take care of itself. In other words, if in the early days of extreme weakness the Bolsheviks' banking on foreign comrades and foreign revolutions to bail them out reflected a recognition of the absence of adequate assets of their own, in time the sense of vulnerability receded as Moscow mobilised and harnessed vast human and economic resources. As a Soviet commentator remarked in 1962, 'Gone are the days when the working men . . . had indeed nothing to lose but their chains'.[5]

This shift in orientation was greatly reinforced not only by Stalin's characteristically pejorative attitude toward those whom he could not fully control or command – foreign communists included – but also by the sequence of revolutionary failures abroad. From the collapse, in the early days, of the Hungarian and Bavarian Soviet republics to the communists' fiascos in Germany in 1918, 1921 and 1923; from the decimation of the Javanese revolutionaries in 1926 and the Chinese communists in 1927–28, to the defeat of the Spanish Republic in the civil war of 1936–39; from the fighting in Greece to Malaya after World War II, Moscow's allies and clients seemed doomed to failure and defeat.

Only after the Comintern was disbanded (1943) were new regimes established that seemed to symbolize the shift in the international balance in Moscow's favour: regimes in Eastern Europe (and North Korea) created or imposed thanks to the presence of Soviet troops. By contrast with the authentic communist regimes (in Yugoslavia, Albania, China, Vietnam and Cuba), it is precisely these derivative communist regimes that proved in 1989 to be remarkably lacking in support at home.

1949–50 saw one more attempt at radicalisation and revolution at the initiative of the Cominform and its Soviet sponsors. The message was received and complied with in the entire arc from Kerala, over Malaysia and Indonesia, to the Philippines and Japan. But, while this episode deserves to be elucidated further, it was ultimately as unproductive as its predecessors.

Thereafter – in the last 40 years – we have little or no evidence that Moscow ever advised/instructed/ordered any foreign communists to attempt to seize power by political revolution, civil war, or coup.[6] Virtually no foreign communist parties came to power on the national level by the ballot box, and a number of non-ruling parties split (e.g. in Finland, Japan, Greece, India). Cuba and later Nicaragua were unexpected windfalls (and costly ones at that, in both instances creating difficult dilemmas of policy for Moscow). Splits with the Titoists in Yugoslavia (1948–55) and later with the Maoists in China and elsewhere (from about 1960 on), and more recently with the Eurocommunists, hopelessly divided and weakened international communism.[7] Even when some of these conflicts were later settled, these splits led Moscow to lower its expectations of 'world revolution' further and further; the term itself was in effect quietly abandoned. In fact, even organisationally Moscow could not properly institutionalise its relations with either the ruling parties (the

---

[5]*World Marxist Review*, December 1962, p. 6, cited by William Zimmerman, 'Elite Perspectives and the Explanation of Soviet Foreign Policy', *Journal of International Affairs*, Vol. 24 (1970), No. 1.
[6]The exceptions to this generalisation appear to be rooted in particular local circumstances, such as the ongoing struggle in Angola, the Yemens and Ethiopia.
[7]For further details, see e.g. Heinz Timmermann, *The Decline of the World Communist Movement* (Boulder, Colorado, 1987).

Bloc) or the non-ruling ones. Meanwhile its hopes for a new phalanx of ruling and dedicated client parties in the Third World proved to have been as misguided as had been earlier bursts of revolutionary optimism. In the end, Moscow was advising the Sandinistas to accept the verdict of national elections that they lost; telling the African National Congress and the Palestine Liberation Organisation to refrain from 'direct action' and instead move to negotiations; and assisting in the settlement of regional disputes, from Namibia and Angola to Cambodia.

Finally, a sequence of experiences strengthened the Soviet inclination to defend, rather than subvert, the existing international order. Among these was the Soviet role as a member of the victorious coalition in World War II and later its image as one of the two nuclear superpowers (with occasional innuendos of a Soviet–American condominium and the demand for 'political parity' once strategic parity was acknowledged by the U.S.A). In the Khrushchev days it was also reinforced by the arguments developed within the Soviet élite in warding off the challenges from the Maoists, whose demands, in the 1960s, for ideological purity – including a clean break with the imperialists rather than attempts to conclude arms control agreements – helped crystallise in a large part of the Soviet élite a sense that, first, nuclear weapons constituted a threat to the survival of civilisation – that in their trajectory atomic bombs 'did not follow the class principle' – and that therefore, second, along with vast areas of conflict between East and West, there were shared interests, beginning with a common commitment to human survival: a perspective that raised doubt about the unconditional validity of the traditional Leninist zero-sum assumption of *kto kogo*.

True, the acceptance of the existing order as a framework for super-power relations implied no assurance of peace or stability. Nor did it preclude the use of troops beyond Soviet borders, though in fact they were used almost entirely on the territory of Soviet allies and clients (or on Soviet soil) rather than against foreign foes.

Moreover, the evolution of Soviet attitudes did not proceed in a straight line. Differences and cleavages within the Soviet élite in the 1960s and 1970s appear to have included arguments – essentially, between proponents of accepting the status quo and advocates of a commitment to change – about which we are still inadequately informed. In retrospect, it may be suggested that they adumbrate some of the rethinking and soul-searching that has characterised the Gorbachev years.

The 'New Political Thinking' of the Gorbachev era, as it gradually took shape, appeared to mark a fundamental break in Soviet policy assumptions and preferences. At the same time, as I have tried to suggest above, some of its themes and orientations may be seen as the culmination of protracted processes of ideological erosion, of changing élite values and perceptions, of adaptation and learning – processes that had been at work, behind the scenes, for a good many years.

The general orientation of the 'new thinking' in foreign policy was to normalise the Soviet approach to, and the Soviet role in, the international system. It involved a fresh look at Soviet security and an unprecedented acknowledgement of interdependence. Most significant for our purposes, it included the explicit rejection of the hitherto mandatory application of 'class analysis' to international relations, and the recognition that global, 'all-human' objectives – beginning with the avoidance of a nuclear holocaust, environmental catastrophe, or massive starvation – had (or could have) a higher priority than traditional class interests. It also laid the groundwork for the rejection of the unilateral use of force in the pursuit of policy objectives, including the application of what used to be called the Brezhnev Doctrine.

One major trigger for the articulation of these views was unquestionably the perception of potentially critical and destabilizing problems within the Soviet Union, beginning with the disastrous state of the economy, and the changing relationship between state and society. Challenges in the Soviet Union's international environment likewise added to the pressures for change. First, all these tension areas showed the Soviet Union to be considerably weaker than had earlier been assumed. Second, at a time of domestic transformation, the Soviet Union had a strong interest in keeping the international environment as stable, predictable, and unprovocative as possible. And third, given the conditions of exceptional tautness in resource allocation, prudence dictated a foreign policy that would require significantly smaller defence and foreign aid outlays.

Ironically, if earlier the sense of power and parity with the 'other' superpower had propelled the Soviet decision-makers toward accepting, and working within, the existing international system, now a sense of weakness and need reinforced the same impulse to an even greater extent. At a minimum, there was now no viable alternative to it; at a maximum, Soviet officialdom felt more comfortable identifying with that milieu.

This was particularly true – in addition to the situational factors listed above – in so far as the 'new thinking' was greatly promoted by a new generation of Soviet international affairs specialists and diplomats who, during the preceding years, had become acquainted with Western thinking and practice and who had, cautiously and sporadically, begun to integrate this experience into their own world view. While this cohort included some older officials with diplomatic experience in the United States or at the United Nations (such as Vladimir Petrovsky) and some 'fast learners' without the benefit of such foreign service (including Edvard Shevardnadze), the bulk of revisionist thinking came in memoranda and briefings from men in their 30s and 40s (mostly in academic institutes, in the foreign service, or in journalism) whose skills, polish and mode of thinking for the first time rivalled those of their Western counterparts, who for many of them did indeed serve as an explicit or implicit reference group. Increasingly accompanied by a sense of shame for the backwardness of their own country and expressions of anger about the sacrifice of generations to a tissue of fictions and falsehoods, these affinities were important for the cadres who pioneered the fresh approach.

Some officials, on the other hand, had difficulty in jettisoning the 'old thinking'; for instance, seeing the world in Manichean terms of 'us' and 'them' has been second nature to many. Others have emphatically disagreed with significant parts of the 'new thinking', such as its Western (and Westernising) orientation. In most instances, an individual's willingness to accept and assimilate the principles of the new thinking correlates positively with his or her favourable orientation toward the general reform outlook of the Gorbachev era.

The 'new political thinking' and its consequences are part of the skein that the orthodox diehards in the Soviet communist party have attacked. Former Politburo member Yegor Ligachev, for instance, voiced his dissent from the priority of all-human over class interests. He and his political allies have accused the reformists of surrendering Eastern Europe and contributing to the disintegration of the Soviet state.

In the Gorbachev years, this was no longer an esoteric debate among a few insiders. One consequence of the political changes in the Soviet Union has been the mushrooming of public opinion research. One survey of 120 international affairs specialists, scholars, journalists and diplomats was published in 1989. A second phase covered a sample of 1,200 persons representing (or intended to represent) all strata of Soviet (urban) society. The data show broad support for the priority of 'all-human' interests and values, ahead of state, class, or other narrower interests. Almost 80 per cent disagreed with the statement that the principal aim of Soviet foreign policy must be to assist the spread of socialism as a system on a world scale. Some 77 per cent believed that the prevention of nuclear war should be the principal aim of Soviet foreign policy, ranked ahead of any 'class' purposes. When the interviewers structured a hypothetical conflict between the interests of proletarian internationalism and all-human interests, only nine per cent of the respondents felt that internationalist help to progressive forces abroad must have the top priority.[8]

Broadly speaking. Soviet published sources, anecdotal and impressionistic findings, as well as a series of interviews, all point to the existence in 1990, side by side, of several opinion groups regarding the 'new thinking', ranging from those who fully accept it (or even go beyond it) to those who resist the ideas and their implications.[9] For our topic the problem is to try to establish in what demographic groups 'revolutionary–internationalist' sentiments are concentrated. It is a good guess that the youngest groups (30s and younger) include the smallest proportion of people giving priority to the spread of socialism abroad. It is also likely that such sentiments are even weaker in the non-Russian areas than in the RSFSR. It is

[8]See Andrei Melville and Aleksandr Nikitin, 'Konets edinomyslia? Sovetskoe obshchestvennoe mnenie po voprosam bezopasnosti i mezhdunarodnykh otnoshenii' (typescript).
[9]For further details, see Alexander Dallin, 'New Thinking About Soviet Foreign Policy', in Archie Brown (ed.), *New Thinking in Soviet Politics* (London, forthcoming, 1991).

probable that they are highly concentrated among party bureaucrats, especially in Moscow and other administrative centers, and among people of 50 and over. Furthermore, it may be asserted that, as material conditions in the Soviet Union deteriorate, fewer and fewer people think of a 'revolutionary' policy for the Soviet Union as a realistic operational prospect.

It would appear that, whatever their profound differences on other scores, a (totally informal and unacknowledged) coalition has developed between the liberals and the nationalist Russian (non-communist) conservatives in opposing the revolutionary–proletarian ideology and its operational translation. It implies the relative isolation of the remaining elements who favour the support of a revolutionary policy (and expenditure commitment) by the Soviet Union. Even these include a substantial number of self-styled Stalinists, whose devotion to foreign revolutions might be no greater than that of their mentor and role model.

As the plural spectrum of Soviet political life widens and crystallises, the space left to the hardcore revolutionaries of the old school comes close to vanishing. And yet this finding does not indicate a similar absence of support for a 'patriotic' Russian (or Soviet) hardline policy, including some expansionist variant: it may well be that some erstwhile 'revolutionary' sentiment has been transmogrified into a nationalist one. This, however, is no more than an idle surmise.

VIII

What then is left today of Soviet revolutionary goals or methods? Changing the international status quo may well remain in the back of some Soviet policy makers' minds. But for the foreseeable future, the task for Moscow is primarily one of damage control – stemming the disintegration of the USSR, maximising foreign aid and involvement in the Soviet economy on tolerable terms, normalizing relations with the West and Japan, complying with new international commitments such as arms reduction. Given the state of Soviet society and economy, given the tensions and fissures within, given the priorities and crises at home, no rational policy will give high priority to a provocatively assertive or expansionist conduct.

For that matter, should the present leadership fall, any other regime in Moscow would also need to take as its point of departure the same dolesome reality of crises, weaknesses, tensions and shortages within the state.[10]

What does remain of course are (1) the rhetoric and (2) the military

---

[10]This discussion does not encompass the possibility of central forces being used against secessionist movements within the present USSR, and its possible international consequences.

wherewithal. But the Marxist–Leninist officialese has an eerie hollowness that has lost the capacity to inspire and lead; and the weaponry looms both incongruous and ominous at once. However we wish to define the challenges of the day – order, food, survival, goods, reform – surely they do not include expansion.

Just as surely, the order of the day is not to bring the benefits of the Soviet system to benighted peoples abroad. Seeking to restructure the world in its own chaotic and failed image would be a lunatic agendum for Moscow to espouse, and there is no indication that any responsible leader seriously harbours such intentions. A series of interviews with journalists, deputies, officials, academics and others in Moscow in 1990 revealed virtual unanimity on this score.

On the other hand (as the first Congress of the Russian Communist Party in June 1990 and other occasions since, have confirmed), there are those entrenched, true believers and diehard politicians who stick to their two-camp view of the world and accordingly find it wise, politic and loyal to give support to comrades and clients abroad, rather than surrender the fortresses of socialism without a shot, abet the rise of Germany and Japan, and make deals with the class enemy. And, as the debates at the twenty-eighth Party Congress remind us, their ranks include army generals and authoritative party secretaries. Still, whatever their chances in élite politics, a 'revolutionary' foreign policy agenda would find few takers in the Soviet Union today.

One may puzzle over the definition of a 'revolutionary power'; one may disagree over the date when the Soviet Union ceased being one (if indeed a specific date for it can be found); one may differ in one's assessment of the role of communist internationalism. But it has clearly been one of the ironies of international discourse that for the past generation the Soviet Union has been perceived, by pundits and politicians, as committed to a radical, revolutionary agenda, when in fact it was in the hands of a conservative gerontocracy that sought to evade and defer the challenges of the real world. Now at last some of its leaders have begun to bring beliefs in line with reality, as they see it. It turns out not to be so easy to jettison the ideological ballast of yester year; it is painful for many to grant that their lives have been spent in pursuit of a mirage; it is natural that some would seek to rescue whatever they can of the old values. But a growing number of Soviet scholars, journalists and politicians, with candor and integrity, now acknowledge that they had been wrong in their beliefs and policy advocacy, including their analysis of the 'world revolutionary process'.

Attacking the notion of historical inevitability, the prominent journalist, Aleksandr Bovin, remarks that 'the ability of capitalism to adapt to new historical conditions has surpassed our expectations. The prospect of socialist transformations in developed capitalist countries has receded indefinitely'. One of the reasons for this, he adds, is the fact that the Soviet Union has failed to provide an attractive model to be emulated abroad.[11] And at a roundtable on the world revolutionary movement, an historian, A.I. Volkov, declared:[12]

> 'A realistic assessment of contemporary capitalism, its development, its vitality, is in fundamental conflict with the assumptions of communists – so to speak, with our genetic code, which consists of the notion that human happiness can be achieved only by means of revolution, which is understood as the forcible redistribution of property and power. This is an illusion . . . . Today's developed societies have demonstrated the possibility, in principle, to solve social problems far more painlessly and more effectively . . .'

There is a logic and plausibility in the process, which might be summed up under the rubrics of value change, learning, erosion of ideological commitment, and maturation. If we think of ideology and learning as reciprocals, learning from experience proceeded – in fact though not always in public, let alone in official doctrine – until, most recently, it has been acknowledged aloud. The vanishing of the utopia, the retreat from blithe and unmitigated optimism, the erosion of the sense of mission and of the faith in having all the answers – these are very much in line with what has typically happened to messianic and revolutionary creeds in other places and at other times. In this regard the Soviet experience has conformed to the pattern.

In the Napoleonic era that transformation from revolutionary visions and virtues to imperial policies and their defeat was accompanied by years of bloody warfare. Costly though it has been, the erosion of Leninist revolutionary power has at least been spared the wars, though apparently not the internal strife and suffering in Soviet society.

[11]*Izvestiya*, 11 July 1987.
[12]*Dialog*, 1990, No. 2, p. 94.

Conclusions

No conclusion can draw together the threads of this book, nor can we summarise the results of a process that is continuing. Instead we asked two eminent authorities on Soviet affairs, both of whom attended our workshop, to record their reflections on its deliberations and on perestroika in general.

I Ernest Gellner

The first thing to say about perestroika is to stress its supreme importance. It is not simply a Soviet or Russian event. It does clearly seem to be one of the major events in world history, like the Reformation, like the French Revolution, like the Industrial Revolution, like the Scientific Revolution. It alters the terms in which we think about the human condition, it transforms our collective social condition. It has rewritten the great historic text, and it will take us a long time to think out the full implications.

It has done it in a number of ways. It provoked a revival of the use of the notion of civil society, and has obliged us to rethink that crucial term: what it means, what it should mean, how relevant is it. All that remains contentious. I happen to think that it was right and proper that it should return to the centre of attention, and I'll try to give some reason for so thinking, because the issue is contentious. Perestroika has also caused us to rethink the notion and ideal of socialism, and this too is well worth spelling out.

I can think of no previous example of a collective self-denigration by a whole social order comparable to that which glasnost' has brought about in the USSR. One can, of course, think of plenty of examples of denigration after a change of power, after foreign conquest or some similar upheaval; but a disavowal of one's own past values and ideas on this scale, not forcibly imposed by new rulers, is something quite unprecedented and enormously significant. That which is being disavowed constitutes the first example in world history of a governing secular ideology. A social order was built on a total theory, and on the idea of implementation of that theory. A theory was treated as revelation, one which defines both fact and norm. In all this it resembled traditional religion, though it uses formally secular elements. Of course, the fact that this particular total secular ideology has failed, does not necessarily mean that no other similarly constructed system may not succeed in the future. The failure of one specimen does not actually entail the failure of all other members of their class, but it constitutes fairly strong evidence, and it does provide very important food for thought. It all supports the hunch that religiously validated societies are followed, not by secular ideocracies, but by ideological compromise, which is what we have witnessed in the West.

And let us speculate a little concerning just why this particular total, but formally secular, ideology has failed so dramatically. And what I am very tempted to do, partly in terms of my past research interests, is to compare the fate of the Marxist total belief system with Islam. They resemble each other in one very important way: both Marxist and Muslim civilisations are marked by very weak civil societies. But there the resemblance ends. One of them has a plethora of faith, whilst the other one has altogether lost its faith. In some ways the Iranian revolution is almost a mirror image of perestroika: economic prosperity and a revolution inspired by religious conviction, whereas the perestroika is an attempt at secular revolution, inspired by economic failure *and* a lack of faith.

Why does one faith work, and the other one not? Of course there is a facile explanation, one which I have already heard propounded by important people. It was: men need religion in the literal sense. I think that is too facile and I am not at all convinced that so simple an explanation will do. There are other explanations, some of which were raised in the course of the conference: for instance, that the Marxist belief system suffered from its empirical refutation. I also find it very difficult to accept that. It was I think Judith Shapiro and others who raised the issue of the failure of prophecy, but it strikes me that when prophecy fails, this does not normally undermine faith. It often strengthens it. The tension that has been generated by the failure fortifies the faithful. Even transcendent religions make a sufficient number of assertions about the world to be refutable within it, and yet they survive this. The fact that this faith is slightly more vulnerable, because it claims to be empirical and scientific and this-worldly, doesn't convince me. Nor do I accept, on its own, the explanation which invokes the corruption of some of the ruling personnel of this creed.

But I am willing to offer a hypothesis with which I am experimenting: the weakness for Marxism is not that it is a total faith, and it's not that it is secular in its construction; its weakness is its lack of a profane sphere. It is not so much that it fails to be a religion, but that it is too total, too all-embracing a religion. It leaves nothing alone. I have in mind the sacralisation of the entire social order, the unification of the political, ideological and economic hierarchy. This unification, which turns out totally disastrous in the economic sphere, has also proved disastrous in the ideological sphere. The extension of the sacred into the economy leaves society no slack, into which it would retire at times when zeal is not at its height. It seems to me the strength of Islam is that, whilst it does provide a handrail, and does pervade social life and does make total claims, it doesn't make any particular economic claim, and although it interferes with the economy a bit, it doesn't interfere with it very much. It does not make it the focus of salvation. It is possible for the individual believer to retreat into the economic sphere, without expecting too much from it. And it is this, the lack of slack, which is crucial in Marxism; the lack of a zone into which human activity can retreat at a time when ideological zeal diminishes, is what destroys it. This seems to me one of the reasons why this particular ideology has failed. In any case, I am putting this forward, as a hypothesis. It is the over-ambitiousness, literally, of this particular messianic expectation, not its earthiness, which proves to be its undoing. A salvation-offering faith which turns the economy into the instrument, the sacrament, of total human fulfilment, can afford a so to speak initiatory, purificatory terror, but it cannot afford squalid, corrupt inefficiency in its productive sphere. In other words, faith can survive Stalin but not Brezhnev. The economy constitutes its weak point twice over: it cannot afford to fail there, and it deprives the man of faith of a temporary refuge, of a surrogate preoccupation, in productive activity.

Now one can also approach this undoing in other ways. It seems to me the modern world lives under the domination of two demanding, exorbitant and merciless masters. Not pleasure and pain – those are a little bit too abstract and tautological. The two masters who dominate industrial and advanced industrial society are consumerism and nationalism: the two preconditions that legitimate a social order are that it should deliver an increasing output of goods, and that it should enable its citizens to identify with a culture, of which the political order is an expression, and which it defends. Now once again, compare this with Islam. Islam does quite well on the identity level: in fact it performs the very same role as nationalism does elsewhere, and at least it does not conspicuously fail in the other, the economic sphere. It remains relatively neutral in its attitude to economy; it hasn't extended its claim in such a way as to make it particularly vulnerable to failure in that area. Marxism has made itself particularly vulnerable by its claims in the economic sphere, and when it attempted to rectify that deficiency and liberalise, it also visibly made itself exceedingly vulnerable on the other score. Liberalisation allowed the spirit of ethnic discontent to emerge, without (as yet at any rate) improving economic performance.

One should also say a little about the way in which the experience of that failure, and the reaction to it, has caused one to rethink, or obliged mankind in general to rethink, both the notion of socialism and that of civil society. The notion of socialism is really very simple. The formal definition is very straightforward: it calls for a shift from private property to communal property. The underlying theory, which is loaded into that otherwise neutral definition, is that this will make human beings nicer: nicer in themselves, nicer to each other, and it will make society fairer. And the original socialists basically accepted both this definition and the encapsulated theory, and other accompanying assumptions which were also built into it. Now, the first refutation of the theory by Stalinism did not shake it at all. My suspicion is that, if anything, it strengthened it. The perversion of the best is worst: there was a kind of double argument from the perversion of Stalinism to the vindication of the ideal. First of all, of course, a transformation of the human condition as radical as this must be heralded by great suffering and very painful birth trauma; also there was the argument that the finest ideal will have the worst perversion. However it did show that it was no longer the abolition of private property as such which would automatically engender the desired consequences; only a subset of property-less societies will have them. Not any society that has abolished private property will display the shining qualities of a brotherly, egalitarian, cooperative order: some other, not closely specified additional conditions, which would prevent pervasion or tyranny, were *also* required. A little additional packing of the definition of the conditions of fulfilment did not need to undermine the vision. All this was still acceptable: socialism will still deliver the moral goods, provided it is not perverted by power-seeking, or by inadequate economic development, or by a great and menacing international conflict, and so forth. The explanations were available, and they were not totally absurd, and they were accepted by many people.

Then, however, comes the second disturbing refutation of the promise: this time it was no longer total terror, but pervasive squalor. Let us think of the concept of socialism as a big circle: *two* big segments have now been taken out. One covers socialism perverted by total Stalinist terror, and the other, socialism marred by Brezhnevite sleazy corruption and ineffectiveness. By the time we have taken two quite different segments of the content of the notion, the burden shifts: and it is no longer the notion of socialism as such which promises salvation in its pristine simplicity, but it's the *differentia*. It is no longer the socialisation of property, exemplified by any part of the large circle, which saves mankind: it is the special, *and above all wholly unidentified*, additional conditions which separate off a "good" socialism from both Stalinism and Brezhnevism which carry the burden. The power to save has really shifted from socialism to an unknown X, whose identity and existence are in doubt. There is a possible society such that it is devoid of private property, *and* has additional unspecified characteristics x, y, z . . . *and* it is good. Unfortunately societies devoid of the additional saving graces x, y, z . . . are common, and those endowed with them have not been found, and moreover, we have no clue as to what x, y and z . . . really are. All that is too much. Credulity does not stretch that far.

This is too much. What is that residue, after you have taken out both terror and squalor? The difficulty of finding and defining that blessed residue in the end exhausts the patience of the faithful. There is some order which is desirable, but actually finding the differentia becomes so difficult that it really strains one's capacity for belief. And of course there is the further argument, which was always available in the abstract, but which was now very vehemently substantiated empirically: there simply cannot be such a residue, because it is a precondition of the non-concentration of power that there should be private property, that there should be centres of independent economic power. Now of course in the abstract form, as presented by Hayek and others, we have been familiar with this argument for a long time. But precisely because it was so uncompromising, because it did not allow for the obvious possibility of a mixed economy, it did not really persuade too many of us. But when the failure of Socialist economies over a whole range of societies, a whole range of diverse cultures, becomes so very conspicuous, you can no longer blame that failure on the national situation, on specific Russian traditions, on backwardnesss, the Cold War, on this, that and the other. This excuse no longer persuades when the failure also occurs in other regions, and under quite diverse conditions.

Well, let me now come to the manner in which the notion of civil society was being revived and refined. Here perhaps the greater range of societies which anthropologists deal with may be of some help. The basic intuition associated with a notion of civil society is the existence of centres of social cohesion and power, which can stand up to the state, and force the state to obey its own rules and not be arbitrary. Now I don't find the notion, when so defined, adequate. It is rather ethnocentric in time: it ignores the fact that there are many civil societies *in this general sense*, which would nevertheless be very unsatisfactory to our own contemporary moral and political sensibility.

Roughly speaking, pre-industrial man had the option of being dominated either by kings or by cousins. There was an alternative to the centralised, normally monarchical state, but it depended on the existence of local communities, usually defined in terms of real or fictitious kinship (of 'cousins' of some kind). These social segments, if they were to be strong enough to maintain order and resist the central power, were however obliged to make and enforce enormous demands on their members. These demands were customarily orchestrated by a heavy ritualisation of social life, the demands of constant orthopraxy, the infectious display of loyalty to unit by comportment in all aspects of life. In other words, these communities constituted a 'civil society' of a kind, but of a kind which would be both intolerably stifling for modern man, and incompatible with that intellectual and economic growth and the openness that we have come to take for granted. Yet only such excessively demanding, stifling sub-units could counteract the logic of centralisation, which, alas, is inherent in politics and in conflict: unless there is some counter-vailing mechanism (and historically, these do not emerge generally or easily), it is always logical for the victor to suppress the loser and to prevent him from trying to win in the next round; and it is always sensible for the mass to rally round the victor and thus strengthen his position. This simple mechanism explains why historically, most complex polities of the agrarian age were authoritarian.

The only counterforce was supplied by subcommunities which were a little too demanding for our taste, and which didn't merely resist the state, but which also imposed all kinds of behavioural prescriptions which would be very disagreeable to us, *and* be incompatible with a modern economy. By civil society, in the sense which is relevant for our purposes, we mean something that helps us to avoid not merely the excessive power of kings or central authority, but also the excessive social power of sub-communities. In other words – a society in which sub-units are strong enough to resist the state, but at the same time mobile, volatile, optional enough not to impose their own tyranny on the individual. And it is very difficult to see how these units could be anything other than economic ones, other than units endowed with *independent* economic functions. *This* is the real argument for the market: not from the premise of efficiency, but from the need for at least a partial market as the only alternative to centralisation. The theoretically attractive notion of collective ownership in practice means that decisions are taken in one centre, and it also brings about the unification of all decision-making in one hierarchy, which then implies both inefficiency (because members of a hierarchy are preoccupied with their position in it rather than with efficiency) and tyranny. This is the argument suggested by the outcome of the great experiment, brought about by the attempt to implement the most elaborate sociological theory, the most persuasive messianic secular promise, of the nineteenth century.

The 'civil society' which has, very properly in my view, become the guiding slogan and ideal of much of the ex-communist world, differs both from the plural, participatory communalism which sometimes managed to resist tyranny in the agrarian world, *and* from that over-centralised and stagnant version of industrial society which resulted from the idea that bourgeois civil society is a fraud, and one that needs to be and can be replaced by something even better, more prosperous, and in the end also more fulfilling and free. But the new East European civil society, if it does succeed in emerging, will also differ from Western society, precisely because its starting point, its historic base-line, is so very different. It will have to separate power from faith and to pluralise both, and its autonomous economic units will have to emerge, not very very gradually in the interstices of 'feudal' society, but very very fast, in the interstices of a fairly modern command-administrative system, and from a disenchanted, previously monolithic ideocracy. Can it be done? How can it be done? Can this forcing-house produce anything better than a *lumpen-bourgeoisie*, crawling out from under the stones, recruited from erstwhile black-marketeers and mafiosi, *and* erstwhile apparatchiks? Only a fool would answer these questions with confidence.

What follows? Perhaps one can put a little bit of meat into what may seem an excessively general abstract, trivial and obvious argument. I'll do so by disagreeing with our chairman John Barber's observations this afternoon. He expressed the fear that perestroika will merely replace one messianism by another. The utopianism, which accompanied and ideologically covered and sustained what is now pejoratively seen as the administrative command system, is being replaced by the utopianism of the market. Is this really happening? I am not sure. This is just an empirical disagreement. My reading of such observation as I have been able to make of perestroika is that this is not what is happening. Some over-enthusiastic expectations from the market might make you think that it is happening. But what seems to me to be really happening is not a revolution of enthusiasm and faith in a *new* utopia, but a different kind of revolution, a revolution of compromise and de-ideologising. The underlying current is not that an alternative total solution is available, but that *no* total solutions are available: it is a revolution of loss of faith, of compromise and pluralism, not of a new faith. This seems to me the direction of today. It is precisely because this is the underlying current, and because it is inspired with the desire to achieve the reconstruction without a cataclysm, that no unified, explicit new messianism is likely to prevail – even if a convincing, ideological candidate were available, which is doubtful. This exercise may provide valuable training in politics without a faith; some might say that this is a form of political education which the Russian soul needs.

Of course there are various trends within perestroika. There is both the revival of traditional romanticism of various kinds, and also an element of excessive emulation of the market, and expectation that it will produce a miracle, which it won't. But the main current of feeling and thought seems to be not to expect too much, and to refuse any one single orthodoxy. Of course, this may only be my wish – but it is also my reading of the facts of the case. In John Barber's case, I think he shares my wish, but his fear is that the other thing is happening. History has not yet decided between us. Fairly soon, it will. But this seems to be one of the crucial issues in the interpretation of perestroika.

II Moshe Lewin

I shall not attempt to sum up or come to any hard and fast conclusions in my final remarks: perestroika is an ongoing, multi-faceted phenomenon, and it is, therefore, only proper that one's thoughts on the matter should be left open-ended.

To begin with, a few methodological statements are in order. In the first place, for me, being an historian means that one does not theorize 'on an empty stomach'. The first task of the historian is to amass as much information from the sources as is feasible. Only then should we begin to play with pet theories. Secondly, it is not very helpful if we try to tackle the problems facing us by starting with ideology. This may well result in us ending up where we started from – with an ideology – which means ending up empty handed. Ideologies are not fixed things independent of other factors. They have their own history. They change, lose some of their content, acquire new meanings and may finally become empty vessels – no more than phrase-mongering in political speeches, for instance. What they express or relate depends on the changing nature of outside reality, and the relationship between ideology and reality can be understood only by using the empirical method. In my work on Russia, for example, it became clear to me that ideological constructs – Marxism, Leninism, Marxism–Leninism, Socialism, and in particular Communism – although legitimate objects of historical enquiry, cannot in themselves serve as useful points of departure in any attempt to grasp their essence. The founding fathers of the USSR were, of course, firmly committed to and guided by their ideological constructs, but they recognised – and said quite clearly from the very beginning – that by itself Russia could not produce socialism. Clearly, then, Russian Marxists had no mandate from history to essay what they believed in. Moreover, some of them were obliged to manipulate the original ideology in order to obscure the fact that they were persevering in a project which the founding fathers considered absolutely untenable in Russia alone.

In contrast to some of the opinions expressed in this workshop, I find it difficult to believe that the leaders of the 'command–administrative system' of the last 20 years and before, including Brezhnev, were even remotely possessed of a 'messianic' ideal. They were not marching towards any vision of 'Communism'. The Soviet Communist Party was an organisation dedicated to the maintenance of the status quo; one which utilised the founding fathers' terminology, but which took great care to ensure that terms like 'Marxism' and 'Socialism' were emasculated and completely destroyed as meaningful ideas. Like every other social philosophy and social theory in the Soviet Union, Marxist thought was sterilised. No-one in the full possession of their faculties would have dreamt of going to Moscow to study Marx or Weber. No one would have gone to Moscow to study the problems of socialism either; firstly, because no serious theory of socialism could even exist in the Soviet Union, and secondly, because the term 'Socialism' in no way corresponded to the nature of the system obtaining in the country. Thinking in terms of 'Socialism' would be of no use in trying to understand the way the Soviet system actually functioned. So much for this aspect of the story.

The onset of perestroika has been so momentous that we have almost forgotten what kind of system and what kind of reality existed in the Soviet Union five years ago. The immediate pre-perestroika years were very complicated indeed, but if we are thinking of a gestation period for perestroika should we be looking to the long or the short term? The first answer must be that we should recognize the novelty of it all, both in internal terms and in international terms. Nevertheless, it is misleading to imagine that a 'new society' came into being almost overnight. Leonid Gordon has emphasized the fact that a new society was in the making in the 1960s and 1970s – a phenomenon of immense importance – and it should be added that this was a society which could not understand itself. It could not understand what it was and what was happening to it because there were no channels for the dissemination of information. Secondly, and crucially, there was no input from the social sciences. Not only was the new society incapable of understanding itself, the political system could not understand what was happening in society, nor could it grasp its own nature. In such circumstances Soviet perceptions of change and development could be no more than partial.

The notion of 'civil society' has interested me for many years in the context of social change, especially when studying urbanization in the post-Stalin period. The idea of civil society allows one to take cognizance of a dual feature of the Soviet Union's development. Here was a political system moving in one direction, obviously stagnating (to say the least); an economy showing growing signs of sclerosis, but a society in the process of profound transformation. Hence all the symptoms of a really profound, systemic crisis: a bewildering situation, especially when the tools necessary for self-analysis were so sorely lacking. One could use the metaphor of a rider who does not notice that his horse is not the same any more, and is ready to throw him off. The chain of events we have been witnessing since the launch of Gorbachev's programme has caused (or more exactly revealed) crisis after crisis in the Soviet Union; an ideological crisis, a nationalities crisis, a crisis in all the institutions and values of the system. Virtually all aspects of life are in urgent need of restructuring. The centre of gravity, which initially was located at the centre and at the top, very much *a la russe,* soon moved down into the constituencies emerging from below. There was one scenario when Gorbachev came to power and launched perestroika, but the position is very different today. The emergence of elected institutions has dispersed over a far broader area much of the power which was once concentrated at the top. All this is new and extremely confusing; disorientating for citizens and politicians alike. So many dangers lurk behind so many corners, so many decisions have to be made from so many choices that could be made that the road ahead is no longer clear. This is creating anxiety, even hysteria, in some quarters.

We are sometimes inclined to blame the current leadership for all the trouble, for the deepening crisis in the Soviet Union, but it is clear that policies alone are not the chief cause of the crisis, nor are they the main factors in the situation. On the one hand are the policy decisions, made by a variety of actors, on the other a range of spontaneous developments. This produces a situation in which it is very difficult to make predictions. Like Madame Tussaud's wax figures, all previous certainties are dissolving, and the question is, what will remain when all the wax has melted away? The Soviet Union is, for the moment, suspended between order and chaos, between democracy and authoritarianism, between USSR and Russia, between capitalism and socialism, and also between Gorbachev and Yeltsin – in that order. It is awesome. In the meantime, as the old certainties continue to dissolve, what we *can* say is that the whole situation should be characterized as *a system of uncertainties:* all the key elements of the system, not just this or that aspect of it, are in flux.

Conclusions

From the Brezhnev period onward two processes were at work, sometimes running parallel to each other, but later tending to bifurcate. The first was located in the state, the specific organizational form of which is appropriately termed the 'command–administrative system'. The command–administrative system was, in many ways, successful, but its very success contained a paradox. It managed, as has no other system in our century, to achieve a completely monopolistic position in the country. It did not have to account for its actions to anyone. It was free from any competitors. It did not have to answer to consumers, it was not accountable to any electorate, and it was not even afraid of the top leadership. There was a time when the party leaders did have control over the bureaucracy, but, as the system settled down and became routine, the bureaucracy absorbed the party and thus rendered control from above ineffective. The party apparatus was, of course, important. It could demote ministers, for example. But it could do nothing to change the manner in which ministerial machines (the *vedomstva*) functioned. Furthermore, the party became addicted to the *vedomstva* since they operated as its main entrepreneurs – the 'makers and shakers' of the system. Over time the entire edifice went into visible decline, looked ever more unreformable, and the party merely presided over this decline.

Many western observers identified the signs of decay, but they concentrated overmuch on events in the Kremlin. They ignored the second set of processes, the remarkable transformations wrought by history; the continual, hectic pace of social change apparent from the 1930s onwards. In the post-Stalin period successive waves of rural migrants transformed the social structure of the country. Even during the Second World War the country was still overwhelmingly rural, but in the 1970s Russia ceased to be a country of *muzhiks,* one dominated by the countryside, and became an urban society. This was no small matter. It was a phenomenon quite new in Russian history, one which I shall elaborate on in a moment.

It should now be apparent why these two processes were tending to bifurcate. On the one hand the administrative planning–controlling system inherited from the Stalin period acquired a 'negative dynamic': it continued to decay. Social change, on the other hand, exhibited a very different dynamic. Social change fundamentally transformed the country and thus accelerated the unfolding crisis of the entire system. This is why it is not really justifiable to speak of some 'sudden collapse' of the system, or of the 'sudden death' of the ideology. Processes and transformations, not events, were at work here, and as far as ideology is concerned, there was a veritable cascade of transformations. Even in the 1960s one could see how the current version of the official ideology was losing its hold on the population: Geoff Gleisner's doctoral thesis, submitted to the University of Birmingham, showed that the party's ideological commission was worried because people were not listening to party propaganda. In fact this was a trend which had started much earlier. In higher education, for instance, compulsory courses on 'Marxism-Leninism' or 'Scientific Communism' bored everyone to death and made no sense to most students:

their only justification was that they gave birth to a great number of good jokes.

Whilst the screen of official ideology was becoming ever more tenuous economic performance was becoming ever more unsatisfactory. On top of it, the party was decomposing from within and was losing all credibility. The party's previous success in so thoroughly depoliticising society – and its own members – now seemed a dubious and ironic achievement. Depoliticisation came to haunt the party. It maimed the organisation. The collapse was not too far off, but it was not sudden.

Why was the West so surprised by the onset of perestroika? Why was it unable to foresee the momentous events which were to unfold so dramatically? Even when Gorbachev began to speak out and break with the past many Westerners remained sceptical. Why was it that all the spy networks, all those satellites and listening devices, turned out to be completely useless when important historical events and processes gathered momentum? This is an interesting topic. To put matters in a nutshell this extraordinary oversight arose from the logic of political and ideological competition between East and West. Each side had an interest in constructing and maintaining an image of the other tailor-made to its own strategic and ideological requirements. The Cold War imposed on both contending blocs the imperative of simplification, while the study of historically rooted complexities – something that demanded a different kind of logic – was discounted. As Russia became ever more complex catch-phrases continued to masquerade as scholarship. The idea of 'totalitarianism', for example, served as one of the great simplifiers, and it still continues to do so today. It is true that from the 1960s onwards an increasing number of Western scholars were abandoning the concept and were searching for some other explanatory model. It is also true that the totalitarian model did have some restricted efficacy in describing some periods of Soviet history, but the main proponents of the idea wanted to begin everything with Lenin. They endowed the system with some 'original sin'. They denied the Soviet Union a history. They ignored change. They overlooked the fact that choices were available and that mistakes were made. One French author who was, for a time, popular in Paris, even went so far as to say that there was no society at all in Russia, merely an army with a society attached to it. In his view there was nothing more to explain.

The system was controlling (or trying to control) everything – that is true – but it ended up doing something else, and it is vital to focus on all those events and processes it could not control. How did a civil society emerge in Russia? Where did Khrushchev come from? Where did the reforms of the 1960s come from? Where did the legion of reformers – many of them party members – and reformist texts come from? How was it, for example, that Shkredov could declare, in his *Ekonomika i pravo,* that the official Soviet claim to 'socialism', based on state ownership of the means of production, was no more than 'Proudhonism', and that the nationalisation of the economy was a premature, and in the final analysis, a pernicious measure? This was a perfectly orthodox Marxist text, but it was completely at odds with current official thinking. The principle that economic agents should be allowed operate in market conditions was advanced as far back as the 1960s, sometimes with doctrinal justifications drawn from the theory and practice of the NEP years, and this could be argued out in strictly marxist terms, as could many other critiques of the prevailing system. This is why marxist theory in particular had to be emasculated in the Soviet Union. Soviet Marxists, if allowed freedom to argue, could not have accepted that the existing system, with its enormous concentration of political, economic and social power, its denial of political freedom and its promotion of ideological mystification, was in any way socialist. I was a worker in Russia for a couple of years during the Second World War, and I did not need any theory to appreciate the real position of working people in the USSR. Who, in his right mind – whether a Marxist-orientated intellectual or ordinary worker – could claim that what existed in the Soviet Union had anything to do with the idea of a 'workers' state'?

Let us move on to the 'historical perspective', which was supposed to have been the main theme of the workshop. Historical perspective must engage, not just with 'the past' in general, but with the relevant past; with those trends which underpin the particular historical turning points in which we are interested.

In the context of a short analysis I can only briefly survey the main aspects of the story. In the first place it is evident that the roots of the Soviet system are buried deep in the soil of Tsarism, and in the crisis that undermined Tsarism. It is also evident that massive imbalances, which rendered the entire system dysfunctional, were responsible for the collapse of Tsarism. What is less evident – and what is hard to prove – is a second series of contentions. The imbalances which sealed the fate of Tsarism continued to dominate the events of 1917. Furthermore, they were also influential in the NEP, and they were still making their presence felt in the 1930s. In each successive period new factors came into play, but this does not diminish the fact that older ones continued to affect matters. Let us take the years 1905–21 as an example. Anyone familiar with the period would probably agree that not everything was due to 'the revolutionaries'. 1905 and 1917 'happened', so to speak, and the revolutionaries joined in the fray. They predicted that revolutions would occur, but they did not make them: they were faced with them.

It is often thought that there were only two alternative futures in 1917, a democratic future and a Bolshevik future. No. There was a third alternative, a third agglomeration of forces, a 'White' reality. The demise of the Tsarist regime was deceptively easy. It gave the impression that the social foundations of Tsarism had been swept away, hence the exhilarating sense of freedom characteristic of the February Revolution. Thereafter the history of 1917 is the history of the disintegration of the Provisional Government, a feeble state form based on the democratic alliance of socialists and liberals which soon fell apart. Most people imagine that the Bolshevik take-over caused the Civil War, but it is worth considering another hypothesis: 'White Russia' was still there. It did not disappear when the Tsar abdicated. White Russia, as we know from the events of the Civil War, passionately hated, not only the Bolsheviks, but also the Mensheviks and Socialist Revolutionaries, and it had little sympathy for the Kadets either. I believe that the Civil War was already inscribed in the events of the February Revolution, and that the Constituent Assembly – if it had survived at all – would have suffered the same fate at the hands of the Whites as is did at the hands of the Bolsheviks. One lesson taught by the Civil War was that the democratic forces of pre-revolutionary Russia were insubstantial. During and after 1917 they simply disappeared. As a result the stage was left open to two contenders, two authoritarian forces of differing complexions. This was a factor of considerable significance for the future.

If the chances for political democracy were slim even in 1917 they were nonexistent by the end of the Civil War, say by late 1920. Interpretations of Lenin's policies and personality at this juncture are matters of perennial interest, but whatever his merits or faults, it was clear that the Russia he presided over in 1921 had regressed some 50 or 60 years in terms of its development; even – measured on some indices – 100 years. De-industrialization, partial de-urbanization, plus all the other calamities which befell the country, turned Russia into a place in which one could only dream of recreating the cultural and material environment of 1914 or 1917. It was a catastrophic point of departure for the new regime, and this must be borne in mind as another important factor conditioning what was to follow. If the Civil War produced War Communism, the NEP produced its antithesis: an official policy of 'down with War Communism'. NEP was a very short period, but one full of interest. We all know (I would even hazard that we can almost hear the echoes of Lenin's voice saying) that no form of communism should be imposed on the countryside by force, and though Lenin was dying there was nothing senile in his view that socialism was, after all, no more than 'a system of civilised co-operators'. He was absolutely explicit. He put it in writing that the party should not rush ahead of the peasants, but should march in step with what the peasants understood to be in their own best interests. The key, salutary slogan guiding policy should be *luchshe men'she, da luchshe*. This was not the only Lenin, of course, or the only form of Leninism. There were several Lenins: the pre-revolutionary Lenin, the Civil War Lenin, the NEP Lenin. It is clear that Lenin learned from experience. He adapted to circumstances, and when his aims and strategies changed, so did his theoretical justifications – the *Leninisms* changed. But by 1929 Leninism was dead. By then the Bolshevik party had been transformed to such an extent that it no longer existed, and this even before the physical annihilation of party cadres during the Great Purges.

How did this come to pass? Throughout the 1920s the Old Bolsheviks still stood at the apex of the party-state organisation. It might have seemed to them that they were running things, but they were being undermined by two developments: the influx of a vast mass of new party members from below and the construction of an apparatus that controlled this mass from above. Whilst those at the top diverted themselves with abstruse debates on industrialization, 'socialism in one country' – or even Einstein's theories – another party kept on growing from below. By 1929 the party was a very different creature from that in evidence at the end of Lenin's life. The new party hemmed in the old, and there was little in common between Bolshevik intellectuals and the rest. In this novel situation practicioners of *realpolitik* – Stalin, for instance – simply accepted the changes, without sentimentalism and without regretting the loss of some imagined paradise, and set about playing a different game.

The specific phenomenon of 'Stalinism', however, was born of the 1930s. There was no 'Stalinism' before then, and even Stalin himself was not a 'Stalinist' in the preceding decade. Stalinism was the unique product of a further crisis (or rather of an avalanche of crises) which began with the procurement difficulties of early 1929 and the *velikii perelom* of late 1929. The situation in which the political system found itself at that moment was one of 'systemic paranoia'. By this I mean that the reciprocal effect of the continual accretion of power and control from above (itself a response to the unintended consequences policy and the chaotic conditions in society at large) was the amplification of a profound sense of insecurity amongst the ruling élite. And as the sense of insecurity prompted a need for still more control, so the phenomenon became ever more complicated – even horrendous, once the process of concentration reached its final stage and converged on one individual. By then a polity of 'systemic paranoia' (troublesome enough for a collective leadership) had fallen into the hands of a personality which was itself paranoid.

The 1930s gave birth to two other things besides Stalinism. The first of these was the future command–administrative system. Notwithstanding the proliferation of bureaucrats, the system could not mature under Stalin's rule; it could not coexist with despotism because no despot would tolerate it. The full elaboration of bureaucratic power would have eliminated despotism, but this eventuality was prevented by the Great Purges; a real bureaucrat is unthinkable without tenure. Bureaucratic power grew and blossomed only after Stalin's death, after the most pernicious features of Stalinism – unacceptable to a ruling bureaucracy – were dismantled. But while the victory of Soviet Bureaucracy in the post-Stalin years gave rise to a uniquely monopolistic and uncontrollable polity, a second motor of change, urbanisation, had been running in parallel. The urbanisation of the 1930s should more properly be called ruralisation, and the ruralisation of the cities was a factor that generated a climate favourable to the emergence of despotism. A huge body of uprooted people flooding into towns whetted the totalitarian appetites of the government. In this context the term 'totalitarian' makes sense. The vast clouds of dust thrown up by mass migration blinded the élite and created a world that was at once threatening and difficult to control. The world was no safer for the country's citizens. There were 'enemies' everywhere, and any citizen could be designated an 'enemy of the people' at the behest of the ruler, who, in the eyes of the population, had assumed the status of a cult figure.

From the social flux of the 1960s and 1970s – a second, spontaneous process of urbanisation – there emerged a further social reality. By then state institutions born of an earlier period, institutions designed very different tasks in a very different society, had lost all vitality. They could neither adapt, nor reform nor respond to new conditions. The stream of history had passed them by. They were doomed to extinction. The onset of perestroika signalled their demise, but they had been succumbing to the attrition of social change for many years.

Index

247